THE REMOTER RURAL AREAS
OF BRITAIN

AN AGRICULTURAL ADJUSTMENT UNIT SYMPOSIUM

THE REMOTER RURAL AREAS OF BRITAIN

Edited by
J. Ashton and W. H. Long

Published for the
Agricultural Adjustment Unit
University of Newcastle upon Tyne
by
OLIVER & BOYD
EDINBURGH

First published 1972 for the
Agricultural Adjustment Unit
University of Newcastle upon Tyne by
OLIVER & BOYD
Tweeddale Court, 14 High Street, Edinburgh EH1 1YL
A Division of Longman Group Limited

ISBN 0 05 002471 X

Printed in Great Britain by
Cox and Wyman Ltd
London, Fakenham and Reading

305661

CONTENTS

INTRODUCTION

IAN F. BAILLIE, C.M.G., O.B.E., M.A.
Senior Research Associate,
Agricultural Adjustment Unit,
Department of Agricultural Economics,
The University of Newcastle upon Tyne.*

The life and character of the countryside are inevitably subject to change—sometimes dramatic in its effects, but more often slow and almost imperceptible. Although the quality of the environment and the amenities of rural areas have in the past been watched over, with varying degrees of success, by a large number of statutory and voluntary organisations, by the Government and local authorities and by individuals in a variety of capacities, there can be no doubt that in recent years interest has quickened. Increasing attention is being given to the many forces which will shape the future of the countryside, and a bewildering variety of arguments and points of view are presented to those responsible for taking the decisions which may affect living conditions and landscape for many decades to come.

The continuing decline in the numbers employed in agriculture has given rise to many problems in rural areas and has often changed the whole character of country life. It has become increasingly difficult and expensive to provide public and commercial services in areas of depopulation, and in many cases the smaller rural settlements are being allowed to run down. In some parts of the country, however, attempts are being made to stabilise the rural population by the introduction of small industries. A growing number of people choose to commute from rural districts or to have week-end cottages there; many retire to the country. Tourism is being encouraged virtually everywhere, and our increasingly mobile society, with greater opportunities for leisure pursuits, will inevitably impose new and far-reaching demands on the resources of rural areas. Yet people in the mass making their way into the countryside can

* Now Secretary of The Thistle Foundation, Edinburgh.

endanger the very things which they go there to seek. A balance must be found which will allow the interests of farmers, foresters, conservationists and others to be integrated with the recreational needs of the urban population.

The pressures are many and diverse. It is not, therefore, surprising that it is difficult to reconcile them in any attempt to propound coherent policies for the future of the countryside. Sound policies are unlikely to emerge if based uncritically on tradition and sentiment; more satisfactory criteria may well be provided by objective economic considerations, tempered by a sympathetic awareness of modern social pressures. Attempts to resist economic and social trends run the risk of leading only to muddle and distress.

Opposition to change may arise from an innate conservatism, which fears any departure from the *status quo*, or from a lack of understanding of the issues involved. Vested interests may support the existing state of affairs. But, on the whole, people fight shy of change because they fear that someone is likely to get hurt in the process. Economic and social changes seem to advance remorselessly; yet, when attempts are made to control and moderate their effects, the institutional machinery is itself sometimes found to be outdated and no longer capable of adjusting to developing circumstances.

Legislation often serves contradictory ends. An Act dealing with economic aspects of agriculture may in the last analysis run counter to accepted social policy. Perhaps it would be better to take a broader view and to legislate for rural communities as a whole, on the basis of an explicit recognition of the social content of certain agricultural support measures. The Rural Development Boards set up under the provisions of the Agricultural Act, 1967, were charged with rationalising the pattern of agricultural holdings in hill and upland areas—a process which would almost certainly lead to further migration from the areas concerned; the same Boards were given powers to improve communications and public services, and to assist in providing tourist facilities in step with 'the need for preserving and taking full advantage of the amenities and scenery'.

The pressures that bear generally upon all rural areas often have a particularly harsh impact on the remoter parts of the country. The problems tend to be more acute, and the resources for dealing with them fewer. Emigration becomes a self-perpetuating phenomenon. Fewer people mean a decreasing demand for services, which are in consequence gradually withdrawn. In turn, the lower level of services reduces the viability of the community; it loses its attractions for those already there and others are discouraged from entering it. The community's will to survive dwindles as the younger and more enterprising elements of the population go elsewhere. Those who remain, particularly the wives and those just leaving school, have increasing difficulty in finding employment.

Large parts of Scotland, Wales, the Pennines and the South-West can, by any definition, be regarded as remote. There are, in addition, many areas which, while not perhaps very remote geographically, share the same problems as the obviously more remote parts of the country. For instance, it is not difficult to find places within 25 miles or less of major conurbations where the declining population is almost wholly based on agriculture and where social services and transport facilities are minimal. Specialised agencies to attack the problems of the remoter rural areas have been established in the Highlands and Islands and in Mid-Wales. The Development Commission also has an important part to play. The whole field of purposive regional development is fluid and experimental with much room for new ideas and thought.*

THE AGRICULTURAL ADJUSTMENT UNIT

The Agricultural Adjustment Unit was set up in 1966 at the University of Newcastle upon Tyne with the help of a grant from the W. K. Kellogg Foundation. It forms part of the Department of Agricultural Economics within the Faculty of Agriculture. Its purpose is educational—in the widest sense—and it is concerned with the means by which the farming industry may adapt itself to changing conditions and to the many pressures upon the countryside. It seeks to bring about a greater awareness not only of the economic factors but also of the institutional and social problems which inevitably arise in a period of rapid change. Amongst other activities, the Unit sponsors conferences and publishes books and bulletins in an attempt to create a wider understanding of underlying trends.

In the course of this work it has become increasingly clear that adjustment to change is not just an agricultural matter, but one affecting the whole rural community. Change tends to produce

* In the event only one Rural Development Board was established (in the Northern Pennines) and it was disbanded following the change of government in June 1970.

dislocation and even hardship in individual cases, and attempts to minimise the social and economic consequences—seldom, unfortunately, wholly avoidable—must largely depend for their success on the smoothness with which adjustment to new circumstances can be achieved. Education—again in its widest sense—can make a valuable contribution towards accommodating change without undue stress by ensuring that people are made aware in good time of the choices open to them.

THE CONFERENCE

It was with these considerations in mind that the Agricultural Adjustment Unit decided to mount a conference on the socio-economic aspects of 'The Remoter Rural Areas of Britain'. Its purpose would be to analyse the nature of the changes that were taking place and to consider what adjustments were necessary. The characteristics of the remoter areas would be described and their present economic, social and institutional framework discussed. It was agreed that the main theme of the conference should concentrate on the following questions:

What should be the longer-term objectives for the remoter rural areas?

How are they affected by the changing demands of the rest of the country (i.e. the urbanised regions)?

To what extent is comprehensive development a desirable and practical means of achieving these objectives?

It was felt that a useful purpose would be served by providing a forum for those responsible for taking day-to-day decisions which affect the lives of people in the remoter areas. Here the points of view of representatives of the various professions—agriculturalists, foresters, planners, economists, politicians, sociologists, conservationists and others, meeting together—could be discussed and an examination could be made of the many economic, social and institutional strands which must be brought together in any attempt to work out balanced and integrated bases for policies for the remoter rural areas. The chapters which follow reproduce the papers presented at the conference, and a résumé of salient points from the discussions is given in the Postscript.

Part 1

THE ECONOMIC AND SOCIAL FRAMEWORK

1 | The Economics of Upland Farming

JOHN R. RAEBURN, Ph.D., M.A., F.R.S.E.
Professor of Agriculture and Principal of College,
School of Agriculture, Aberdeen.

Climate affects nearly everything that farmers can do in their farming. But climates are complex and difficult to define adequately. The pattern of them on the ground can be very intricate. And how reliable they are in comparison with each other, year by year, is a complex question. So we tend to map not climates themselves but their consequences in the distribution of plant populations and the patterns of actual land use. Thus we run the risks of arguing: '*What is* measures climate, since climate has fostered it most, and nothing else can be, because climate will not foster it sufficiently'. In fact, other determinants of 'what is' are not to be ignored: (a) the parent materials from which soils have been derived, (b) topography directly, and (c) men and markets. What we should know are the costs and benefits of altering the basic effects of climate. In estimating these costs and benefits, location by location, ecological and land use maps are guides, but we need also at least some of the direct measures of climate that characterise the 'uplands'.

For forestry we may need a set of values different from that for farm costs and yields. And the conservers and promoters of amenities and recreation in the countryside will need yet another set. But in relation to agricultural production the set that can most readily be assembled[1,2] is summarised in Table 1.1 for selected areas we may well call 'upland'. The climates of these compared with 'lowland' climates have higher rain-falls, more days with rain, later and shorter and cooler growing seasons, more snow, more wind, and higher humidities in summer. There are some notable exceptions to these tendencies (e.g. Shetland, Orkney, the Hebrides and Cornwall all have long, frost-free periods). In general, however, upland climates are relatively unfavourable to the growth of tillage crops and grassland, to the conservation of grass and the harvesting of

3

Table 1.1. Some indicators of climate. Selected Upland and Lowland areas, Great Britain

Area	Elevation	Rainfall	Rain-days, June to September	Frosts, screen — Date of last	Frosts, screen — Days without	Temperature, mean daily — April Min.	April Max.	Temperature, mean daily — July Min.	July Max.	Sunshine, bright (a)	Snow: mornings with snow lying	Wind: days with gale	Humidity: relative humidities, June–August (b)
	feet	inches per year	number		number per year	degrees Fahrenheit				per cent	number per year	number per year	per cent
Upland													
Shetland	200	40	68	April 15	207	37	46	48	56	30	10	33	83
Orkney	150	37	66	April 8	211	38	47	49	58	30	10	20	83
Sutherland, centre	1000	60	80	May 8	145	34	47	46	58	28	40	20	75
Inverness:													
Aviemore	740	39	72	June 1	92	34	49	47	63	27	40	8	67
Source of Spey	1500	80	65	May 15	123	31	46	45	61	24	80	9	71
Uists	80	50	73	March 20	259	39	50	51	61	34	4	38	80
Selkirk:													
Ettrick Forest	1000	50	72	June 1	114	33	49	46	64	28	50	12	66
Westmorland:													
Shap	1000	60	71	May 15	128	35	50	49	65	32	30	14	64
Merioneth, centre	1000	90	69	May 1	168	37	49	51	62	34	40	8	73
Radnor, centre	1000	60	64	May 20	113	35	49	49	65	34	24	8	68
Cornwall, (c)	500	43	60	March 15	260	41	52	54	65	44	2	20	69
Lowland													
Scotland (d)	200	29	64	May 2	173	37	50	50	63	31	15	9	70
East England (e)	150	26	53	April 23	172	38	53	53	69	38	13	2	66
Cheshire Plain	200	34	62	May 1	175	39	53	53	68	34	8	5	66

Source: Based on: Air Ministry; *Climatological Atlas of the British Isles,* HMSO, London, 1952.
(a) Mean of actual bright sunshine hours in May and July as per cent of theoretically possible (which is in the May–August period some 2 per cent greater at 58°N than at 52°N).
(b) Mean at 1300 hours corrected from sea level by coefficients related to elevation and mean daily maximum temperature in July.
(c) West of Falmouth.
(d) Averages for Moray Firth, Buchan and East Fife.
(e) Averages for east side of Trent in Lincolnshire and Norfolk.

cereal crops,[3] and some because of snow cover in late winter are unfavourable to out-wintered sheep and cattle.

_Upland soils are generally also unfavourable to plant growth for agricultural production (including grazing). The high rainfalls and humidities, together with poor natural drainage through rocks, have led through the centuries to accumulations of deep acid peat in some areas, and in others to very shallow acid soils with heavy badly drained subsoils. Naturally poor water relationships and deficiencies in soil nutrients are substantial obstacles to plant growth. Indications of this are set out in Table 1.2, although in interpreting this it should not be assumed that exactly the same definitions were adopted in each county, or in Scotland as against England and Wales, nor that how particular parcels of land were classified depended only on their natural endowments.

Table 1.2. *Areas of each class of land*
Selected parts of Great Britain 1946

			'Agricultural value'					Portion with low or poorest 'value'
	High	Medium	Low			Poorest	Total	
			Heavy	Mountain Moor	Light			
Class	1–4	5–6	7–9	8H	9H	10		
Upland counties			*thousand acres*					*per cent*
Shetland	3	23	—	326	—	—	352	92
Orkney	85	64	—	92	—	—	241	38
Sutherland	—	92	19	1183	4*	+	1298	93
Inverness	69	258	—	2364	4*	—	2695	88
Selkirk	6	46	—	118	—	—	170	70
Westmorland	54	213	1	226	—	1	495	46
Merioneth	23	104	2	283	—	7	419	70
Radnor	2	140	35	122	—	—	299	52
			million acres					
England	17·3	9·4	0·6	2·8	0·8	0·1	31·0	46
Wales	0·5	2·5	0·2	1·7	+	0·1	5·0	40
Scotland	4·0	2·9	0·1	12·0	0·1	+	19·1	64

Source: Research maps of Ministry of Town and Country Planning—as quoted in Stamp *op. cit.*, pages 518–520.
* Including 'machairs' (sea sand areas) in the west.

Topography is less important overall than climate or soil but it does seriously increase the costs of using many upland areas because of difficulties in the use of machinery, and in supervision and stockmanship, and because areas facing 'away from the sun' have less favourable climates.

Thus we might well define the uplands as those areas where the growth of plants for agricultural production (including grazing) tends to be depressed below average levels, by climatic conditions, particularly short and cold growing seasons, and/or by soil conditions, and/or topography. So defined, the uplands will include some areas that are in fact not high above sea level (e.g. Shetland, the Hebrides). The important characteristic is not elevation but the generally unfavourable nature of output–input relationships for inputs added per unit area of land. In general upland areas have under a particular set of price relationships, a lower capacity per acre for labour and other inputs to secure livestock and crop outputs.

Remoteness we also need to consider and define. Remote from what? The lowest contours on maps of prices of products are remote from the highest because of marketing charges of all kinds related to the locations of production, imports, storage, processing and of demands for consumption; and perhaps, also because of certain other attributes of the market structure. On maps of the prices of factors such as feeding stuffs, fertilisers, imported seeds, fencing and building materials, machinery, the highest contours are divorced from the lowest in a similar way, (Table 1.3). But the use of land itself, and labour, management, and capital are different matters.

Table 1.3. *Transport and handling charges on some farm inputs and outputs from or to Perth or Leith, Scotland, May* 1969

	To farms		From farms	
	Feed or fertiliser	Fencing wire etc. (c)	Stirks	Store lambs
	£ per ton		£ per head	£ per head
Farms in (or near):				
Shetland	(a)	(a)	(d)	
Lerwick	4·1	11.3	2·3	0·45
Yell	8·1	16·6	4·0	0·70
Orkney				
Kirkwall	3·7	7·9	3·5	0·60
Westray	6·2	12·4	5·3	1·00
Banff, Tomintoul	6·3	10·6	2·0	0·25
Aberdeen	2·5	4·1	1·2	0·20
Lewis	(b)	(b)		
Stornoway	4·1	9·7	4·5	0·55
West coast	7·1	14·7	5·1	0·70
Inverness,				
Spean Bridge	3·0	3·0	1·5	0·15

Source: Data provided by Regional Directors of County Work—North of Scotland College of Agriculture.

(*a*) Quotations relate to loads of 6 tons or over.
(*b*) Quotations are for full loads and return loads. Return loads are often difficult to obtain, and where not obtained almost double would have to be charged for transport.
(*c*) Variable depending on volume: weight.
(*d*) Stirks assumed to weigh 5 cwt. live.

Particular parcels of land have fixed locations. Supplies (in the form of vacancies for use) can only be increased at any one time by inducing existing users to give up occupancy. Remoteness here tends to operate by keeping relatively low the prices (rents) that other users would pay if they have crop and stock production only in mind. If they have recreation and amenities also in mind their offer prices may be depressed less, and for some land remoteness may indeed have a substantial value. Some bidders obviously also try to seek out high percentage rates of increase in land values resulting from amenity and recreation demand, and favour some remote areas for purchase.

On the supply prices of farm labour and management as factors of production remoteness has complex effects. Most upland farming is family farming, and family homes and histories have to be taken into account in interpreting human behaviour in relation to apparent incomes.

To boys leaving school practical training in local farm skills, but few others, has been available along with cheap family living, and the boys' physical energies for farm work have been valued comparatively highly, although not always in cash. Propensities to leave home, and net income differentials to induce them to do so, rise from about 17 onwards so that much of the rural depopulation has been due to the leaving of 19–25 year olds. And the early leaving of girls and young women, unable to find paid employment near enough, has had a not inconsiderable effect on the boys and young men. In more recent years older age groups have also left increasingly as net income differentials have widened, doubts about the future of upland farming have increased, and opportunities in the towns and elsewhere have seemed more certain. Remoteness in this context is not simply a matter of mileage or marketing costs. It is much more a matter of communications and confidence. The sea-faring world from Glasgow and beyond is to the crofter's son in the Hebrides not remote. The small farmer's son in upland Aberdeenshire may through relatives be equally close to Canada. The obstacles to transfer, including uncertainties, can be the more easily surmounted.

But for those who continue to stay in remote areas, remoteness may be judged as aggravating such obstacles still despite the influence of schooling, closer communications through television and motor vehicles, etc., labour exchanges, and further education. Also for those rearing families, or older people, country living in their old homes may be substantially cheaper and in several ways more attractive than urban life in perhaps some council house or flat, and wage-paid employment. The whole-life advantages of the son who carries on in an upland farm are not to be lightly accounted for even though they cannot easily be valued in money. And those who have left for seafaring, soldiering, police work, or other strenuous employment, when they reach the age of 35 or later, may often see real net advantages in returning to their 'calf-ground' if no other son has carried on as the parents aged and died.

Thus it is that the supply prices of family labour and management for upland farming tend still to be relatively very low if measured in the ordinary ways in cash terms. (See Table 1.4 for the number of farming units and Table 1.5 for land used and stocking in Scotland.)

Table 1.4   *Classification of farms Scotland, 1962*

			Full-time farms					
	Hill	Upland	Rearing, with		Other	Total	Part-time units	Spare-time units
			Arable	Pigs, Poultry				
			thousand units					
All Scotland	1·4	3·8	5·7	1·7	15·6	28·2	11·8	20·9
Regions:								
Highland	0·6	0·8	0·5	+	0·9	2·8	5·8	12·3
North-east	+	0·9	3·7	1·4	3·6	9·6	3·4	3·7
East-central	0·2	0·4	0·6	0·1	3·3	4·6	0·8	1·3
South-east	0·2	0·4	0·5	0·1	1·6	2·8	0·4	0·8
South-west	0·4	1·3	0·4	0·1	6·2	8·4	1·4	2·8
			units					
Counties:								
Shetland	20	34	4	—	11	79	1072	1784
Orkney	—	373	384	248	132	1137	745	739
Sutherland	50	53	43	1	25	172	601	1219
Inverness	144	280	192	15	153	784	2098	3560
Selkirk	52	39	26	2	22	141	18	49

Source: Scola, P. M. (1965) in *Scottish Agricultural Economics*, Vol. XV.

And because livestock and other forms of capital are obviously needed along with this family labour and management, the supply prices of family owned capital are also comparatively low—low rates of return are accepted on such amounts as are both available and regarded as rightly related to the farming system and family's way of life. We shall have to consider this point more fully later. Here we

Table 1.5. *Distribution of land, crops, livestock, labour tasks and labour force by class of farm, Scotland, June 1962*

	Hill	Upland	Arable	Rearing, with Pigs, Poultry	Other	Total	Part-time units	Spare-time units
			Full-time farms					
			thousand acres					
Land								
Total area	5828	2920	1542	147	3052	13489	860	1300
Tillage and grass	79	507	813	113	2434	3946	190	179
Cereals	4	64	209	37	673	987	35	13
Potatoes	1	2	11	2	119	135	4	3
			thousand head					
Livestock								
Dairy cows	2	8	7	1	334	352	7	2
Beef cows	21	100	91	9	157	278	19	7
Other cattle	32	215	273	52	700	1272	58	22
Ewes, breeding	1194	798	512	36	708	3248	275	115
Pigs	1	10	31	74	326	442	22	2
Fowls, over six months	39	199	563	546	1906	3253	480	140
			million standard man days					
Labour								
Tasks	1·3	3·4	5·0	1·1	21·7	32·5	1·5	0·6
			thousand					
Force (a)	3	7	10	2	50	72	3	2

Source: Scola, P. M. *ibid.*
(a) Excluding farmers and their wives, but including other family workers and casual workers at the time of June census.

need only note that remoteness, if it is depressing the supply prices of family labour and management, may also be depressing the supply price for the use of *limited amounts* of family capital in farming.

The position of paid farm employees who are not in farming families is obviously different from that of family workers. There are few such employees in most upland areas: they have had fewer advantages in staying. But some are still very important: for example, shepherds on large hill sheep farms. The effect of remoteness on the supply price of such men in the future needs careful consideration especially when State investments in remote areas, for example for roads for tourists, raise local wages well above those payable to young shepherds.

To sum up our brief consideration of remoteness, we can note that it tends to make price relationships between products and factors unfavourable, depressing particularly the local prices of products which are bulky, difficult to transport, are perishable, and raising particularly the prices of inputs with similar characteristics and those difficult to provide because few are needed per square mile (e.g. veterinary services). For these reasons, and because physical output–input relationships are comparatively unfavourable in upland areas most of which are 'remote', land-use costs per acre are generally lower, but amenity and other values not directly related to farm production are influential in raising land values, although not necessarily rents. The supply prices of farm family labour management and capital tend to be relatively low, but for the future not enough capital may be available from families themselves, and family labour and management may be increasingly attracted elsewhere. The amount of ordinary employee labour in remote areas is small and may be increasingly attracted away from farming. Much depends on trends in the productivity of management, labour and capital in remote upland farming as against other activities, but in defining productivity and the costs of transfers—individual, family, and general social—we have to be especially careful.

CHOICE OF PRODUCTS

Turning now to the influence of remote upland conditions on decisions about farming systems, we can clearly expect climates, soils, topography, and price relationships to limit the range of activities that can be economically combined into farming systems. Cash crop production cannot be important except in particular pockets of land favourable to special crops (e.g. flower bulbs in small parts of the Hebrides). Trees, of course, are a cash crop and others will be dealing with forestry as an activity. I would only note here that many upland climates and soils do not limit tree growth so much as that of tillage crops and high quality pasture swards. We must not forget, however, that at the higher elevations and in the wetter and windier areas trees are not favoured by climates and soils and for this and other reasons we should consider whole water sheds and the various alternative 'mixes' and 'layouts' of forestry and farming within them rather than farming and forestry separately. The best use of land for these purposes and for recreation and amenity is not always achievable when the various parties taking decisions cannot or will not do this. What, of course, aggravate the difficulties are:

(a) the very different flows of expenditures and incomes over time in producing timber as against farm products, and, therefore,

(b) the very different finance required,* and

(c) the very different taxation arrangements.

But upland farming, excluding farm forestry, is largely the use of grazing and winter feeding stuffs (largely hay, but with some grain, straw and turnips and even grass silage in some areas). These winter feeding stuffs are in physical terms comparatively costly to produce, and the hay of low quality. The grazings, too, are fibrous and the grazing season generally short, although a limited proportion of lower ground, the in-bye land, may have better grass. These are conditions that largely prohibit commercial dairying and cattle fattening, limiting livestock production mainly to those systems that will use the limited winter roughage feeds and in-bye grazings to best advantage without over-dependence on the rougher grazings, but using them as fully as possible in the short growing season. Ewes can do this with their growing lambs grazing the rough in summer. When the lambs are weaned and set off—many for fattening elsewhere—the demands on grazings are reduced markedly again. The ewes can be maintained cheaply much of the rest of the year on these grazings and only allowed to use in-bye grazings, and expensive feeding perhaps at flushing and tupping time, in late pregnancy, and for a few weeks after lambing. So sheep are the main users of the roughest land in agricultural use. The production of single suckled weaned calves for growing on and finishing else-where for beef, is similar in the seasonality of its demands but requires better conditions for plant growth and winter feeding-stuff production. In Scotland, it is common to refer to these somewhat better conditions as upland, as against the hill conditions where sheep predominate. Better again than the upland are rearing farms, with less rough grazing, more of their land tilled, and on some, particularly in Aberdeenshire and Orkney, pigs and poultry.

* These difficulties are not so great in much of Sweden, where the forests were not so fully converted long ago into farms lands, where farmers have been able to practise continuous forestry with more even flows over the years of expenditure and income, and where there is good training in the work for them. In Britain in contrast, where a large initial investment is required to establish a forest but the major benefits will not be forthcoming for perhaps 30 years, the financing problem is substantially different.

The official classifications of farms according to the total standard man-day tasks indicated by their June census statistics of land use and stocking, and the distribution of these tasks amongst the different crops and stock, permit some statistical assessment of choices of product on what we have called remote upland. Summaries for Scotland are set out in Tables 1.4 and 1.5. If for our present purposes we include the rearing classes indicated as well as the hill in what we call upland, it appeared that upland farming covered 77 per cent of the agricultural land area of full-time farms, but had only 12 per cent of the potatoes, 5 per cent of the dairy cows, and 26 per cent of the pigs. But they had 57 per cent of the beef cows and 22 per cent of the ewes. The part and spare-time farms are mainly in our upland areas. They are numerous but had in 1962 only the following percentages of the totals on full-time farms:

Total area	16	Dairy cows	3	Pigs	5
Potatoes	9	Beef cows	9	Fowls	19
		Ewes	12.		

Trends in land use and stocking are of importance to our discussion because they indicate responses to changing technical knowledge, market prices, and government interventions, and we can compare these responses in the uplands as against those in other areas. Table 1.6 summarises briefly trends in Wales and the Highlands of Scotland, and in the north-east of Scotland which includes substantial areas of upland and rearing farms. Trends are also shown for all Scotland and for England. The trends most significant in relation to our present purposes have been the decreases in the uplands of the area tilled, with no marked increase in the grass area—even a decrease in the Scottish Highlands. Increases in the upland have been substantial in beef cows and other cattle, although in Wales and the Highlands these have been smaller than in Scotland as a whole. Increases in sheep in the upland have been smaller than those for cattle but markedly greater than increases in sheep elsewhere. Pigs and poultry have tended to fall as compared with numbers elsewhere although the north-east of Scotland has greatly increased pig production.

The basic price changes causing these responses are, in essence, summarised in Table 1.7. Fat cattle have risen in sale value to farmers more than agricultural products as a group but have fallen much in value in terms of urban labour. Fat lambs have since the mid 1950s maintained their value in terms of agricultural products

Table 1.6. *Trends in land use and stocking, Great Britain 1938 to 1967* (a)

			Scotland			
		Wales	High-lands (b)	North east (c)	All	England
			index numbers, 1938 = 100			
Land use—areas						
Tillage	1953	183	91	112	114	146
	1967	107	76	94	101	153
Grass	1953	85	96	87	88	80
	1967	96	92	103	91	76
Stocking—numbers of stock						
Cows	1953	124	111	120	122	109
	1967	152	143	176	161	119
Other cattle	1953	116	119	121	126	122
	1967	150	139	160	157	138
Ewes	1953	89	114	77	93	67
	1967	126	130	100	104	106
Other sheep	1953	96	113	87	96	78
	1967	148	129	101	108	110
Pigs, total	1953	106	184	215	194	110
	1967	119	116	388	204	164
Poultry, total	1953	116	127	158	125	121
	1967	89	56	98	116	184
Land use in 1967			*million acres*			
Tillage		0·32	0·11	0·49	1·52	10·00
Grass		2·31	0·28	0·73	2·78	11·70
Stocking in 1967			*thousand head*			
Cows, dairy		348	18	40	330	2281
Cows, beef		138	66	111	354	458
Other cattle		802	121	447	1401	4903
			million head			
Ewes		2·56	1·14	0·40	3·51	5·42
Other sheep		3·72	1·29	0·62	4·73	8·78
Pigs, total		0·27	0·01	0·23	0·51	5·51
Poultry, total		4·01	0·34	2·91	8·93	95·20

Sources: *Agricultural Statistics for Scotland*, and *Agricultural Statistics for England and Wales*.

(a) So far as possible the livestock data are three-year averages centred on the Junes of 1938 1953 and 1967.
(b) Argyll, Inverness, Ross and Cromarty, Sutherland and Shetland.
(c) Kincardine, Aberdeen, Banff, Moray, Nairn, Caithness, Orkney.

as a group but are now valued at only half as much urban labour as during the mid 1950s. So cattle have been favoured through prices more than sheep, but the output of both have become cheap in terms of urban labour.

The Government interventions have tended to reflect these basic

Table 1.7. *Values of gross returns to farmers for fat cattle and lambs, United Kingdom*

	In terms of:		
	Agricultural products	Manufactured goods, wholesale	Men's weekly earnings in manufacturing industries
	1954–5 to 1955–6 = 100		
Fat cattle			
1965–6	123	101	70
1966–7	120	97	68
1967–8	126	102	69
Fat lambs			
1965–6	101	83	57
1966–7	99	80	56
1967–8	99	81	54

Sources: Index numbers from *Agricultural Statistics* and *Annual Abstract of Statistics*.

Table 1.8. *Government payments, to farmers, crofters and agricultural estate owners, in relation to sale value of agricultural output, Scotland 1966–7 to 1968–9*

	Cattle	Sheep, wool	Cattle, sheep, wool	All Agriculture
	£ million per year			
Sale value of output	48·3	19·8	68·1	188·0
Deficiency payments	4·7	3·7	8·4	22·7
Total	53·0	23·5	76·5	210·7
Other Government payments for current operations (*b*)				
Wholly or mainly for hills and uplands				
Cows, ewes	4·39	3·39	7·78	7·78
Winter keep	1·63	0·43	2·06	2·06
Crofters cropping, etc.	na	na	0·50	0·50
Ploughing up grass	na	na	0·79	0·79
Calf rearing (*a*)	3·02	—	3·02	3·02
Sub total	9·04+	3·82+	14·15	14·15
General				
Calf rearing (*a*), lowland cows	2·43	—	2·43	2·43
Small farmers scheme	na	na	na	0·34
Fertilisers, lime	na	na	na	5·98
Other 'relevant'	na	na	na	0·16
Sub total	2·43+	na	2·43+	8·91

Improvement and other grants				
Wholly or mainly for hills and uplands				
Crofters	na	na	0·29	0·29
Livestock rearing and hill land	na	na	0·44	0·44
Sub total	na	na	0·73	0·73
General				
Farm improvements	na	na	na	1·73
Drainage	na	na	na	0·31
Structure improvements	na	na	na	0·03
Other	na	na	na	0·10
Sub total	na	na	na	2·17
Total Government payments				
Wholly or mainly for hills and uplands	9·04+	3·82+	14·88	14·88
General	na	na	na	11·08
Total	na	na	na	25·96

Sources: Based on Department of Agriculture for Scotland—*Annual Reports* and *Scottish Agricultural Economics.*

(*a*) The total payments have been allocated here to hills and uplands according to the ratio of cows eligible for hill cow subsidy to total calves on which subsidy was paid. This ration was 3 : 5.
(*b*) Counted in February reviews of agricultural incomes and prices.
na Amounts not available.

price movements. Deficiency payments have been relatively high on sheep compared with other products. And for sheep and cattle together, and particularly for those in the hills and upland, the share of other grants has been exceptionally high (Table 1.8). Improvement grants largely for longer-term capital assets have been much smaller than other payments. Total Government payments have become a large part of the gross income of hill, upland, and rearing farms and a still larger part of their net farm incomes (Table 1.9). Without these interventions the marked increase in stocking that have taken place, and particularly the increase in cattle (Table 1.6), would probably not have been brought about.

No major change in price trends for beef and lamb are expected by 1975.[4] But it has to be recognised that in this country the price elasticities of demand for fat cattle and lambs are low.*

* Thus fat cattle prices fall by about 0·8 per cent when a 1 per cent increase in supplies is to be absorbed.

Table 1.9. *Outputs, grants and costs on different types of farm*
'Hill Sheep, 'Upland' and 'Rearing Farms', Scotland 1966-7 and 1967-8
Livestock Farms, England and Wales 1967-8

	Hill sheep	Upland	Rearing, with		Livestock	
			Arable	Intensive livestock	Mostly sheep	Cattle and sheep
Number of farms	72	70	95	18	99	237
Acreages			*acres per farm*			
Crops, Grass	58	167	160	89	117	179
Total	3238	1004	278	102	459	270
			days/farm/year			
Standard man day tasks	871	893	856	637	826	709
Gross output (d)			*£ per farm*		(a)	(a)
Cattle	505	1553	2041	1090	1139	3078
Sheep, wool	2854	1806	1004	229	2048	1520
Other livestock	55	109	655	2612	604	374
Crop and miscellaneous	81	507	1208	1094	532	1018
Total	3495	3975	4909	5025	4323	5990
Production grants (e)						
Hill cattle	227	584	276	82		
Calf	135	362	278	124		
Hill sheep	997	294	51	11	(a)	(a)
Winter keep	133	228	103	32		
Ploughing up	12	47	59	28		
Fertilisers, lime	64	172	189	114		
Other	18	64	68	94		
Total	1596	1751	1024	485	42(c)	36(c)
Total	5091	5726	5932	5510	4365	6026
Costs						
Fertilisers	206	620	691	422	215(a)	351(a)
Feed	858	721	850	1458	838	866
Seed	33	154	158	137	97	129
Rent and rates	421	427	393	322	415	623
Machinery and power	512	1002	1018	894	694	974
Labour (b)	1394	1266	1141	678	651	896
Other	612	635	604	442	382	514
Total	4036	4825	4855	4353	3292	4353
Net farm income	1055	901	1077	1157	1073	1673
To tenant's capital at 5 per cent	468	516	442	291	331	451
Remainder for farmers and wives work and management	587	385	635	866	742	1222

Sources: Based on data in *Scottish Agricultural Economics* and *Farm Incomes in England and Wales*.

(a) Most grants included in output of cattle and sheep. Fertiliser subsidy deducted from fertiliser costs.   (b) Excluding that of farmer and wife.   (c) Based on capital estimates for 1967-8 only.   (d) Including deficiency payments.   (e) For current operations, see previous table.

FACTOR COMBINATIONS

Increased productivity in British agriculture as a whole has been achieved largely by the use of more and better machinery, fertilisers, seeds, and other inputs such as pesticides, veterinary preparations etc. Between the mid 1950s and late 1960s the *quantum* of such inputs was raised 26 per cent and, if we include imported feeding stuffs and related services, 30 per cent. The *quantum* of gross output was raised 32 per cent, and the net output 44 per cent. Yet a large part of the total labour force on farms was released. Comparable statistics for upland farming are not available during this period but it is clear that, despite Government interventions and the increases in cattle and sheep numbers (Table 1.6), the net returns to farmers are still relatively low (Table 1.10). At first sight the inputs

Table 1.10   *Cost structures in upland farming and all agriculture*
Two-year average 1966–7 and 1967–8

	Purchased inputs (a)		Rent and Rates	Labour (b)	Net farm income	
	Excluding feeds	Including feeds			Return to tenant's capital (a)	Return to farmer and wife (d)
Scotland (g)		£ per £100 gross output (e)				
Hill sheep	26	43	8	28	9	12
Upland rearing	40	53	8	23	9	7
Rearing, with:						
Arable	40	54	7	20	8	11
Intensive						
livestock	33	60	6	13	5	16
England and Wales—						
Livestock (f) (g)						
Mostly sheep	32	51	9	15	8	17
United Kingdom						
All agriculture	27	50	8	16	6	20

Sources: As for Table 1.9 and *Annual Abstract of Statistics.*
  (a) Machinery use costs (excluding interest on capital) fertilisers, seeds, feeds, and other.
  (b) Excluding farmer and his wife.
  (c) Calculated simply at 5 per cent. Total for U.K. based on ratio of tenant's capital in Farm Management Survey Scheme reports to net output and to 'labour' costs.
  (d) Remainder figure as return to management and manual labour of farmer and his wife.
  (e) Excluding from gross output purchases of livestock bought and transport costs thereon.
  (f) 1967–8 only.
  (g) Farms in Farm Management Survey Scheme.

(including feed) used per £100 gross output may look quite up to modern standards—indeed higher than in U.K. agriculture as a whole—and rents not too high. But overall efficiency is relatively low as shown by small net returns to farmers and their wives for labour and management when 5 per cent is accounted as return on their capital. At higher returns allowed for capital, the net returns for labour and management would be even smaller. The basic data for these conclusions refer to full-time farms studied by the Scottish Agricultural Colleges: they are not as a group small nor badly run farms.

Two conclusions emerge (a) that it is especially difficult in practice to apply modern scientific knowledge and new agricultural techniques economically in farming the uplands and (b) despite high rates of saving-investment by farmers and substantial grants and other interventions from Government, the uplands have tended not to keep pace in international competition and inter-regional competition within the UK.

Nonetheless it is equally clear that substantial improvements in overall efficiency are possible, and at least as much by more knowledgeable, able and close management* as by major increases in the total of costly inputs. The climatic and other basic conditions of production outlined at the start of this chapter limit the economic capacity per acre for inputs and require such management. Many

Table 1.11. *Comparison of high and low performance farm businesses*
Scotland two year average 1966–7 and 1967–8

	Hill farming		Upland rearing		Rearing with arable	
	Low performance	High	Low performance	High	Low performance	High
Number of farms (a)	18	18	18	18	23	23
Size of business						
(Standard man days)	787	826	892	878	854	923
Area of farm (acres)	2639	3972	1204	829	244	291
Rent, rates (£)	423	355	498	383	397	393
Labour employed (b)(£)	1402	1176	1503	964	1333	1214
Other inputs (b)						
Excluding feed	1155	942	2540	1721	2340	2552
Including feed	2072	1452	3247	2465	3018	3497
Net output	3166	4233	3897	4804	3885	6030
Net farm income	218	1778	−469	1852	−23	2045

Source: As for Table 1.9.
(a) Farms grouped by two year averages.
(b) Excluding work and management of farmer and wife. Fertiliser costs net of subsidy.

* Skilled and close management includes, for example, careful decisions on (a) what qualities of weaned calf and lamb to aim at, (b) types of breeding stock, (c) grazing densities and control, (d) in-bye land fertilisation and use, (e) flushing and spring feeding of ewes, separate arrangements for older ewes, (f) fencing and handling equipment, (g) parasite control.

farmers have already shown what it can achieve (Table 1.11), and special knowledge to help them is slowly increasing.

SIZE OF BUSINESS

Table 1.4 shows that large numbers of the agricultural units in upland areas are part-time and spare-time, i.e. not requiring the year's work of one man working under more normal conditions. Table 1.12 indicates briefly in other ways the structure of upland agriculture.

Table 1.12. *Frequency distributions according to sizes of ewe flock, beef cow herd and numbers of full-time workers*
Highland region Scotland, June 1967

Breeding ewes per holding range	Number of holdings	Beef Cows per holding range	Number of units	Full time workers per holding range	Number of holdings
	hundred		*hundred*		*hundred*
Nil	79	Nil	128	Nil	173
1– 24	41	1– 5	39	1	9
25– 49	31	6– 9	8	2	5
50– 99	21	10–19	8	3	2
100– 199	9	20	4	4	1
200– 299	3	30	2	5– 6	1
300– 499	4	40	1	7– 9	1
500– 699	2	50	1	10–19	+
700– 999	1	60	+	20 and over	–
1000–1999	1	70	+		
2000 and over	+	80	+		
		100 and over	1		
	192		192		192

+ Less than 51.
Source: DOAFS *Agricultural Statistics*, 1967.

Most data relate to 'full-time' units and as mentioned earlier these are responsible for most of the total production.

The larger the full-time farm businesses as measured by the labour required for normal working (standard man days) the greater the net return to farmers and their wives for their labour and management (Table 1.13), but the greater also the requirements of capital, management, and risk and uncertainty bearing. We must tread carefully if we are to judge from the cross-sectional data available the extent to which, under different policies, changes in structure

Table 1.13. *Relation of net returns to size of business*
Scotland 1967–8

1 Size of Business	2 Hill sheep	3 Upland rearing	4 5 Rearing. with Arable Intensive livestock		6 Mixed (b)	7 Averages Columns 2, 3 and 4
Standard man days			*standard man days*			
275–599	465	439	456	415	542	453
600–1199	793	857	845	1222	880	832
1200 and over (c)	1638	1937	1942	—	1474	1839
1800 and over	...	...	...	...	3092	...
			£ tenant's capital per farm at 5 per cent			
275–599	228	255	218	182	274	234
600–1199	432	501	461	573	490	465
1200 and over (c)	904	1101	1001	—	730	1002
1800 and over	...	...	...	...	1641	...
			£ return to farmer and wife (a)			
275–599	725	383	788	749	1321	632
600–1199	789	940	844	1552	1335	858
1200 and over (c)	1161	465	1183	—	3268	936
1800 and over	...	...	...	...	4967	...

Source: Scottish Agricultural Economics, Vol. XIX, 1969.

(a) For labour and management.
(b) England and Wales from *Farm Incomes in England and Wales 1967*.
(c) 1200 to 1799 for mixed group.

(i.e. in the distribution of upland farms according to size groupings) would be achievable and economic. Considering together the data for 'Hill sheep', 'Upland rearing' and 'Rearing with arable farming' groups in Scotland (Table 1.13), to expand from an average small full-time business with standard man day requirements of 453 days to a larger one requiring 1839 days (306 per cent more) would require some £15,360 (330 per cent) more tenant's capital but raise net returns to the farmer and his wife for labour and management from £632 a year by only £304 a year (48 per cent) to £936. Even this would be substantially less than the net returns to farmers and their wives for labour and management on the smaller 'mixed' full-time farms in England and Wales (Table 1.13). And if more than 5 per cent is accounted as annual return on tenant capital, increasing sizes of upland farms would look less attractive. Also, the additional capital required in reasonable amalgamation arrangements would be substantial, as is now recognised in Government grants. These are basic reasons why the changes in structure are fairly slow (Table 1.14). If they are to be speeded, more positive steps will be

Table 1.14. *Reductions in numbers of agricultural holdings and workers*
Selected Areas, Britain, June 1965–8

	Full-time (a) workers	Holdings
	per cent per year (b)	
Scotland		
Regions		
Highlands	8·4	0·8
North-east	7·5	1·3
Counties		
Shetland	9·7	1·0
Orkney	8·5	0·8
Inverness	9·4	0·4
Selkirk	7·8	1·0
England and Wales		
Counties		
Merioneth	7·7	3·1
Radnor	2·8	2·8
England	5·8	1·9
Wales	4·2	1·5
Scotland	7·8	0·6

Source: Agricultural Statistics for Scotland, and Agricultural Statistics for
England and Wales.
(a) Excluding farmer and wife.
(b) For workers, one third of the 1965 to 1968 change as per cent of 1965 figure. For holdings
one half of the 1965 to 1967 change as per cent of 1965 figure.

required in appropriate finance and estate management. But these
alone may not be enough. Better and more closely applied skills in
management are desirable on many farms apart from changes
simply in size of business.

There is not time enough here to discuss adequately the large
numbers of part-time and spare-time farms of upland Scotland. A
recent study[5] has shown that of the holdings with between 100 and
350 standard man days labour requirement 64 per cent were occupied
by persons aged 50 or more.[6] The comparable percentage for all
agriculture and crofting in Scotland is 52. Over half the holdings
(54 per cent) were considered incapable of 'giving full-time employment to at least one man', but of this 54 per cent only about half
(48 per cent) were occupied by persons with any work other than
farming. Thus it is clear, first, that the scales of value of many
present occupiers are reflected in a comparatively low demand for
material incomes. Second, to attempt to raise material incomes to
commoner levels by agricultural activities alone would require
major structural changes and much depopulation. What must need

development are the job opportunities outside agriculture, and very careful thought about their type and location and training for them. Some at least may enable rural folk to remain in rural homes if they so wish. Lewis and the Harris tweed industry with others have pioneered the way.

SOCIAL ASPECTS

These matters bring us to problems in logistics. But because of the wide variations in the productivity and capability of land and related climates, average input and output data per square mile may be very misleading for agricultural and pastoral production.

Table 1.15 *Input and output data for full time farming*
Hill sheep, Upland and Rearing Farms, Scotland 1966–7 and 1967–8.
Livestock Farms, England and Wales 1967–8 (a)

	Hill sheep	Upland	Rearing, with		Livestock:	
			Arable	Intensive livestock	Mostly sheep	Cattle and sheep
	number per 500 square miles (b)					
Number of farms (a)	99	319	1150	3109	697	1186
	£ thousand per year per 500 square miles					
Machinery use, power	51	320	1171	2780	486	1159
Fertilisers (c)	20	198	785	1312	150	418
Seed	3	49	182	4262	68	153
Other, excluding feed	61	203	695	1375	267	612
Feed	85	230	978	4534	586	1031
	220	1000	3811	10,427	1557	3373
Social Output						
Rent and rates	42	136	452	1001	290	741
Labour—paid (d)	138	404	1312	2109	456	1066
—farmer and wife	58	123	730	2693	519	1454
Tenant's capital at 5 per cent	46	165	508	905	232	537
Total	284	828	3002	6708	1497	3798
Gross output	504	1828	6812	17,135	3054	7171

Source: Based on data in *Scottish Agricultural Economics* and *Farm Incomes in England and Wales.*

(a) Based on data for full-time farms in Table 9 and subject therefore to any sampling errors.
(b) 320 thousand acres. If there were one 'centre' for each 500 square mile unit, centres would be fully 22 miles apart on average.
(c) Gross cost.
(d) I.e. excluding farmer and wife.

Moreover, the local activities economically related to this production (e.g. transport, marketing, machine repair services, banking, etc.) are difficult to assess reliably. Some indications for full-time farming are, however, set out in Table 1.15. These are from the farm management scheme data and so refer to the farm position and not to that of the whole locality and community.

SUMMARY

Upland farming in remote areas has achieved during the last fifteen years substantial expansion of the outputs of cattle and sheep of importance in the total fatstock and meat industry of the UK. But the present state of upland farming is not to be judged sound by ordinary economic criteria. In particular, some sections appear to be heading towards a shortage of wage-paid employees, and the material incomes of self-employed farmers and their wives are relatively low despite heavy government payments and intervention.

For the future there are major opportunities to improve the economic performance of full-time upland farms through more able, tighter management and the development of new knowledge for use in such management, but unfavourable natural endowments and price relationships limit the economic capacity per unit area for greater inputs.

Higher material incomes, if they are to come from upland farming itself, would therefore have to depend quite largely on reducing the number of farmers, i.e. on amalgamations of farms. In this, however, the net gains in the short-run may not be judged attractive enough to secure the finance required and induce the additional work and uncertainty bearing on the part of the remaining farmers. Much turns on the supplies of family labour, close management, and capital: outside capital is unlikely to be forthcoming, except through Government intervention.

Neither amalgamations nor closer management, even with some additional inputs, will provide major increases in the average material income of the bulk of the total populations of the remote upland areas, including crofters and other part-time farmers. Shifts out of farming will continue. But further increases in job opportunities, correctly located and serviced with appropriate training, etc., as in Lewis and Harris, may well be judged important to the welfare of remote areas, and probably to our nation as a whole.

B

Comparisons of farming and forestry and services to tourism, etc., have not been made here. Sharp, meaningful comparisons are particularly difficult because of measurement, heterogeneity, and time scale problems, and because little of the countryside is likely to be best used economically and socially if in single-purpose use.

REFERENCES

1. Air Ministry, *Climatological Atlas of the British Isles*. HMSO, London. 1952.
2. Stamp, L. Dudley, *The Land of Britain: its use and misuse*. London, Longmans, 1962.
3. The decrease in the 'length of the growing season' is given for North England and South Scotland as 4 days per 100 feet rise in elevation (Coloyne, R. W. (1951) *Agriculture Memo 18* (Paper in Meteorological Office), but there are variations in this ratio with the aspects, etc.
4. *Agricultural Commodities Projections for 1975 and 1985*. FAO, 1967.
5. Dunn, J. M., 'Some features of small full-time and large part-time farms in Scotland.' *Scot. Agric. Econ.* XIX, pp. 205–220, 1969.
6. Averages for Shetland Orkney, Caithness, North-West, and Argyll.

2 | Forestry and the Forest Industries

PROFESSOR J. D. MATTHEWS, B.Sc., F.R.S.E.
M. S. PHILIP, M.B.E., M.A., B.Sc.
D. G. CUMMING, B.Sc.
University of Aberdeen, Department of Forestry

In his paper for the conference mounted by the Agricultural Adjustment Unit in January 1967, Grayson[1] (1967) described forestry in Britain and gave facts and figures to demonstrate the economic status of the industry. This chapter will attempt to add to the information provided by Grayson and to answer several questions about forestry in the remoter rural areas of Britain, namely:

1. What is the national policy concerning forestry and the forest industry in the remoter rural areas?
2. What area of land is available for afforestation and what is a suitable rate of planting?
3. What are the requirements of manpower for forestry and the ancillary industries?
4. What has been the experience with forest villages?
5. What are the present and future relationships between agriculture and forestry?
6. What future developments in forestry and the forest industries are needed?

THE EVOLUTION OF FOREST POLICY

Two lessons of the First World War were the importance of wood to the modern industrial economy and the need for home sources of wood in an emergency. The Forestry Commission was formed in 1919 to create new forests, encourage private forestry, and help to maintain an efficient timber trade; and thus the rebuilding of the depleted forest resource began. During the Second World War further massive fellings of mature and semi-mature trees to meet the demands of the war effort re-inforced the argument for replanting to maintain a strategic reserve of wood in Britain. The work recommenced in 1945, and 1969 marks the completion of fifty years of planting and replanting by Forestry Commission and private foresters in the remoter rural areas of Britain. This is, therefore, a good time to review the past and present role of forestry and the forest industries in the development of the remoter rural areas, and to make proposals for the future.

Forest policy has been examined on several occasions since the report, 60 years ago, of the Royal Commission on Coast Erosion[2] which criticised the unsatisfactory state of British woodlands and proposed a programme of afforestation to convert 'comparatively unprofitable lands into forests' and 'stem the tide of rural depopulation'. The Forestry Sub-Committee appointed in 1916 to consider and report on the best means of conserving and developing the forest resources of the nation, recommended the afforestation of 1·77 million acres to safeguard the supplies of timber in time of war and 'cause large areas of the United Kingdom, now almost waste, o be put to their best economic use'.[3]

Coming forward to the Second World War, the Report on Post-War Forest Policy[4] asserted 'It is necessary to envisage what area of forest Britain requires and how it should be managed. The Report proposes that the Nation should make up its mind at this stage to devote five million acres to the purpose. That area is required for national safety and will also provide a reasonable insurance against future stringency in world supplies. There are also valuable contingent advantages associated with forests, such as the development and settlement of rural Britain'. The Report goes on 'The five million acres should not merely be planted with trees but also systematically managed and developed. This conception entails among other things the continuous application of good silviculture, the development of markets and internal transport and the settlement of forest workers in a good environment.'

A report published in 1957[5] examined the problems relating to forestry and agriculture in our marginal lands, and advocated 'the integration of agriculture and forestry' and 'structural improvement in agricultural units.' The report also drew attention to 'the growing importance of recreation and tourism in the countryside and the need for more advice and general knowledge about forestry matters to be brought to bear upon the farming community.' It considered that 'It is in the marginal hill areas that suitable tracts exist for the afforestation which is required in the national interest.'

Nine years later the Natural Resources (Technical) Committee re-examined the question of forestry, agriculture and the multiple use of rural land (Department of Education and Science, 1966) and concluded: 'Defence considerations have faded but an expanding and vigorous private and national forest estate is important to home industry, especially in view of the forecast of world shortage of timber by the turn of the century.'[6]

The Report[7] of the Advisory Panel on the Highlands and Islands of Scotland (D.A.F.S., 1964) emphasised that 'Agriculture and forestry remain the vital "key" means of achieving economic improvement and providing local employment. They must be co-ordinated,' and later, 'An imaginative and sustained programme of afforestation over the next twenty years is not only possible, but necessary.'

In 1958 and 1963 the size of the Forestry Commissioners programme and the structure of grants to private woodland owners were reviewed. After the 1963 review and the Minister of Agriculture's Statement in Parliament, the Forestry Commissioners published the following summary of their policy[8]:

1. To increase the production of wood as a raw material for industry by extending the area of their forests at a steady rate, in accordance with sound land use; and by making each forest as productive as possible.
2. Within the limits set by their other objectives to manage the forest estate as profitably as possible.
3. To provide employment in rural areas, especially those affected by depopulation, and in so doing to maintain a skilled labour force.
4. To help in maintaining an efficient home timber trade.
5. To give due attention to the aesthetic and protective roles of the forest and to encourage open air recreation.
6. To foster industrial and social development ancillary to forestry.
7. To encourage the orderly development of private forestry and specifically to assist in creating conditions in which produce from private as well as Commission forests can be marketed to best advantage.

The Forestry Act of 1967[9] consolidated the Acts enacted between 1919 and 1963 and charged the Forestry Commissioners with the general duty of promoting:

1. the interests of forestry;
2. the development of afforestation;
3. the production and supply of timber, and other forest products; and
4. the establishment and maintenance in Great Britain of an adequate reserve of growing trees.

Thus the main role of forestry and forest industries in Britain is to contribute to the National need for wood and wood products but modern forest policy also recognises the need for close integration of forestry with agriculture and other forms of land use, and the value of forests in providing employment, giving shelter against wind and snow to men, crops and animals, protecting water supplies, offering facilities for sport and recreation, and improving the amenity of the countryside. All these benefits can be seen to best advantage in the remoter rural areas of Britain.

LAND AVAILABLE FOR FORESTRY AND RATE OF PLANTING

Many estimates have been made in the succession of Government reports since 1909 of the area of land that could be planted to trees in Britain. Because this section of the chapter deals with the land available for forestry in the remoter rural areas and must therefore include consideration of land known as 'rough grazing' the discussion which follows is based on the summary analysis of the major uses of land given in the Report of the Land Use Study Group.[6] The figures are presented in Table 2.1.

Table 2.1. *Major uses of land in Britain, 1960*
Millions of acres

Type of use	England and Wales	Scotland	Great Britain
1. Agriculture	(29·4)	(16·9)	(46·3)
(i) Arable	13·7	3·4	17·1
(ii) Permanent grass	10·7	1·0	11·7
(iii) Rough grazing	5·0	12·5	17·5
2. Forests and woodlands	2·5	1·6	4·1
3. Urban development	4·0	0·5	4·5
4. Other	1·2	0·1	1·3
Totals	37·1	19·1	56·2

Source: Based on data from Report of the Land Use Study Group, Forestry, Agriculture and the Multiple Use of Rural Land. Department of Education and Science, H.M.S.O., 1966.

The recent analysis of agricultural statistics for Great Britain during the period 1866–1966[10] describes the changes in the estimated area of 'rough grazing' as being mainly due to variations in classification, but the currently accepted figure for rough grazing, mountain, heath, moor or down land in England and Wales lies between 4·8 and 5·0 million acres. In Scotland with a harsher climate and steep terrain two-thirds of the land is in 'rough grazings.' The term covers land with a wide physical range from the gentle, grassy hills of the Borders to extremely exposed bare rock in the West Highlands and the area of 12·5 million acres includes mountain, hill, moor and deer forest.

The authors of the Report of the Royal Commission on Coast Erosion[2] in 1909 considered that the approximate area available for afforestation 'without material encroachment upon agricultural land' was 8·5 million acres but the Sub-Committee on Forestry[3] which reported in 1918 thought that an area between 4 and 5 million acres was more realistic. The experience gained by the Forestry Commissioners between the two world wars enabled them to be more precise in their estimate and in the Report on Post-War Forest Policy[4] they considered that '5 million acres of effective forest can be secured, as to 3 million acres by the afforestation of bare ground and as to 2 million acres from existing woodlands.' The year 1947 was the first year of this programme which was to be completed in fifty years, that is, by the end of this century. By 1957 however the planting programme of the Forestry Commission was being delayed by the difficulty of acquiring suitable land, and the Natural Resources (Technical) Committee re-examined the situation. They estimated that 'More than 4 million acres of rough grazing are suitable for afforestation. Much of this is on livestock hill farms, but areas of coppice and commons also provide opportunities for forestry.'[5]

Table 2.2 summarises the distribution of productive forests in Britain in 1966. Seventy per cent of the Forestry Commission plantations have been formed on upland heaths, moors and bogs, that is, on land classed as 'rough grazing.'

Unfortunately it is not possible to give a close estimate of the area of privately-financed planting on such land but it can be suggested that the total area of plantations on land formerly bare of trees and originally classed as 'rough grazing' is at least 1·25 million acres.

Thus if we accept the opinion of the Natural Resources (Technical)

Table 2.2. *Distribution of productive woodlands in 1966*
Millions of acres

Country	Forestry Commission	Private Woodlands	Totals	Land area	Per cent Forested
England	0·58	1·14	1·72	32·0	5·4
Wales	0·29	0·14	0·43	5·1	8·4
Scotland	0·75	0·50	1·25	19·1	6·6
Great Britain	1·62	1·78	3·40	56·2	6·0

Source: Grayson, A. J. (1967), 'Forestry in Britain' in *Economic Change and Agriculture*, Oliver & Boyd, p. 171.

Committee in 1957[5] that 4 million acres of rough grazing are suitable for afforestation, there is still a very large area of land that can be planted in the remoter rural areas of Britain. Moreover, the target of 3 million acres of afforestation of bare ground proposed in the Report on Post-War Forest Policy[4] appears practical and feasible, especially because it includes the assumption that 'The loss to food production would be relatively small'.

It is appropriate at this stage to introduce a brief outline of forestry in different parts of rural Britain because the present situation and future prospects for planting differ greatly from one area to another. The mountainous parts of Western Scotland, the Lake District, Northern Wales and Dartmoor together form the *Western Mountains*. The rainfall is very high, the soil tends to be acid, shallow and infertile, and deposits of peat become more extensive and frequent the farther north one goes. The upper limit for planting is usually fixed by exposure to wind. Sitka spruce is the most important species and Lodgepole pine is useful on the poorer soils, but a wide range of conifers can be grown on the more sheltered and fertile sites. Sites in the *Western Mountains* are often expensive to plant and forest roads also are costly, but tree growth is good and markets for the wood exist in the forest industries. Attention must be given to landscaping when forming plantations in the *Western Mountains* and there is a rising demand for recreational facilities in these forests.

The 'upland' as distinct from the 'mountainous' parts of Britain must be divided into three main areas because of important differences in climate, soils and vegetation. The *Drier Uplands* include much land in Northern, North-eastern and Central Scotland, the eastern parts of the Scottish Border country, the Pennines and some of the drier parts of Central Wales and the Welsh Marches. The rainfall does not exceed 40 inches and the vegetation usually consists of poor mountain grassland with fescue, *Agrostis* and *Nardus*. Much of the ground is too dry for spruces and the main species are Scots pine and the larches. Douglas fir is common on the best sites. There are very extensive areas of land in the *Drier Uplands* that could be afforested but hill sheep and cattle farming are well established, and although sawlogs can be marketed the outlets for small roundwood are often limited at present.

Where the rainfall exceeds 40 inches and the parent material consists of shaly rocks of the Silurian and Carboniferous systems, a situation very favourable to the growth of extensive spruce forest exists. The rolling grasslands of the *Moister Uplands* are found on the Scottish border and in central and Southern Wales. The soils are rather clayey, the vegetation is dominated by *Molinia* grass and drainage is very important. A good deal of this land has fallen out of sheep pasture and large areas of readily plantable land have been taken over by the Forestry Commission and private forestry companies drawing their funds from syndicates of owners. The *Moister Uplands* are not very remote from good roads and markets and spruce plantations are recognised as a good investment. The main hazard is premature windthrow.

The *Upland Heaths* form a special and important type of site which is most extensive in North-East Scotland. The soil is usually acid and often very compacted and the dominant element in the vegetation is *Calluna vulgaris*. The *Upland Heaths* require cultivation by ploughing to suppress the heather, open up the sub-soil and break any pan. Pines are the principal species either pure or in a mixture with spruces. The most fertile *Upland Heaths* are also the best grouse moors and the lower sites are often ploughed and reseeded for agriculture. Thus in North-East Scotland the allocation of land to agriculture, forestry and sport has been almost static for many years and any expansion of forestry must be at the expense of agriculture or sport or both.

In summary it can be said that the value of forestry in the *Western Mountains* and *Moister Uplands* is well recognised and much land has been transferred from agriculture to forestry in these two areas. The allocation of land on the *Upland Heaths* appears static, although in North-East Scotland there are 0·75 million acres classed as 'rough grazing' and lying below 1,500 feet some of which could be planted with trees without serious loss to hill farming and grouse shooting.[10] It is in the *Drier Uplands* that the role of forests is less clear cut and much depends on the future development of hill farming.

Concerning broadleaved forests there are small stands scattered throughout the remoter rural areas of England, Wales and Scotland. If the timber is of good quality it can readily be marketed but lower grade material can only be sold as sawn mining timber, motorway fencing, flooring blocks and the like.

The area afforested has been greatest on land previously used for hill sheep farming (as already noted 70 per cent of Forestry Commission forests are on upland heaths, moors and bogs). The experience of the last fifty years has shown that afforestation in the *Western Mountains* and upland areas can usually be done without reduction of the numbers of sheep or cattle. Indeed the improvements in management of *Upland* farms have revealed ways of increasing the stocking of animals and in many remote rural areas the old antagonism between farmer and forester is being replaced by new patterns of integrated land use of benefit to both parties and the nation.

Between 1920 and 1939 the total area planted by Forestry Commission and private foresters increased steadily from 4,000 to 40,000 acres each year. There was a sharp drop to 10,000 acres during the war years 1939–45, followed by a steep rise after the Second World War. In 1961 the record figure of 100,000 acres was achieved. Since then the rate of planting has remained steady at around 88,000 acres each year.[11]

The area planted between 1920 and 1939 by the Forestry Commission alone rose steadily from 1,000 to 28,000 acres and then dropped to 6,000 acres during the Second World War. After that came a steep climb to around 70,000 acres in 1954 followed by a steady average of 55,000 acres since. Planting by private owners averaged 5,000 acres each year from 1920 to 1946 and then increased rapidly to 37,000 acres in 1961. The current figures average 37,000 acres. The rapid increase in planting by the private sector is believed to be mainly due to the system of grant aid and a helpful tax structure which gives an improved rate of return on the investment in plantations.

The current figure for total planting in Britain (around 88,000 acres) includes the restocking of cleared woodland, which is about

6,000 acres in Forestry Commission forests and about 20,000 acres on the private estates. Allowing for this the Forestry Commission adds each year around 49,000 acres to the total area under trees, while the private estates add 17,000 acres. The total annual addition, therefore, averages 66,000 acres.[11]

The Prime Minister announced in October 1967 that the planting programme for Scotland would rise from the then current level of 34,000 acres each year to 50,000 acres a year by 1976. Rankin[12] recently proposed the afforestation of 2·5 million acres of marginal hill land at about 70,000 acres annually for thirty-five years. The afforestation of 1·75 million acres of rough grazing land in the remoter rural areas of Britain at 60,000 acres annually for thirty years would take us to the target of 5 million acres proposed in the Report on Post-War Forest Policy in 1943.[4] The experience gained during the past half-century of forestry suggests that a sustained programme of afforestation by Forestry Commission and private foresters of between 60,000 and 70,000 acres each year would bring very great and lasting benefits to the remoter rural areas of Britain.

THE SUPPLY OF WOOD AND THE FOREST INDUSTRIES

Perhaps the strongest proof of the success of the forest policies conceived in 1918 and 1943 can be seen in the new pulp, paper and board mills and the enlarged sawmilling industry based on Britain. There are five major and several other centres where home grown wood is being processed into wood-based products on a large scale. In Scotland there are the pulp and paper mill and related sawmill at Cropach near Fort William in Inverness-shire, the long-established sawmilling industry throughout the country and the wood chipboard factories at Irvine and Annan. Moving south into England, there are in the north-west the mechanical pulp mill with integrated board and sawmills at Workington in Cumberland, the ground-wood pulp and paper mill at Ellesmere Port in Cheshire and, near by, the fibre building board mill at Queensferry. In the north-east of England, three wood chipboard factories (at Hexham, Wallsend and Stockton) draw their supplies of wood from the forests of the Border country and the Pennines. Farther south, the forests of South Wales and South-West England have markets for both broadleaved and coniferous roundwood in the semi-chemical hardwood pulpmill at Sudbrook in Monmouthshire, the St. Ann's board mill at Bristol, and three smaller plants producing moulded wood chipboard (at Coleford), wood chipboard (at Monmouth) and moulded wood fibre products (at Bristol). There are other industrial plants using home-grown wood but these do not necessarily draw their supplies from the remoter rural areas of Britain.

The building of the new pulp, paper and board mills noted above and listed in Table 2.3 has been closely tied to the present and potential production of the forests and for some years the Forestry

Table 2.3. *Industrial plants using home-grown wood*

Owners and location	Type of product	Source of wood
Scottish Pulp and Paper Mills, Corpach, Fort William	Chemical pulp mill with fine paper mill and sawmill.	Highland forests and imported hardwood chips.
Scotboard Ltd., Irvine	Wood chipboard.	
Airscrew Weyroc Ltd., Annan	Wood chipboard.	
Thames Board Mills Ltd., Workington	Mechanical pulp mill with board and saw-mill.	South Scotland and Northern England.
Airscrew Weyroc Ltd., Hexham	Wood chipboard.	
Tyboard (Formica Co. Ltd.), Wallsend	Wood chipboard.	
Hills Ltd., Stockton		Scottish Borders and the Pennines.
Bowaters (Mersey Division), Ellesmere Port	Groundwood pulpmill with newsprint mill.	South Scotland, North England and North Wales.
Powell Duffryn Timber Industries Ltd., Queensferry	Fibre building board (insulation board).	
Formwood Ltd., Coleford	Moulded wood chipboard.	
Flakeboard Ltd., Monmouth	Wood chipboard.	
Ashton Containers Ltd. Sudbrook	Semi-chemical hard-wood pulp mill with fluted paper mill.	South Wales and South-West England.
St. Ann's Board Mill Ltd., Bristol	Mechanical pulp mill with paper board mill.	
British Moulded Fibre Ltd., Bristol	Moulded wood fibre products.	
Airscrew Weyroc Ltd., Thetford and Marks Tey	Wood chipboard.	
P.I.M. Board Co. Ltd., Sunbury on Thames	Fibre building board.	East Anglia and South England.

Source: Dickson, J. A., 'Utilisation of Britain's Timber Resources', *Commonwealth Forestry Review*, 46, 2, 112–124, 1967.

Commission have prepared forecasts of the yield of wood in a manner that can be used by industrialists in designing and siting new plants and expanding existing ones.[13] The forecasts of production of small roundwood and sawlogs are based on sixteen regions[14] and these could be useful for the further planning of forestry development in the remoter rural areas.

It is of the nature of forestry that the future output of wood from Forestry Commission and private forests can be estimated with some certainty. Similarly the consumption of the pulpmills, chipboard mills, divisions of the National Coal Board and other users of roundwood can be predicted. The causes of uncertainty on each side of the account do not overlap and a balance between the two can be drawn. Three tables presented by Richards[15] summarise the situation during the next ten years in a very convenient way. Table 2.4 gives the potential production of softwoods (coniferous wood) during the decade 1970–1980.

Table 2.4. *Potential production of softwoods*
Million cubic feet (Hoppus)

Source	1967 (Actual)	Potential	1970	1980
Forestry Commission	(31)	32	37	72
Private forests	(16)	30	37	45
Total	(47)	62	74	117

Source: Richards, E. G. in 'Fifty Years On'. Supplement to *Forestry*, 53–55, 1969.

It will be seen (1) that the present production of softwood by private forests is about half the estimated potential production, and (2) the production of Forestry Commission forests (which are mainly in the remoter rural areas) will almost double between 1970 and 1980.

It is important in planning and supplying forest industries to know how much of the total production will be suitable for the sawmills (Sawlogs) and how much will be smaller material (Small roundwood). Table 2.5 shows the division expected during the decade 1970 to 1980.

Turning now to the needs of existing industrial plants and markets for small roundwood, reference back to Table 2.3 will show that industrial plants exist for the manufacture of chemical pulp for fine paper, mechanical pulp for newsprint, mechanical pulp and paper-

Table 2.5. *Division between small roundwood (R) and sawlogs (L)*
Million cubic feet (Hoppus)

Source	1967 (actual)			1970 potential			1980 potential		
	R	L	Total	R	L	Total	R	L	Total
Forestry Commission	(24)	(7)	(31)	25	12	37	45	27	72
Private forests	(7)	(9)	(16)	14	23	37	20	25	45
Total	(31)	(16)	(47)	39	35	74	65	52	117

Source: Richards, E. G. in 'Fifty Years on.' Supplement to *Forestry,* 53–55, 1969.

boards for cartons and for the manufacture of chipboard. To these
can be added the markets for pitwood, fencing wood, and other
small roundwood with the results shown in Table 2.6.

Table 2.6. *Needs of existing industrial plants and markets for small roundwood.*
Million cubic feet (Hoppus)

Market	1970	1980	Notes
Pulpwood	20	27	30 per cent increase 1970–80
Chipwood	6	8	30 per cent increase 1970–80
Pitwood	6	5	Greater use of home-grown wood will offset fall in total demand
Miscellaneous	6·5	7	Includes fencing wood
Totals	38·5	47	Potential production in 1980 65 million cubic feet

Source: Richards, E. G. in 'Fifty Years on'. Supplement to *Forestry,* 53–55, 1969.

It will be seen that the existing industrial plants and markets can
absorb 47 million of the 65 million cubic feet (Hoppus) of small
roundwood that will be available in 1980. The demand for small
roundwood in new industry or by expansion of the existing industry
is potentially very great and can easily absorb the surplus of 18
million cubic feet.

Attention must now be given to the potential markets for the
increased quantities of softwood (coniferous) sawlogs that will
become available between 1970 and 1980, especially from forests in
the remoter rural areas of Britain. Several important developments
must be noted. On the production side there are the improvements
in sawmilling technology (which permit acceptance of smaller
sawlogs) and the easier integration of sawmilling with pulp or chipboard manufacture. On the consumption side, factory mass-
produced roof trusses, partitions and structural components are

now in common use. This, when combined with the very great consumption of sawn softwood in Britain, means that the saw-millers who use home-grown softwood sawlogs will have a big opportunity to expand between 1970 and 1980.

The final point for discussion here is the importance of an improved system of roads for forestry in the remoter rural areas. Rankin[12] points out that seventy per cent of the cost of pulpwood into the mills consists of the cost of felling, extraction and delivery. Only 30 per cent remains for the grower. The proper siting of industry and the provision of adequate roads are thus vital to the economies of growing wood. Davidson[16] provides an analysis of how more efficient use can be made of existing roads but also reveals the low capacity of roads in the remoter rural areas of Britain.

THE DEMAND FOR MANPOWER

It has been customary in the past to base calculations of the number of people, including supervisors, directly employed in planting, tending and harvesting forests in the ratio of 10 men per 1,000 acres (or 1 man per 100 acres). This ratio is applicable to fully productive forests where plantings are balanced by fellings of mature trees, but because the productivity of woodmen engaged in planting has risen in recent years and our forests are relatively young and still producing well below their potential yield of wood, the current figure in Britain is nearer 7 men per 1,000 acres (1 man per 140 acres). This is a possible ratio to use in the remoter rural areas of Britain but although this ratio is useful, the actual figures for individual forests and regions of Britain deviate greatly from it and the main causes of this variation are described by Jeffers,[17] Wardle[18] and Philip.[19] The important factors influencing the number of men employed on a forest unit include:

1. the size of the unit and especially the area under plantations, the reserve of land still to be planted, whether the plantations are in large blocks (fewer men) or smaller scattered blocks (more men) and the amount of tending required;
2. the size of duration of the planting programme, the nature of the terrain (whether flat and easy or steep and difficult) and the mechanisation of ground preparation and planting;
3. the volume of timber to be cut and whether it is to be sold

standing to a merchant or harvested by the forest or estate staff;

4. the size of nursery or sawmill or other additional enterprises associated with the forest unit.

Jeffers shows figures for Forestry Commission forests ranging from 5 to 10 men per 1,000 acres while Philip *et al.* examined the records of a stratified random sample of fifty private estates in Scotland and obtained figures ranging from 4 to 8 men per 1,000 acres. One very important feature which emerges from these investigations of the manpower requirements of forestry is that estimates of the demand must be made for each afforestation scheme and a generalised ratio such as that suggested in this chapter (7 men per 1,000 acres) can lead to over- or under-estimation of the value of forestry as a source of employment in the remoter rural areas. Thus Steven[20] shows that on the change from extensive pastoral agriculture to forestry in the North-West Highlands of Scotland, employment increases five to six times, but there may be little alteration in the number of men employed per 1,000 acres in the change from agriculture to forestry in some parts of Central Wales.[6]

A second important point is that the decline in population can be reversed by large concentrated blocks of forest. This is demonstrated by two examples from Galloway[21] and the North Cheviot[22] hills respectively. The Forestry Commission's Glentrool Forest Park is situated in the district of Galloway in the South West of Scotland. The Park contains five forests and extends to 130,723 acres or about 205 square miles. The Forestry Commission started buying land in 1921 and almost all the land acquired for planting consisted of hill grazing. In the 1920s the principal land use in the Park was sheep-farming and the human population was decreasing. Now the principal land use is forestry but 40 per cent of the land is still used for sheep-farming, and in addition the beauty and amenities of the Glentrool Forest Park draw a rapidly rising number of sportsmen, hill walkers, and lovers of wild country. (Each year more than 30,000 people use the Camp site at Caldons Farm at the South-Eastern end of Loch Trool). In 1966 the Forestry Commission employed 213 people and owned 146 houses. In addition 18 smallholdings were let to forest workers. Forty-six of the houses, together with a shop and school, were concentrated in the new village of Glentrool. Glentrool village and most of Glentrool forest lie in the Parish of Minnigaff and this is one of the few rural parishes of Kirkcudbrightshire in which the population is increasing, the figures being 1,144 in 1931, 1,251 in 1951 and 1,342 in 1961.

In the North Cheviot hills forestry has a strong social role. This area offers a combination of cheap establishment costs and soils good enough to grow the high-yielding species. Rowan records[22] that many of the upland parishes lost 30 per cent of their population between 1931 and 1961 and the sole exception was the forest lands in Bellingham Rural District comprising the great forests of Kielder, Redesdale and Wark. Here the fall in population has been dramatically reversed due entirely to forest employment.

Turning now to the demand for manpower in the industries based on forestry, experience in this and in all other countries shows that the contribution of forestry to employment is not only in the growing of wood but also in its processing and utilisation, the generally accepted ratio between these two parts of the industry being about one to four or five. Thus if the wood-using industries are sited away from the forest much of the potential benefit of increased employment in the remoter rural areas is lost. Conversely the greatest gain is seen when an integrated industry comprising primary wood processing (such as a pulp mill, board mill or sawmill) and secondary processing (such as paper making or container making) are sited near to the forests. The siting of wood-using industries requires consideration of the quantities, nature and costs of transport, labour, power and raw material; optimum situations are rare, but the example of the pulp and paper mill and associated sawmill at Fort William shows that suitable sites can be found in the remoter rural areas.

THE FOREST VILLAGES

Until the arrival of the Forestry Commission, in many parts of the remoter uplands of Britain there had been a steady exodus of the young and active inhabitants to the towns, leaving behind them an ageing population, derelict homesteads, chapels and schools, even whole hamlets and land going back to wilderness. When the population of an area begins to fall the social services—schools, shops and roads—inevitably begin to be neglected or abandoned: and this in turn accelerates the drift from the land. The increase of population following large-scale planting creates both a need and a justification for improvements and this tends to reverse the process.

In their Annual Report for 1959[23] the Forestry Commissioners struck an optimistic note about their forest villages. For example, to provide a stable labour force for the forest of Inverliever beside Loch Awe in Argyllshire a new forest village of 47 houses was built at Dalavich. In 1908 when there was no forestry activity the resident population of the area was 55, of whom only 11 were children under the age of 18. The population in 1959 was 318 and there were over 125 schoolchildren for whom the County Council built a new school in the village.

The forest villages have had their critics both inside and outside the State Forest Service. Ryle[24] records that the decision to form forest villages came after the Second World War '. . . and so there appeared in the heart of several of the larger forests, groups and terraces of new houses. . . . Each house was good and well planned with up-to-date amenities for townsfolk. Each house was just like its neighbour. Each tenant had the same job and the same wage packet and the same boss as his neighbour.' In spite of all this many of the forest villages have been successful and a strong community life has developed in them.

However, there are plenty of degenerating or static small towns and villages in the remoter areas of Britain and in 1954 the decision was taken in Wales to site new woodmen's houses where they could help to put new life into existing villages. This policy gradually became general and an example of the kind of settlement with people of varied employment, skills and interests which is now favoured is provided by the village of Llanwddn on the Lake Vyrnwy Estate in West Central Wales.[25] The Lake Vyrnwy Estate of 22,800 acres was acquired by Liverpool Corporation from several owners between 1880 and 1887. The reservoir constitutes an important supply of water to the City of Liverpool. Four thousand acres of plantations have since been managed by a joint scheme agreed between the corporation and the Forestry Commission under which costs and receipts are shared equally between the two parties. Prior to acquisition of the land between 1880 and 1887 some 260 people were supported by the remote upland farms and the original village (which was submerged by the reservoir). In 1961 more than 500 people were supported by the improved farms, small holdings, forestry and water works and this number was being increased constantly by the employees of timber merchants. In 1961 the replacement village of Llanwddn acquired a new school and community centre of advanced design, and tourist traffic had 'reached embarrassing proportions.'

THE INTEGRATION OF FORESTRY AND AGRICULTURE

So far relatively little mention has been made of forests on private estates in the remoter rural areas but this is an appropriate point to emphasise the size and importance of the private sector of forestry and also draw attention to the fact that many fine examples can be found of integrated land use on private estates, in which forestry, agriculture and sporting interests are combined in a carefully balanced way.

Having said this, it is necessary to return to the main theme of this section, which is the integration of forestry and agriculture over large areas owned or tenanted by many people. Although the principles of integration are the same whether one or several owners are involved a single owner has the simpler task.

The 1957 report of the National Resources (Technical) Committee[5] presented a strong case for the integration of forestry and agriculture, while a later report[6] emphasised that 'integration means the co-ordination of multiple uses of land and associated activities within a given area of land.' Much can be learned from the attempt being made to integrate forestry and agriculture in the remoter rural areas and two examples can be quoted here, one from Scotland and the other from Wales.

In 1948 the Advisory Panel on the Highlands and Islands suggested that the Forestry Commission and the Department of Agriculture for Scotland might undertake a joint survey of the Strathoykell area in the counties of Sutherland and Ross and Cromarty. The two departments surveyed some 250,000 acres of land comprising 17 estates, with a total of 150 agricultural sublets, the great majority of which were crofts with common grazing. There were several farms in the area, some tenanted but mostly in hand and worked by the owners. The aims and objects of the survey were to increase cattle production, create economic sheep-farming units, improve grazing areas by shelter blocks, drainage and land improvement, replant old woodland and plant new forests on those areas suitable for the production of wood.

The plan suggested that some 22,000 acres could be used for commercial forestry and the land planted to trees in 1967 was just over 18,000 acres, made up of a large number of plantations spread over the 17 estates and ranging from extensive blocks down to 100-acre plantations. The progress of agricultural development has also been 'quite considerable, if less spectacular.'[26] The number of breeding cows and breeding ewes increased substantially, even though 18,000 acres of grazing land had been taken up for forestry. Twelve schemes under the Hill Farming and Livestock Rearing Acts contributed towards achieving the economic hill farm units envisaged under the plan. Less satisfactory progress has been made in developing the crofting settlements but the difficulties may well be overcome in time. Sport was also included in the original report. Fishing continues as a high-value attraction and the main deer forest areas are untouched.

In assessing 18 years of work in Strathoykell, Macdonald wrote . . . 'the plan is not completely fulfilled but this is inevitable without imposition. In one sense it was perhaps as much a strategy as a plan and, if so regarded, the results must be considered satisfactory. It has demonstrated that a large increase in total production from the land can result from planning in this way. It has shown that dying areas can be revived and that renewed life and employment can be brought to the countryside. It has shown that these benefits can be the result of looking at a large area as a whole, collecting and assessing all the necessary information and planting, without sentiment or prejudice, to achieve the best land use.'[26]

A second, smaller, example of joint planning by foresters and agriculturalists can be found at Myherin and Tarenig forests in Mid-Wales where the Forestry Commission and the Ministry of Agriculture got together in 1956 and allocated about 4,000 acres of rough grazing land from the recently acquired Pwllpeir Estate.[27] Some 1,900 acres were allocated to forestry and 2,100 to agriculture, using as criteria the stock-carrying capacity of the land, the need for shelter for stock and crops, the provision of roads for forest and farm purposes and the sharing of labour and equipment.[27] By the end of 1961, some 1,800 acres of plantations had been established and six shelter belts planted on the land allocated to sheep. Despite the loss to the farm, of plantable land, the stock of ewes remained the same, at around 2,000; in addition, it became possible to winter 300 lambs and a herd of 60 Welsh black cattle was established. The labour employed before integration was 4 men, wholly on agriculture. In 1961, 5 to 6 men were employed on the farm and

18 to 20 by the Forestry Commission on the area afforested. The forest labour was available to help with seasonal tasks on the farm and the work of the shepherd had been greatly eased by the construction of over 8 miles of forest road leading through the forest to the grazing areas beyond.

THE MULTIPLE USE OF FORESTS

Quantock forest in Somerset is a productive forest of 2,232 acres backing on to open moorland in an area of great beauty in the southwestern peninsula. In 1968 the annual cut was 5,700 tons of wood; this means that two lorry-loads of wood were leaving the forest each day for consumption in the mines, pulp mills and sawmills.[28] By 1985 the allowable cut will be 10,400 tons each year, equivalent to almost four lorry-loads of wood each day.

Quantock forest is an important employer of local labour and provides work for 15 men per 1,000 acres in the growing, harvesting and primary conversion of wood and if it is accepted that each man may have a wife and one child, the forest supports 45 people per 1,000 acres. Moreover, the wages that are earned in the forest are spent in the village shop, post office, garage and village church. Thus Quantock forest is truly part of the rural economy. It is also the home of a herd of Red deer, a haven for the naturalist in search of rare plants, a gathering ground for an important source of water supply and a resort for the public. The forest is host to some 14,000 visitors each year, who are attracted to an area of such outstanding beauty. They also include members of the armed forces engaged in training, youth organisations, school parties, pony trekkers, car rallies and the stag and fox hunts. Quantock forest and the adjoining moorland are enjoyed by a very wide variety of people and organisations. For some the forest is the main attraction; for others it is the combination of forest and open moors that attracts the visitors. Other examples of the multiple use of Forestry Commission and private forests are numerous and need not be added here. There is no doubt that the general public are discovering the attractions of forests and it is estimated that close to 1 million people stay overnight at camping and caravan sites within State and private forests.

THE FUTURE DEVELOPMENT OF FORESTRY

It is now desirable to summarise the benefits of establishing forests in the remoter rural areas. These according to Wardle[17] are:

1. forestry provides a higher rate of employment per unit area where the alternative is extensive pastoral agriculture. In all areas forestry increases the diversity of employment and if developed on a sufficient scale, provides openings for woodmen, civil and mechanical engineers, technicians of many kinds, accountants, managers and general office workers;

2. expenditure on forest operations is largely on staff and labour living in the forest area. Sixty to seventy per cent of the expenditure of the Forestry Commission and private owners on commercial forestry is spent locally;

3. when the plantations become productive they produce wood which can form the basis of local manufacturing industry, thus making a further contribution to the multiplier;

4. employment in forestry does not require that the worker lives remotely or in isolation. He can live in the local community and travel to work daily;

5. the planting, tending and harvesting of forests require the construction and maintenance of a network of roads which can be of value to neighbouring farmers and provide access routes for sportsmen and visitors. In addition the interests of forestry, farming and sport can be served by jointly agreed and well-sited fences;

6. afforestation can contribute in major ways to the landscape by improving the amenity, providing more diverse habitats for plants and animals, and increasing the opportunities for sport and recreation;

7. the improvements in landscape and recreation make the area more attractive to tourists. This in turn benefits those who accommodate the tourists and further broadens the economic base of the area;

8. if the work of afforestation proceeds at a steady and sustained rate the improvements in housing and social services— schools, shops and roads—can proceed at a predictable rate. The yield of wood also rises at a predictable rate and the

forest and public roads can be made ready for the increased traffic in good time.

The cost of obtaining these benefits is known. The natural average cost of forming plantations in Britain is[29] £98 in the private sector and £130 if done by the Forestry Commission.[30] The costs of roads and other capital works must be added to the former figure in order to make the two comparable. As there are no published figures we estimate their cost at £10 per acre.

The returns are less well known. We reject the current means of assessing the profitability of the investment in forestry in terms of the revenue derived from wood alone. The benefits are not reflected by 3 per cent, which is the generally accepted rate of return from such calculations.[31] To this return must be added the savings in the social costs of maintaining both the population and social services within the dwindling rural community and re-settling the emigrants. We know of no comprehensive review showing the comparable cash flows for a rural area and its community under the two contrasting regimes of progressive economic depression and economic expansion, but the University of Aberdeen intends to undertake such a study as soon as funds are available.

FOESTRY DEVELOPMENT AREAS

As we have seen, many Government reports have stressed the potential value of forestry and wood-based industries to the future development of the rural areas but little has been done to exploit the obvious advantages of afforestation of compact blocks of country. The present piecemeal development is unsatisfactory because the use of land, labour and capital—all of which are highly priced— tends to be dispersed. Therefore we consider that the concept of specially designated development areas similar to those employed to draw industry away from the South, should be used to concentrate the nation's afforestation effort, and thereby meet modern industrial and social requirements.

The benefits and nature of forestry development areas can be illustrated by means of an example. Argyllshire with ten per cent of the total land area under trees is now the most heavily afforested country in the Highlands of Scotland. In 1930 the Forestry Commission employed 95 forest workers and the wage bill was £7,000. By 1961 the Forest Service had planted 105,000 acres of forest and employed 900 workers. The wage bill was £480,000 most of which was being spent in Argyllshire.* Five hundred houses had been built (most of them since 1945), village halls provided, and community life fostered. Three hundred and thirty miles of new forest roads permitted the extraction of 50,000 tons of timber each year, and a modern sawmill had been built to convert the harvested stems into constructional timber. The timber merchants who bought, extracted and converted part of the annual yield of wood employed some 300 people, so, after thirty years of planting, forestry had provided direct employment for 1,000 more people than in 1930. The yield of wood is still rising rapidly and by 1980 will reach 200,000 tons each year. The pulp and paper mill at Fort William lies to the north, the conurbation of Glasgow forms the largest single market for sawn timber in Scotland and the future market for the wood produced by Argyllshire forests is assured.

The objects of Forestry Development Areas may be defined as:
1. to stimulate greater economic activity in remoter rural Britain;
2. to provide employment and especially to broaden the range of skills required in the area;
3. to produce a sustained supply of wood of value to a range of wood-using industries;
4. to raise the level of economic activity in the forestry sector by establishing wood-using industries within the Forestry Development Areas;
5. to improve the use of the land, maintain or improve the fertility of the soil, protect water supplies, and increase the aesthetic value of the landscape;
6. to encourage where appropriate ancillary activities such as sport and recreation.

The incentives which the Forest Development Areas could provide to the development of the community would be similar to those provided by Industrial Estates in the field of manufacturing industries. For example these would:
(a) programme and construct roads designed primarily for the transportation of timber within the area as a whole and not confined to a single ownership;
(b) similarly provide regional deer fencing in a manner which will enable development in both these forms of land use;
(c) provide fiscal relief in the capital cost of machinery and

* In 1969 the Forest Services' wage bill reached £1 m.

equipment utilised in the area for the development of forestry and forest industries;

(d) provide essential services of electric power, water and housing at competitive rates;

(e) and eventually provide advance factory facilities or comparable financial assistance to wood-using and other industries.

Forestry Development areas will be located where:

(a) the site and climate are favourable to the rapid growth of high-yielding coniferous trees, especially the spruces and Douglas fir, and extensive hill farming has less economic viability;

(b) a central site exists which is suitable for an integrated wood-using plant consisting of sawmill and pulp, paper and board mill (that is, there should be sufficient water, a cheap source of power and good transport links with large markets);

(c) a small town or large village exists which can be developed as the main settlement and is already equipped with social services including a school.

We feel that suitable sites could be found, in such areas as the Dee and Don valleys, in the Cromarty/Moray Firth neighbourhood, and in Dumfriesshire at, for example, Moffat.

In each Forestry Development Area, forestry will be closely integrated with agriculture, sport and tourism but it will be the main land use. The area planted will be at least 30,000, and preferably 50,000, acres and the planting programme will be sustained for a sufficient period to permit adjustment of housing, schooling and other social services to create a permanent force of skilled labour for forestry. The present pattern of land ownership will normally be maintained so that the Forestry Commission and private owners both form plantations. Roads will be improved and joint fence lines devised to meet the needs of all the users of land. The area of forest (at least 30,000 acres) will, when productive, be sufficient to supply a wood-using industry.

CONCLUSION

The experience gained by foresters can now be brought to bear on the questions put to this conference.

First, what should be the long-term objectives for the remoter rural areas? Fifty years of experience suggests that much of the land which has been under-used for so long can yield wood in economically valuable quantities, provide steady employment, and increase the wealth of the nation.

Second, how are the long-term objectives affected by the changing demands of the rest of the country? The evidence is clear that there is a huge demand for wood and also a rising demand for the sport and recreation available in the remoter rural areas. Forestry can supply part of both these needs.

Third, to what extent is comprehensive development a desirable and practical means of achieving these objectives? The main conclusion of this chapter is that forestry development plans are both desirable and practical and that land, labour, and capital should be allotted to them.

REFERENCES

1. GRAYSON, A. J., 'Forestry in Britain' in *Economic Change and Agriculture*, edited by J. Ashton and S. J. Rogers, pp. 168–89, Oliver and Boyd, 1967.
2. ROYAL COMMISSION 'Second Report (On Afforestation) of the Royal Commission on Coast Erosion', Command 4460, London, HMSO, 1909.
3. MINISTRY OF RECONSTRUCTION, 'Final Report of the Sub-Committee on Forestry,' Reconstruction Committee, Command 8881, London, HMSO, 1918.
4. FORESTRY COMMISSION, 'Post-War Forest Policy', Command 6447, London, HMSO 1963.
5. LORD PRESIDENT'S OFFICE, Natural Resources (Technical) Committee, 1957.
6. DEPARTMENT OF EDUCATION AND SCIENCE, 'Report of the Land Use Study Group, Forestry, Agriculture and the Multiple Use of Rural Land, London, HMSO, 1966.
7. DEPARTMENT OF AGRICULTURE AND FISHERIES FOR SCOTLAND, 'Land Use in the Highlands and Islands,' Edinburgh, HMSO, 1964.
8. FORESTRY COMMISSION, Forty-Fourth Annual Report of the Forestry Commissioners, London, HMSO, 1964.
9. Forestry Act 1967, London, HMSO, 1967.
10. M.A.F.F., 'A Century of Agricultural Statistics, Great Britain, 1866–1966', London, HMSO, 1968.
11. EDLIN, H. A., 'Timber. Your Growing Investment,' Forestry Commission Booklet 23, London, HMSO, 1969.
12. RANKIN, K. N., 'The Economic Problems of Private Forestry,' 1968, *Forestry, 42*, 1, 28–36, 1969.
13. HOLTAM, B. W., 'Home-Grown Roundwood, Forestry Commission,' Forest Record 52, London, HMSO, 1966.
14. 'Pulpwood Supply and the Paper Industry,' Forestry Commission, Forest Record 68, London, HMSO, 1969.
15. RICHARDS, E. G., 'Now and the Next Ten Years. Using the Wood' in *Fifty Years on*, Supplement to *Forestry*, 53–5, 1969.

16. DAVIDSON, J. L., 'Road Haulage of Scottish Pulpwood,' *Scottish Forestry*, *21*, 3, 145–52, 1967.
17. JEFFERS, J. N. R., 'Relationship between Staff and Work-load in Individual Forest Units,' Forestry Commission, Report on Forest Research for 1965, London, HMSO, 1966.
18. WARDLE, P., 'Land Use Policy,' *Timber Grower*, *19*, 18–25, 1966.
19. PHILIP, M. S. *et al.*, 'The Economic Survey of Private Forestry,' University of Aberdeen, Department of Forestry, 1969.
20. STEVEN, H. M., 'The Beneficent Forest,' *Forestry*, *37*, 1, 2–12, 1964.
21. FORREST, G., 'Multi-purpose Land Use in a Forest Park,' *Scottish Forestry*, *20*, 1, 10–16, 1966.
22. ROWAN, A. A., 'Forestry in the North Cheviot Hills,' *Forestry*, *36*, 1, 21–36, 1963.
23. Fortieth Annual Report of the Forestry Commissioners, London, HMSO, 1960.
24. RYLE, G. B., *Forest Service*, David and Charles, Newton Abbot, 1969.
25. BEST, F. C. and HAMPSON, J. R., 'Forestry in West Central Wales,' *Forestry*, *34*, 1, 1–13, 1961.
26. MACDONAND, T., 'The Strathoykell Plan. Scottish Agriculture 1967,' Reprinted in *Journal of the Forestry Commission* No. 35, 1966–67, 115–118, 1967.
27. THOM, J. R., 'Forestry and Multiple Land Use in Wales,' *Quarterly Journal of Forestry*, *54*, 2, 1962. 101–9, 1962.
28. BANISTER, N., 'Quantock Forest: an Example of Multiple Land Use,' *Forestry*, *41*, 1, 15–26, 1968.
29. LORRAIN-SMITH, R., 'Economy of the Private Woodlands in Great Britain,' Institute Paper, Commonwealth Forestry Institute, University of Oxford, 1969.
30. JOHNSTON, D. R. *et al.*, *Forest Planning*, Faber & Faber, London, 1967.
31. MUTCH, W. E. S., 'Accountability in State and Private Forestry,' A Report to the British Association for the Advancement of Science, 1968.

3 | *The Establishment of New Industries (With Particular Reference to Recent Experience in Mid-Wales)*

D. P. GARBETT-EDWARDS, F.C.I.S.
Secretary,
Mid-Wales Industrial Development Association

It is fundamental to the success of any rural area attempting to attract new industry that it should consider what it is trying to achieve. What kind of countryside and what kind of rural society is it in fact trying to create? However altruistic this may sound it needs to be said, for far too many people concerned with the country-side are carried away by the excitement and hidden possibilities of the very phrase 'industrial development'. They look upon such development as the panacea for all the economic and social ills of the countryside without giving much thought to the countryside they want to create nor why they want to create it. The provision of new forms of industrial employment in the rural areas inevitably changes both the pattern and the pace of life in the countryside. It is as well, therefore, that those concerned with the attraction of new industry to the countryside should undertake their work neither ignorant of its objectives nor blind to its result.

In the absence of any regional or national policy to guide it, any rural region seeking to maintain or revitalise its economy by attracting industrial development may find that its best starting point is to consider three simple but searching questions—why it wants industry, what kind of industry it wants, and exactly where it wants it.

In most cases a rural area seeking to attract industry will answer with speed and conviction that it does so because a diversity of employment is necessary to the economic and social well-being of the countryside. But quite apart from high-sounding reasons of this kind, or even reasons of national significance, there are usually

50

important local reasons for action. An area may, for example, need to absorb some of the run-off from its declining agricultural labour force: it may even want to encourage the movement of labour from the land so as to help rationalise and strengthen the agriculture of the area. Alternatively, it may be intent on stemming migration by providing more and better local employment opportunities for school leavers: there may be a specific unemployment problem due to the decline of a traditional industry or the completion of a major capital works scheme. Then again, because of its demise as a market or service centre, a town may need new employment if its economy is to be maintained. The real strength and stimulus for action will, generally, spring from the special characteristics of the region or locality.

Mid-Wales is an area comprised of the northern districts of Breconshire and the counties of Cardiganshire, Merioneth, Montgomeryshire and Radnorshire. It covers over 40 per cent of the surface area of Wales and has some 7 per cent of its population: it also has 5 county councils and 43 county district councils. Well over half the area's population of 178,500 live in minor villages or scattered hamlets and farms. Sixty-three thousand people live in 21 small towns (i.e. Fourth order or ordinary regional centres) which, generally some 10 to 15 miles from one another, vary in size from Aberystwyth, which has a resident population of a little over 10,000, to Newquay, an urban district of some 900 people. The area's population has fallen by 37,000 (17 per cent) since 1901, and by 96,500 since its peak population in 1871. (Table 3.1).

Table 3.1. *Mid-Wales population enumerated census*
Figures for peak population years, 1901, 1951 and 1961

	Peak Population	Date	1901	1951	1961
Breconshire	61,627	1861	54,213	56,508	55,185
Mid-Wales Counties	275,000	1871	242,325	217,234	209,779
Wales	—	—	1,943,648	2,598,675	2,640,632
England and Wales	—	—	32,527,843	43,757,888	46,071,604
Mid-Wales survey area	*		215,492	185,729	178,546
Breconshire (part)	*		27,380	25,003	23,952
Cardiganshire	73,441	1871	61,078	53,278	53,648
Merioneth	52,038	1881	48,852	41,465	38,310
Montgomeryshire	69,607	1841 (a)	54,901	45,990	44,165
Radnorshire	25,430	1871	23,281	19,993	18,471

Source: Registrar-General, Census of Population.
    * Not calculated.
    (a) A secondary peak of 67,623 was reached in 1871.

Mid-Wales has a simple concept of regional development: it aims to create a vigorous and developing community which will not only benefit Mid-Wales but will contribute to the progress and well-being of the United Kingdom as a whole. Faced with the run-down of the area following years of heavy outward migration, Mid-Wales has sought to encourage industrial growth as a means of raising income levels and living standards and thereby encouraging more of its young people to remain in the area. Its practical efforts and its publicity have been designed to achieve that end.

Having satisfied itself *why* it wants to encourage industrial growth, an area must then decide on its policy for locating new industry. This means simple deciding upon the places to which new firms are to be attracted. The question has to be decided whether industrial growth is to be concentrated in selected places or whether it is to be spread generally throughout the area. In Mid-Wales during the past decade it was felt that every effort must be made to spread new industry and employment as widely as possible. Perhaps the prime reason for this was that morale was low and, in many parts, the future bleak: there was a need to carry the fight against depopulation on as broad a front as possible. Nevertheless, there was a sound base for action because, with substantial under-employment and hidden unemployment, there was throughout the area a good deal of slack in the economy.

It was in 1957 that the five Mid-Wales County Councils formed the Mid-Wales Industrial Development Association to act as their spearhead in the attack on the economic and social problems which have for so long manifested themselves in depopulation. Financed by the Counties and grant-aided by the Development Commissioners, the Association is an organisation with no direct powers. Its role has been to stimulate action by the area's Local Authorities and by Government alike, and to bring together industrialists wishing to expand with areas wishing to develop. Since its formation the Association has been the means of attracting 53 new industrial projects to Mid-Wales. Of these projects, 38 are now in production and 15 factories are under construction. The 38 factories in operation provide 2,500 jobs. As the remaining factories are completed and factories already operating reach their minimum labour figures, a further 1,500 jobs will be available. Within a decade the number of manufacturing industries in the area has more than doubled. Now a total of 94 firms (Appendix 1) are operating in Mid-Wales: all the area's small towns and several of its villages as well have one or more manufacturing industry.

Up to the present time the Development Commissions and the Board of Trade have financed the building of 24 factories in Mid-Wales. Including extensions built and others being constructed, these factories constitute over 450,000 square feet of factory space. Four Government factories are now in the course of construction: of the other 20 which have been in production for some time, no less than 13 have already been extended to twice their original size. The Mid-Wales New Town Development Corporation, to which reference is made later, is now building three factories.

Following the scheduling of the area as a Development Area in 1966, the Board of Trade is now responsible for building factories for specific tenants, but because of the over-riding social implications, the Development Commissioners using the powers available to them under the Development and Road Improvements Fund Act, 1909, are still responsible for the advance factory building programme.

The purpose of Government factory building in Mid-Wales has been to 'prime the pump' in the hope that private industrial development will follow. Although slow to start, private development is now moving forward. It has been stimulated by the scheduling of the area as a Development Area and by the fact that with growing confidence in the future, local authorities are also beginning to give their support through the powers (e.g. Local Authorities Land Act 1963) available to them. Up to the present time 22 new factories have been built by companies establishing in Mid-Wales.

Although prepared to follow a policy of widespread industrial dispersal, Mid-Wales nevertheless attempted to concentrate development in the area's 21 small towns. Whatever their size, these towns were usually the focal point of their areas and as such commanded a labour catchment area of some size. Moreover, these were the towns which could best offer the facilities and services likely to be required and which had the best prospect of attracting industry. Even if desirable, to carry industry into every corner of the countryside is unlikely to be practical. The average industrialist looks for a location which can provide him with the services, housing, schools, transport and the amenities he requires: he certainly looks for an area where he is likely to attract the labour he needs. And he expects to see some sign of 'life' in the town if he and his family or those of his key-workers are to live there. Industrialists are not much interested in places which are static.

Early consideration will need to be given to the type of new

Table 3.2.   *The Source of new factories in Mid-Wales 1957–69*
June 1969

Government financed factories			
For Rent			
Development Commission			
Purpose-built factories	10		
Advance factories	11	21	
Board of Trade			
Purpose-built factories	2		
Advance factories	1	3	24
Mid-Wales New Town Development Corporation			
For rent			
Purpose-built factory		1	
Advance factories		2	3
Privately financed			
(where applicable with grant, etc., from			
Board of Trade)			
New factories		15	
Financed with local authority loan assistance		5	
Existing building acquired		2	22
Existing buildings rented			4
			53

industry to be attracted. In this the assessment of why the area needs industry will play an important part. Obviously the industry needed to absorb redundant quarry workers will be different from that required to attract boys and girls leaving school. In its desire to retain its bright young people the countryside usually sets its sights on skilled employment and research. This is admirable, but development of this kind is more likely to be attracted when there is an industrial base on which to build—and in the creation of such a base the clothing firms and the light engineers can be invaluable.

It is not difficult to obtain information on those sectors of industry which in present economic conditions have the best prospects of growth. From this information it is then merely a matter of assessing which industries are likely to provide the type of employment the area needs and which would benefit from the facilities the area itself has to offer. It is almost inevitable that the facilities and the labour force which an area has available will dictate the type of industry which can be attracted.

Generally only light manufacturing industry can be expected to establish in the outlying rural areas. Industries such as engineering, packaging, electronics, plastics, office equipment, food manufacture are amongst those which might be attracted. From the area's point of view it is usually an advantage if incoming firms have a high labour content in their products and offer training for skilled employment. Firms in the luxury or semi-luxury class are always attractive for with them fractional production cost considerations, whilst important, are often not vital. Firms on mass production which attracts low transport costs may also be attractive.

Table 3.3. *New industries attracted to Mid-Wales 1957–69*
June 1969

Industry	Year factory constructed										
	1957–60	'61	'62	'63	'64	'65	'66	'67	'68	'69	Total
Clothing	1	1	1	3	2					1	9
Engineering		3		2	1	1	4		4		15
Packaging									1	1	2
Plastics								1	1		2
Office equipment							1			1	2
Others (1)	1		1	2	2		2	3	4	3	18
Advance factories (to be let)										5	5
	2	4	2	7	5	1	7	4	10	11	53

1 Perfume
Glassware
Musical instruments
Timber processing
Pottery
Horticultural products

Building components
Candlewick textiles
Furniture
Needles
Ornaments
Concrete products

Shoes
Animal feeds
Printing
Yarn spinning
Fishing tackle
Floor tiles

In Mid-Wales industrial development has been mainly of three kinds—the establishment of branch factories by well-established companies (27); the complete removal to the area of small or medium-sized firms (16) and the location in the area of new companies (5). Many people speak of the danger of establishing branch factories (e.g. in times of economic difficulty they will be the first to close) but, whilst not ignorant of them, Mid-Wales has not yet encountered such difficulties. It could be that in the more remote rural areas the establishment of branch factories is the most likely form of development. It has the advantage that the larger firms involved have greater resources, both human and financial, to enable them to overcome the problems of development in a country and non-industrial area. For the small man the removal of his factory to a new location is a very personal matter: it is a matter of moving his business and his home. It often means starting his business all over again.

It is inevitable that at some stage consideration will need to be given to the attraction of industry using the natural resources of the area or the products of its forests and agriculture. That industry attracted to the rural areas should be industry 'ancillary to agriculture' is usually the theory of the protectors of the countryside. It is a theory which in Mid-Wales has caused us to spend a good deal of time to no purpose. It is usually assumed that such industry will reflect its benefits throughout the area's agriculture—and so it may in a horticultural or livestock rearing area. In Mid-Wales we have found such industry hard to identify and experience suggests that the output of areas of marginal farming (coupled with problems of distance from markets) is unlikely to be sufficient to attract processing firms. The products of the area's forests are not yet sufficiently mature to attract timber-using industry and presently, doubting the possibilities for a new pulp mill (with two on our borders, north and south), we are not yet convinced of the contribution in terms of new employment which 'forestry' and its ancillary industries are likely to make.

It is at this point when it has decided broadly why it wants industry, what industry it wants, and where it wants it, that an area is ready to proceed. Its most prudent next step will be to set about providing the facilities which incoming industry will require. A survey of what the area has to offer, and an enquiry into what the industrialist is likely to want, is essential.

It is now a matter of history that in 1957 there were in Mid-Wales just three acres of land allocated for industrial use. The County Development Plans were of little help for they did not then even reflect the area's desire to attract industry. Later when industrial land began to be allocated it was important always to ensure that it was something rather more than a pleasant colour on a map! There was a tendency to allocate land for industry only on the grounds that it was not suitable for anything else and often land was allocated completely regardless of whether it could actually be acquired or not.

It is a pre-requisite to any effort to attract industry to a rural area that attractive industrial sites must be available in all the towns chosen as the locations for industrial expansion. Initially for a town with a population of 1,000–3,000, a site of five acres may be sufficient. This should allow for three 10,000 square feet factories and ensure space for their further expansion. Sites should be flat, well drained, and have all the services readily available. Ideally the site should be acquired by the local authority. Not only does this give the authority some control over its development but it also assures any potential industrialist that, subject to negotiation on price, the land can be made quickly available. Even though allocated for industrial use in a County Plan, the sale of land in private ownership is always subject to the decision of the owner who, farmer or landowner, cannot always be relied on. It is significant that the areas of Mid-Wales which have been most successful in attracting industry have been those where the local authorities have been bold in providing industrial land.

The reason why a site must be available is entirely simple: an industrialist considering expansion wants to think in *actual* terms. He wants to see where he can develop and is rarely impressed with an area which may or may not be able to offer him a site. He will know full well that if one area cannot offer a site there are plenty of other areas which can!

In advocating the area of land to be acquired for industry, the size of commitment which the local authority is being asked to make has to be borne in mind. To a small authority with a low penny rate product, the acquisition of land (at say £1,000 per acre) constitutes a sizeable investment and the whole issue is one which in Mid-Wales even now generates spirited discussion as to (*a*) whether the ratepayers' money should be invested (others say speculated) in the acquisition of industrial land which may or may not be used, and (*b*) how far the ratepayers of a small authority can reasonably be expected to finance expansion which will probably be of benefit to future generations and maybe incoming population rather than to themselves.

With the passing of time Mid-Wales, like many other areas, has become more and more sophisticated and competitive in its provision for industry. It is no longer sufficient to provide isolated sites but rather, small industrial estates, where access roads and the main public services are already provided. There is much to be said for the attraction of a rural trading estate which might be located so as to serve the interests of a number of areas. A handicap here is the intense rivalry between authorities to attract industry and it may be that the trading estate concept can only be implemented by an authority which has the finance and powers to allow it independence of action.

Whilst the availability of an industrial site is an important factor in the location of industry in the rural areas, experience again suggests that the availability of an existing building (e.g. a church hall, or old school) can be an even more important factor. It is the experience of most people concerned with the practical aspects of industrial development that every industrialist wants his new factory 'yesterday'. Perhaps for good reason the smaller industrialist (and some larger ones also) looks for new space generally when demand is upon him and not much before. For the reason that it will allow speed, therefore, the industrialist is often much interested in an existing building in which he can establish *now*. Further, remembering that he has probably never developed before, his decisions may be easier when he can see something in bricks and mortar rather than when based on the impression of how a new factory will look on a green site. Finally, the availability of an existing building which he can lease enables the industrialist to limit his initial capital investment and to make a practical assessment of the area's suitability for his project before he makes any longer or lasting commitment.

In any review of the basics which must be provided before any attempt to attract industry should begin, the provision of main services must be considered. The provision of electricity, water, and main sewerage is essential and can probably be offered by every country town. Gas is often an added advantage. The main problem in respect of services in the countryside is that of effluent disposal. In an area where there is little industry the disposal of effluent via the sewers and into the river can be a problem—and with few other firms about, an obvious one! However, with the installation of a new treatment plant on the one hand and goodwill on the other, industry and the local authorities in Mid-Wales have usually reached a satisfactory understanding.

If an area is to attract industry it must not only be able to offer sites for new factories but new housing for its workers. The readiness to provide housing quickly is one of the more important ways in which local authorities can encourage new development. It is unlikely that a firm will find all the skilled workers it requires in the rural location in which it proposes to establish. It will probably have

Table 3.4. *Size of manufacturing units attracted to Mid-Wales 1957–69 as at June 1969*

Industry	Size of factory ('000 sq. ft.)							
	Up to 5	5/10	10/15	15/20	20/25	25/50	50+	Total
(a) *Government-financed factories*								
Clothing	1		4	1				6
Engineering			2	3	1	1	1	8
Packaging			1					1
Plastics								–
Office equipment					1	1		2
Others		2	2			1		5
Advance factories (to be let)			5					5
	1	2	14	4	2	3	1	27
(b) *Privately financed factories*								
Clothing	1	2						3
Engineering	1	4			1		1	7
Packaging				1				1
Plastics	1			1				2
Office equipment								–
Others	6	1	3		1	2		13
	10	9	17	6	4	5	2	53

(a) Includes factories built by Mid-Wales New Town Development Corporation.
(b) Includes existing buildings acquired (2) and rented (4).

to import its key workers and this move should be encouraged, for the attraction of men and women with new industrial skills is an essential part of providing the diversity of employment necessary for the development of the countryside. Local authorities must give a clear and decisive undertaking to help and this may well be a problem, for, on account of its inadequate financial resources, the small authority is rarely able to keep abreast of local housing needs. Moreover, because of the high cost of building in some rural areas, housing costs tend to be above the yardstick and even with government subsidies the rents move to a level which incoming workers are unwilling to pay.

Many authorities in Mid-Wales have provided housing for incoming key workers—Newtown and Welshpool have each provided over 50 houses—and many other small towns have provided anything up to 12. At Rhayader 40 houses are now being built 'on spec.' by the local authority with a view to attracting people to the employment provided by the town's industries. Everything possible needs to be done to synchronise the building of houses and factories, for the one without the other creates problems and friction. Perfect synchronisation of houses with factories is probably rarely achieved —but much can be done by a regional body acting as co-ordinator between the various bodies responsible for building.

It may well be that the main reason for an industrialist's interest in a relatively underdeveloped area will be not so much the advantage of that area itself as the disadvantage of his current location. If situated in an industrial area he may be experiencing severe labour problems such as heavy turnover and excessive wage rates. His interest in a rural area may quicken if he can be convinced that it is free of such conditions. It cannot be emphasised too strongly that the greatest care and responsibility must be exercised in helping the industrialist to assess both the present and likely future supply of labour. Indeed, of *all* responsibilities carried by those concerned with the attraction of industry to the countryside, the assessment of labour supply is the heaviest: it is also the most critical.

If an area is suffering from high unemployment, the provision of a substantial labour force may be no problem. But as everyone has long since recognised, at face value unemployment figures are grossly misleading. On the one hand, some Labour Exchange areas in Mid-Wales may have unemployment of eight per cent—which, in fact, represents only a little over 200 people, including the aged, infirm and unemployed. On the other hand, although this cannot be proved there are probably areas with unemployment rates where a worthwhile labour force can be recruited nevertheless. In the small towns the only way we have found of assessing the potential labour supply, particularly of females, is to undertake advance advertising, organise a local door-to-door canvass, or hold a public meeting. To build up a list of would-be immigrants or exiles anxious to return is an attractive idea and certainly provides excellent publicity. Its effect depends largely upon the availability of housing, and unless and until there are specific and substantial schemes for the expansion of certain towns within an area, the results of such publicity can probably have only marginal effects on the recruitment of labour to firms establishing in the small country towns.

In respect of the availability of male labour, the unemployment figures are generally more important—not that they always represent the true position but because the industrialist himself tends to believe that if a man is available for work he must be registered as unemployed. This is not necessarily true, for there remains in the countryside a good deal of under-employment, and the movement of labour from industries with depressed wage levels is to the general advantage of the rural areas.

It is well worth saying that it is the *availability* of labour rather than the possibility of paying lower wages which has been of greatest interest to the industrialist looking at Mid-Wales. Moreover, if he feels that by his early establishment in an area he will be able to command the labour supply for some time to come, the industrialist may well be interested in a location which presently seems remote and is distant from centres of population and industry alike. Most industrialists are anxious not to upset any existing wage levels in the area in which they establish themselves. Their concern is commendable, but it is not always in the area's best interests. In most cases, the introduction of new industry and the element of competition it brings is to an area's advantage: without competition wage rates may be artificially low and it is not unknown for existing employers to have informal agreements whose effect is to force a man to first register as unemployed if, without the employer's agreement, he wishes to leave one firm for another. Maybe this creates stability in the employment situation: it also kills initiative and stultifies personal progress.

The future supply of labour is all-important and a careful assessment needs to be made of the number and location of the school-leavers who will be available each year. In Mid-Wales we found that there were only some 2,500 children leaving school each year and that of these about 30 per cent were destined for some form of further education and 20 per cent were committed to agriculture— usually on the family farm. There is hardly need to point out that the balance left, if all available to local industry (and they were not), was small and very thinly spread over five counties. The final figure produced by an assessment of future school-leavers may not have any very fine accuracy but in the absence of anything better it does provide the industrialist with a worthwhile guide.

The Youth Employment officers and Headmasters of the schools are usually most helpful, and their interest and enthusiasm for country-based industry grows as it is introduced and their own

Table 3.4. *Jobs provided by industries attracted to Mid-Wales 1957–69, June 1969*

Industry	No. of firms	Male	Female	Total
(*a*) *Factories in production*				
Clothing	9	60	500	560
Engineering	12	1020	440	1460
Others	17	240	260	500
	38	1320	1200	2520
(*b*) *Factories under construction*				
Clothing	—	—	—	—
Engineering	3	210	50	260
Others	7	250	150	400
Advance factories	5	100	100	200
	53	1880	1500	3380

a) Estimated labour force in June 1969.
b) Estimated labour force within 12 months of commencing production. Normal expansion of the labour forces of these 53 units will probably provide a further 500–800 jobs.

understanding of its possibilities and opportunities increases. Their struggle is usually one of balancing their duty to provide vocational guidance with the needs of the countryside to retain more of its brighter young people. Initially the 'respectability' of industrial employment may be doubted by schoolmasters and some parents alike. This stems from the old out-of-date thinking that the boy or girl most suited for industry was one 'not much good at school but wonderful with his hands!' With an academic education the best passport to a standard of living which the country areas could not provide, education (certainly in Mid-Wales) has been slanted towards the arts. Moreover, even with the youngsters themselves, the tradition that the best people go away dies slowly. If efforts to attract industry to the rural areas are to succeed, a major job has to be done to bring home to the area's people themselves the advantages and opportunities of the new forms of employment now being provided. In this the schools have a leading part to play.

It is not possible to talk about the 'ideal' size of firm for a country town because size depends largely on the size of the town and the supply of labour available. It is always surprising, however, to find the size to which, given two or three years, a firm can develop. As it settles in a town, local confidence grows and people become the more ready to change their jobs and to move into industrial employment. In Newtown, a town of 5,500 people, there are five manufacturing industries: one of them employs 650 and altogether they have little short of 1,000 employees; there are a number of major service industries as well. In Rhayader, a town of 1,200, five new industries—precision engineering, light engineering, furniture, musical instruments and pottery—have recently been introduced: these industries now employ 200 people and all are growing.

In general, for towns with a population of between 1,000 and 5,000, the best size of firm to attract appears to be one which offers 40/50 jobs and has good growth prospects. A firm of this size is big enough to make an impact on the employment position, probably big enough to be resilient in the initial period of establishment and yet is small enough not to overtax local resources, is small enough to grow, and small enough to identify itself with the area. Within reasonable limits, towns require to satisfy themselves of the strength of management of incoming firms and of their financial status. Care in this direction is well worth-while for failures always generate a lot of noise and emotion. In Mid-Wales, in twelve years, only three newly established firms have failed and a further two, both associated with the use of the area's natural resources, never got off the ground. There is much to be said for taking the calculated risk of including a few firms with new ideas amongst the industries to be introduced to any region: in terms of growth the interests of some firms and the small towns in which they establish may be synonymous.

The size of catchment area from which a firm can draw its labour depends of course on its precise location and its situation in relation to other towns. It also depends very considerably on the availability of public transport. There is so little such transport available in Mid-Wales that employers tend to look on it as an unexpected bonus. A number of firms run their own works transport; others make a contribution to the cost of travel. In either event these costs are a significant factor when operating a country-based factory and may be the transport costs of which the industrialist will be most aware.

In respect of travel-to-work distance, labour can generally be recruited from a radius of up to 10/15 miles. In a study of travel to work in Mid-Wales,[1] it has been found that a reasonable rule of thumb figure for calculating labour catchments for new industrial enterprises is fourteen miles. The bulk of the factory labour force in Mid-Wales tends to be comprised of employees drawn from the surrounding countryside rather than from the town in which the factory is located. We have not studied the matter and it may be

Table 3.6. *Size, by labour force, of industries attracted to Mid-Wales 1957–69*
June 1969

Industry	Size of Labour Force					
	1/25	25/50	50/100	100/150	400	650
In production						
Clothing	2	1	5	1		
Engineering	4	3	3		1	1
Packaging		1				
Plastics	1					
Office equipment				1		
Others	6	7	1			
*Under construction for**						
Clothing						
Engineering	1		1	1		
Packaging			1			
Plastics	1					
Office equipment				1		
Others	1	1	2			
*Advance factory**						
(to be let)		5				
	16	18	13	4	1	1

* Estimated minimum employment to be provided.

simply that there are more people in the catchment area from whom to recruit: but in the light of all the travel-to-work problems, it might have been expected that small firms would have drawn more employees from the towns where they were established, rather than from the surrounding country districts. It may be that this is where the human and social factors come into play—inasmuch as those who live in the country towns are more aware of the wider range of employment opportunities available and themselves look outwards (out of the area) for their progress—whilst in the same sense, the rural dweller first looks to the near-by town.

Much has been talked about the low female-activity rates of the rural areas and it may be that these are explained partly by the scatter of population and the problem of actually getting people to work. Certainly to increase activity rates in Mid-Wales it may now be necessary to consider carrying development deeper into the countryside. It is an attractive theory that, apart from tapping further unused sources of labour, an industrialist establishing in one of the smaller villages may recruit the labour he wants on the basis that by working in the village employees are relieved of the cost of travel-to-work in the near-by town. The saving involved might often amount to about 30s. per week. Again the human factors come into play. True, some of the older women who are working because they want the money may be attracted in this way but 'the kids' who live in the village may still prefer to work in the near-by town where there is the life, the atmosphere, the coffee bar, the company which they do not have at home.

C. D. Harbury[2] found that rural labour was no less productive than its industrial counterpart. Experience in Mid-Wales shows that labour turnover in the rural areas is lower than that experienced by firms in the industrial areas. These two facts may do something to offset the disadvantage that, generally, people available for employment by industries establishing in the rural areas have no industrial skill and require training. This is not necessarily a difficulty and it is well known that some firms find it an advantage to train green labour whose outlook is not based on out-dated methods or restrictive practices. In some cases the lack of industrial background and tradition can be a handicap to rural-based firms. It is a disadvantage which manifests itself in the difference of 'pace' and the lack of urgency on the part of the countryman or woman. With wage rates and standards of living usually lower than those acceptable in the industrial areas, the country-based firm sometimes finds it a problem to make its employees *want* to earn and thereby reach the standards of productivity which are necessary to its own success.

By providing technical education there is much the local Education Authority can do to introduce new skills and to create an awareness of industry. Faced with their own problems, the Education Authorities are sometimes a little slow to identify themselves with the countryside's objective of development and have not moved to anticipate its new industrial needs. The ideal must be to create within the countryside a reservoir of skill which will itself be an attraction to industry: this is no gamble with limited resources for if the skills cannot be used in the countryside they will still equip those youngsters who possess them for employment in the conurbations.

Communications are always posed as one of the major handicaps to industrial development in the remoter rural areas but in Mid-Wales we have not found this to be the difficulty we expected. Obviously on account of distance actual transport costs are likely to be higher. But actual costs are not the only criteria. The roads in the rural areas are far less congested and as a result, allowing speed and flexibility, they can to some extent balance the disadvantages. It is as the countryside develops and congestion threatens that major road schemes will be required.

Finally, in attracting new industry an area must necessarily consider the financial inducements which can be offered to incoming firms. It is important to record that during the first nine years (1957–66) in which the Mid-Wales Industrial Development Association was at work, Mid-Wales was *not* scheduled as a Development Area. During the early part of this period (which fortunately was at the time the Association was undertaking its initial survey into the area's resources) the area was without any special aid and it was quickly apparent that unless *some* inducement could be offered the task of attracting industry was going to be so slow as to have no effect on the problems it was intended to relieve. In 1958 the Association made out a case to the Development Commission that they should provide financial assistance for new factories to be built in Mid-Wales for lease to incoming firms on attractive terms. In other words, although not able to offer full Development Area facilities, Mid-Wales sought to provide some inducement by offering Board of Trade factories at subsidised rents. The Commissioners not only accepted the Association's application but also the principle that rural depopulation constituted grounds for action by them to encourage the establishment of new industry in the countryside.

From a position where, initially, the Commission would only build to meet a specific requirement, in 1963 it accepted an application from the Association for the building of an *advance* factory— that is to say a factory built before a specific tenant had been found for it. The application was made on the grounds that it was easier to attract industry to a building than to a green site and that the availability of premises had already proved to be a significant factor in deciding the location of new industry. The Commission accepted the Association's application for the first advance factory: since then it was approved the building of a further ten. The Board of Trade has built one advance factory in Mid-Wales at Blaenau Ffestiniog. Tenants were found for the first eight factories before building even started, and for the ninth before the building was completed. The remaining three factories are now being built.

Once it came to grips with the problems of the area it was to serve, the Mid-Wales Industrial Development Association brought mounting pressure on to the Governments of those days for Mid-

Wales to receive the same measure of assistance as was given to areas of high unemployment under the provisions of the Local Employment Act. Most of the arguments were on social grounds but the Beacham Report, 'Depopulation in Mid-Wales' (HMSO 1964) showed that there was a wider economic argument in favour of great support being given and, not least, that the cost of housing people in Mid-Wales might well be less than providing for them in the conurbations. Subsequently Mid-Wales was scheduled as a Development Area and it would be dishonest to suggest (particularly to any area not so scheduled) that the area does not consider this aid to be essential both to its maintenance and certainly to its future growth. None the less, it is equally true to say that the foundations for development were laid and significant progress achieved in earlier years before full Development Area status was achieved.

Throughout its work the Association's relationship with Government Departments has been excellent, though this is not to say that there have not been, and will not be, times of strain! But there has always been an understanding that it is the role of the Association to make the area stretch forward to development and of the Government to give it increasing support in its effort to do so. Initially, apart from benevolent encouragement, the area received little positive assistance from the Board of Trade; recently, as some Welsh problems move nearer to a solution, and Mid-Wales itself has shown evidence of what can be done in the countryside, this Department has begun to fulfil a more positive role. It will be no surprise to anyone concerned with rural development to learn that the main problems come from lack of any real co-ordination of Government policy on the development of Mid-Wales; new organisations continue to spring up, all seeking the same objective but rarely by the same route.

When it has gathered together all the information on the facilities it can provide, an area is in a position to sell itself to industry. The precise method of attracting industry is something which will vary from one area to another and one town to another. So much depends upon the type of industry required, what facilities the area can offer, and whether the area is one in which publicity is likely to bring the best results. The amount of money available for publicity is, of course, a vital factor but useful results can be achieved with as little as £2,500 per annum. The main methods of publicity are the distribution of leaflets, booklets, etc., advertising in newspapers and journals and on television, films, exhibitions and a host of variations.

Mid-Wales has found that it achieves the best results from direct mailing of literature to industrialists, backed by some newspaper advertising. With only modest resources at its disposal it concentrates its publicity on a specific area each year and also on a specific number of firms, usually about 5,000, which are of a kind most likely to be interested in expansion and whose development would be most likely to benefit Mid-Wales. The Association further concentrates its efforts by sending these firms a series of booklets rather than a single publication. Results are by no means immediate: one industrialist admitted that he had been 'throwing the Association's books away for years', but when he needed to develop he remembered Mid-Wales and ultimately transferred his company's entire production from Birmingham to Radnorshire.

From the 5,000 firms circularised there is perhaps a one per cent response. From this response and enquiries drawn from the Board of Trade, other development bodies and, in particular, from personal recommendations, the Association is now able to attract between 5 and 10 new firms to Mid-Wales each year.

In preparing booklets for circulation, attractive pictures of the area's scenery are helpful for they help to interest people in the area, especially those who may have to live there. But it is really most unlikely that an industrialist will select a location for his new factory *merely* because the location is a pretty one, or because there is a good golf course. It may be that there will be considerations of this kind, and it is accepted that the Managing Director's wife will have her say, but these considerations are marginal. If the industrialist is worth having he will be much more interested in the economic reasons of why he should come. And any booklet should tell him what those reasons are. Mid-Wales has little time for the industralist who professes that his main motive for establishing in the area is to 'help' it; he can best help it by making sure the area is one in which he will make a profit.

The purpose of industrial development in Mid-Wales has been to stimulate the economy as a means of stemming depopulation. In the absence of an obvious alternative the level of population may well be the yardstick by which to measure the success of the efforts which the area has achieved. For that reason the results of the 1971 Census of Population are keenly awaited. Already it is safe to say that if no industry had been attracted Mid-Wales would have been in a worse plight than it is. As it is, the Association's experience has shown that in Mid-Wales the scatter and sparsity of population precludes the attraction of industry at the speed and scale necessary to stem depopulation, and that the industrial and general development of the area are inter-dependent.

To put two or three firms into a small country town may provide much-needed employment and give a boost to the economy, but if it is a small town, once two or three firms (say 300 jobs) have been introduced most of the labour force will be absorbed. Moreover, to retain a cross-section of the population, particularly the better educated and more able, the provision of a diversity of employment is as essential as the actual amount of employment. There comes a time when to introduce more employment without more people creates the kind of competition for labour which firms were probably trying to escape in the first place by coming. If the growth of the small country towns is to be dependent upon natural increases only, with too few people in the reproductive age groups already, it will probably be found that if growth is achieved at all, it will not even offset outward migration.

Whilst the economic benefits of industrial development (such as additional purchasing power and rate revenue) are eagerly anticipated, many authorities overlook the fact that having the effect of retaining or attracting people, the attraction of industry imposes significant responsibilities for the provision, not only of sites and services, but of houses, roads, schools and the strengthening of the infrastructure as a whole. For the small authority expansion can be a heavy responsibility and a costly business.

Like so many rural areas, Mid-Wales has a settlement pattern long since out of date. Small towns are scattered about ten or fifteen miles apart and few of them are of a size or have the financial resources for significant growth. As indicated in the Beacham Report, there is little doubt that the area would benefit substantially if its existing scatter of population was reduced by nucleation into fewer and larger settlements. Such a policy of re-organisation poses many human and social problems. At best it is a long job for communities cannot be written off and they wither only slowly.

Unless carefully planned and controlled, the introduction of industry into a rural region may only serve to retain a settlement pattern which the economic and social planners know has no useful contribution to make (and probably little hope of survival) in the 21st Century. In fighting their own cause the rural areas have for years made good use of the argument that industrial dispersal must be used as the tool of the economic planners in their attempt to achieve a better balance of growth. Now those concerned with the rural regions should be prepared to use the location of industry as one of their sharpest tools in reshaping the economic and social framework of the countryside.

In Mid-Wales there is now a move towards the concentration of industrial and general development in fewer centres so as to achieve the maximum advantages of scale and the concentration of investment. The building of advance factories will, in future, be used more to encourage growth than to stem decline. Moreover, the decision to build an advance factory in a particular location will be influenced by the readiness of the local authority concerned to build some 'advance' houses as a means of attracting people to the employment which the new factory will offer. To provide houses in advance of any known demand involves some financial risk: the houses may stand empty for some time. For a small Mid-Wales authority the cost of having, say, 15 houses standing empty for 12 months would amount to some £4,000, or a rate of about 1s. 6d. Presently discussions are being held to establish if that risk can be minimised by the Development Commissioners undertaking to 'insure' the authority concerned against any loss of rent revenue for an agreed period.

In recent years Mid-Wales has also given careful consideration to the possibility of basing regional development upon the planned expansion of a number of its towns. After discussions with the area's County Planning Officers and Government Departments the Association itself recommended that studies should be undertaken into the feasibility of expanding seven of the area's small towns. Its choice of towns was based on a wide range of physical, social and economic factors: in the absence of any better guidance it suggested that the target should be to double the size of the towns within a decade.

On a practical basis the growth town policy provided the opportunity to encourage the area's towns to think in terms of development and for an assessment to be made of the adequacy of normal local authority sources of finance to meet the costs of relatively substantial development. It may be said that the concept of growth towns drew initial support from the opposition which had been shown in Mid-Wales to the then proposed New Town of 70,000 people at Caersws. Generally speaking, public opinion in Mid-Wales appeared to favour 'the expansion of existing towns' as opposed to a new town, preferring to retain both a settlement pattern and a social and cultural pattern with which it was familiar.

The growth town policy has been carried forward in Mid-Wales by simple economic and planning studies of five towns, Rhayader, Bala, Lampeter, Builth Wells and Brecon (all of which have populations of between 1,000 and 5,000). The studies have been intended to examine the feasibility of growth and how physically it might be achieved. If judgement is to be made now after some two years, it would have to be said that whilst a small authority's powers may be adequate enough to enable it to undertake expansion, its financial resources are not. Of the greatest significance and importance also is the evidence which has been forthcoming that the small authority has difficulty in bringing to future planning the objectivity and resolve which is necessary. Future prosperity tends to succumb to present interests. Issues as to the line of a road, the use of certain bits of land and even the possible introduction of people of a different culture, assume locally such enormous proportions that the objective of the town's development is lost sight of and is not pursued.

These factors combine to raise again the need for regional agencies which working within the framework of national policy, can make objective decisions as to a region's development and can have the powers and means to carry them out. The type of agency required and the means and powers it should have are a matter for detailed study.

Despite the fact that Mid-Wales has innumerable bodies concerned with its development, a substantial step forward was taken in 1968 with the formation by the Government under the powers of the New Towns Act 1965, of the Mid-Wales New Town Development Corporation. Formed specifically to strengthen the economy of the region by creating new centre of population the first task of the Corporation is to expand Newtown, Montgomeryshire, from its present population of 5,500 to 11,000 by the end of the 1970s. When forming the Corporation the Secretary of State for Wales said it would be open to him to extend its remit in the light of its progress at Newtown. Clearly with the limits of speed and scale which are imposed upon the expansion of existing towns, the future strengthening of the area's settlement pattern and thereby the strengthening of its economy must depend largely on the extension of the Corporation's work.

The Mid-Wales Industrial Development Association was one of the first organisations formed to promote the development of a rural region. Its formation drew on the spirit and determination of the area to solve its own problems. It has no powers. Its only weapon has been persuasion. Its strength has been its belief in its purpose. It has shown what can be done. Through the provision, so far, of 53 new factories and 4,000 new jobs it has helped to create in Mid-Wales a demand for people. And in an area which for years has only known a decline, to have created a demand for people means that conditions are being created in which the solution to depopulation and progress towards modest but nonetheless significant growth is feasible. Perhaps best of all the Association has helped to create a situation where, now more concerned with the problems of how it is to grow, the area no longer looks over its shoulder at the shadows of past decline but ahead at the brightening sky of the future.

REFERENCES
1. *Geography at Aberystwyth*, Chapter XXI, University of Wales Press, 1968.
2. HARBURY, C. D., *Productivity of rural labour*, University of Wales Press, 1958.

THE ESTABLISHMENT OF NEW INDUSTRY – APPENDIX I
MANUFACTURING INDUSTRIES OPERATING
IN MID-WALES
JUNE 1969

Animal Feedingstuffs	3
Brickworks	2
Carpets	1
Clothing	2
Concrete Products	1
Engineering	23
Explosives	1
Fishing Tackle	1
Food Products	6
Furniture	1
Glassware	1
Horticultural Products	1
Leather	3
Leather Goods	1
Musical Instruments	1
Needles	1
Office Equipment	2
Ornaments, etc.	1
Packaging	3
Paint	1
Plastics	3
Perfume	1
Pet Foods	1
Pottery	1
Printers	7
Shoes	1
Tar Distillers	1
Textiles	3
Timber Products	9
Tyre retreading	1

TOTAL 94

Qualifications: 10 employees.
Bakers have been excluded.

4 | Amenity and Tourism in the Countryside

MICHAEL DOWER, M.A., A.R.I.C.S., A.M.T.P.I.
Director,
Dartington Amenity Research Trust

'Amenity', by the dictionary, means pleasantness. In this chapter it is taken to cover those sides of social and physical planning which contribute to the pleasantness of life rather than to its basic functioning as do jobs, food or timber. It covers leisure, holiday-making, the beauty of our surroundings, the protection of our cultural heritage. Thus it takes us at once into fields of *development* —for tourism and recreation—and of *conservation* of our scenic, natural and historic heritage—a duality to which I shall return.

Within this, I take 'tourism' to mean travelling away from home for one or more nights, for purpose of change, refreshment, curiosity or education. 'Recreation', which forms a part of tourism, is also distinct from it; and includes the leisure activity of the residents within, and of day visitors to, any area, for example those who come from Glasgow to Aviemore to ski on a winter Sunday.

'The countryside', for this chapter, means the remoter rural regions of Britain, namely much of Scotland, Wales, the Pennines, and the south-west. Some examples are also taken from Ireland. The subject of amenity and tourism in the countryside can be considered under four headings:

1. the trends of tourism, recreation and related activity;
2. the combined demands which they place on remote rural areas;
3. the impact of these demands on the economy and land use of these areas;
4. the implications for planning and action.

TRENDS OF TOURISM, RECREATION AND RELATED ACTIVITY

Tourism in Britain has two main elements—holidaymaking by British people within this country, and visits by foreigners.

Total holidaymaking by British people grew steadily from 1950 to 1960, but has been roughly constant at 35 to 36 million holidays a year during the last decade. Of these, about 5 million holidays a year are spent abroad, leaving 30 to 31 million holidays (defined as four nights or more spent away from home) per year in Britain. Of this 31 million total, about 5 million are on second holidays, of which 70 per cent take place outside the peak months of July–August (against only 36 per cent of main holidays).[1] There is in addition an unknown total of week-end and other short trips away from home.

The future prospects for British holidaymaking are uncertain. Rises in population, in average income, car ownership, paid holidays and in numbers of school and university students and retired people over the last decade have *not* produced any increase in the number of holidays. One may guess that people are preferring to spend time and money on, in, and from the home rather than to face the cost, traffic and other uncertainties of a holiday away. As incomes and other factors rise further in the future, we *may* see another swing upwards in holidaymaking. It has been estimated, by reference to these factors, that total British holiday trips at home might rise to about 40 million in 1975 and 48 million in 1985.[2] My own view is that such growth is unlikely to occur unless our national economy takes a steady upwards course, and unless major improvements are made to the communications to and within our holiday regions. Meanwhile, we should remember that those on holiday at home are nevertheless on holiday, spending money and seeking recreation, often over quite a wide area.

Visits by foreigners to Britain (including those for business and similar purposes as well as holidays) have been rising sharply since the war, from 203,000 in 1946 to 1·7 million in 1960 and 3·6 million in 1967. The figure is likely to rise to 5 million in 1970[1]; and heavy promotion, plus falling group travel costs, should ensure that it continues to rise thereafter, possibly to 7½ million in 1975 and 12 million in 1985.

Tourism on this scale, of course, has major economic significance to the country. British people now spend on holidays within Britain at least £560 million a year, of which part might otherwise be spent abroad; and foreign visitors to Britain spend over £250 million a year, plus at least £85 million in fares paid to British carriers, a substantial 'invisible export'.[1]

Table 4.1. *Trends of Tourism in Great Britain, 1946–67*

	1946	1951	1960	1964	1967
		millions (to nearest 100 thousand)			
British holiday-makers:					
Holidays abroad		1·5	3·5	5	5
Main holidays in Britain		23·5	26	26	25·5
Second holidays in Britain		1·5	5·5	5	5
Total holidays		26·5	35	36	35·5
Foreign visitors to Britain:	0·2	0·7	1·7	2·6	3·6
Expenditure in Britain by:		£ million (to nearest million)			
British holiday-makers		320*	400	430	560
Foreign visitors†	12	75	169	190	236
Total		395	569	620	786

* Includes expenditure on day trips.
† Includes expenditure by visitors from the Irish Republic, who are excluded from the visitor numbers earlier in the table.

What do these figures mean to the remote rural regions? Because of the contrast they offer to life in urbanised lowlands, these regions attract a handsome share of the British holiday market: the South-West and Wales in particular, have markedly increased their shares since 1950. The South-West now attracts 20 per cent of British holidaymakers (some 6 million people) each year; Wales, Scotland, and North-East England each 12 per cent; North and East England each 9 per cent.[1] The bulk of each region's visitors still come from within that or immediate neighbouring regions,[2,3,4] but the sense of mobility is increasing, with an even higher proportion travelling by car and moving about between regions while on holiday.[1]

For foreign visitors, the picture is less clear. We know that about 80 per cent of all foreign tourists visit London; and that large numbers go to Windsor, Stratford, Oxford, Cambridge and Brighton.[1] Certain centres within the remoter regions are also strong magnets, notably Edinburgh; but generally these regions form only secondary elements in the visits of those who come, with Scotland as the possible exception. Thus, the indications are that Scotland and the South-West each attract some 15 per cent of foreign visitors to Britain; Wales and the Lake District about 10 per cent; but that the average nights per person spent in any one of these regions is low.[5]

The post-war growth in *recreation* springs from the factors I have mentioned for tourism—the rise in population, income, car owner-ship, paid holidays, education—and from changes in communication and technology, notably the impact of television. These have led to rapid growth in almost every type of recreation activity, both at home and away from home. For the remoter regions, the most significant increases have been in pleasure driving, particularly at weekends, with ever-growing numbers pouring out of cities on to coast and countryside for a change of scenery; in active individual sports such as golf, riding or skiing; in fishing, swimming and all kinds of water sport; and in the distances people are prepared to go for these activities.[6,7] Thus, not only holidaymakers, but day-visitors from considerable distances, are now coming into the remoter regions for recreation. Day visits from Glasgow to Aviemore, from Manchester to the Lake District, Birmingham to Mid-Wales, Bristol to Dartmoor, are now commonplace.

Thus the remoter regions are under growing pressure of recreational demand from holidaymakers, from day visitors from outside their area—and, let us not forget, from their own residents. The space for recreation which such regions offer can have real force in holding, or attracting, people to live and work there—hence the proper emphasis on recreation, and indeed on their region's landscape, in reports by Economic Planning Councils and other bodies.[8]

A further related field is in demand for *educational* activity in the countryside. The rise in field studies, the growing interest in wild life, in history and in regional culture, all imply demands of high relevance to the scenic, natural and historic heritage of the remoter regions.

The general impression must be of a steady growth in demands for tourism, recreation and education of which the remoter regions can aim to attract a share, not only for their own benefit, but to take pressure from some of the better-trodden routes.

DEMANDS PLACED ON REMOTE RURAL AREAS

There are three broad types of demand:
   (a) for attractions and facilities;
   (b) for accommodation;
   (c) for communications and services.

Attractions and facilities
These are fundamental. Tourist accommodation may seem more central, but it cannot alone draw people to an area. They come

because they can see things, do things they want to see and do. Expressed in economic terms, these are the 'products' they want to buy; and an area which wants such customers must know the products it can offer in a competitive world.

There are perhaps five main types of effective attraction, each presenting a main appeal to different markets. First, the traditional one of sun and sea, still a strong draw for British people who do not want to travel far on holiday, but not a serious magnet for overseas visitors: an asset to be safeguarded and developed, but not a universal attraction. Second, scenic driving by car or coach, a major interest since car-ownership became widespread, still a novelty and favourite holiday or week-end activity for millions, but likely to decline somewhat in future as the novelty wears off and road congestion gets worse. Third, sightseeing, that is, visiting historic houses, castles, battlefields, monuments, gardens, wild-life parks, beauty spots, the homes and graves of ancestors. This is a real growth sector, still rooted in curiosity, but with a growing search for real understanding and information; it is popular among foreign visitors, and it presents a challenge to the managers of manifold key features in each region. Fourth, active sports, no longer just for John MacNab with his rifle or the local poacher with his gaff, but for hundreds or thousands in fishing, sailing, canoeing, skiing, pony trekking, walking and climbing—all demanding space, clubhouses, stables, equipment, approach roads. Last, educational activity, from field studies in botany to summer schools on art, language courses, conferences, National Trust cruises, children's summer camps; a growing market not confined to the summer season; requiring imagination to launch and run.

Together, these attractions make a clear-cut physical demand upon a region, varying with the emphasis between them. They require limited areas of land and water in sole or dominant use for recreation, such as golf courses, beach access areas, historic sites or the country parks for which the Countryside Acts provide; a system of routes to link these, mainly roads, rights of way and waterways; and the secondary or sporadic use of areas of moor, wood or farmland for walking, riding, picnicking, shooting and so on. But they also increasingly demand the skilled conservation of resources and of heritage. Thus the angler must have pure water and healthy fish, the naturalist needs the osprey, others need the historic site and the scenery itself. This does not imply 'no change'; but it is a growing factor in land management—a point to which I shall return.

Second of the demands, *accommodation*. British and foreign holidaymakers together spend some 360 million bed-nights on holiday away from home in Britain each year. Of this total, just over 81 per cent is in the four months of June to September, just over 55 per cent in the two peak months of July and August,[1] with a peak demand for about 2¾ million beds at one time. Since the average peak occupancy is probably 75–80 per cent,[9] this means there may be some 3½–4 million beds available for holiday use in Britain.

These range from the traditional 'with-catering' forms such as hotels, guesthouses and cottages, through 'all-in' holiday camps, to the more informal 'self-catering' types such as holiday flats, chalets, caravans and camp sites. Since the war, there has been a marked increase in the proportion of holidays by British holidaymakers spent in the higher grades of hotels, in holiday camps and in most of the 'self-catering' types, with a decrease in that spent in the lower grades of hotels and in guest-houses.[1,4,10] Foreign holiday-makers, who tend to move around more and to be less self-catering, have greater emphasis on hotels and guest houses.

The changes in demand have been reflected in the trends of accommodation, with marked increase in total beds in the 1950s and since then slow total growth, improvement in quality but not much in quantity of hotel accommodation, and a strong swing towards self-catering types, which have a relatively short season and therefore are proportionately higher in number. Since they involve less capital than the hotels, these self-catering types can expand easily as demand grows; and this expansion has been particularly sharp in some of the remote regions. In the south-west, for example, 41 per cent of the 643,000 beds in the whole region are now of the self-catering type; and the Kingsbridge area, in which the number of visitors at peak exceeds the number of residents, has 65 per cent of its 20,600 beds in this category.[7]

It is in hotels that the shortages are now beginning to become serious. Only 26,500 new hotel beds were built in the decade ended 1966.[11] The prospect of an extra 500,000 foreign visitors each year, with an average stay in Britain of 17 nights, led the Hotel and Catering Economic Development Committee to press for Government encouragement of hotel building, and hence to the provisions

of the Development of Tourism Act. The E.D.C. believe that much
of the growth in the demand for bednights, and in hotel building,
could and should come to the remoter regions.[11] I shall comment
later on the economic implications of this.

The third demand is for *communications and services.* I have
mentioned the swing, in holiday transport, towards the car.
Nationally, 67 per cent of main holidays and 70 per cent of second
holidays by British people at home are taken by car.[1] For holidays
to remote regions, the proportion is even higher, for example 80
per cent for visitors to Devon and Cornwall.[3] In these regions, with
little public transport, the car is clearly needed by most visitors,
both to get there and to get around. Thus, good roads to and
within the regions are vital—roads able to cope in many areas with
a sudden doubling, or more, of the local car population in the
summer;[10] and in places such as Aviemore with year-round recreational traffic. Local life and traffic can adjust a bit, but it cannot
disappear: visitors are tolerant of road congestion, but only to a
certain point. In many areas, the inadequacy of roads is becoming a
serious impediment to the growth of recreation and tourism, and
road improvements are a major item of cost to cater for them, as is
well shown by the report on the Cairngorms area.[12] As a corollary,
of course, good roads may bring more visitors than you can cope
with (witness the effect of the M6 upon the Lake District): and
unimproved roads may be the best way to maintain the character
of the place and of the recreation experience, and to keep the number
of visitors within reasonable bounds (witness, again, the policy on
local roads in the Lake District.[13])

Visitors who do *not* have cars, of course, need a combination of
private and public transport, which may be readily available in
populous regions and main resorts, but is by no means always so
in the remoter regions. The decline of rural bus and railway services
since the war is a real drawback.[12] One could wish that the Barbara
Castle policy of social subsidy had come earlier and done more to
slow down the Beeching-type process of closure. The private railway
lines such as the Ffestiniog and the Dart Valley Railway, and the
serious hopes for similar initiative on the Edinburgh–Carlisle line,
show something of the potential and of the imaginative flair which
is needed.

We must, in fact, increasingly gear our communications to the
needs of the visitor—and use him to help to sustain and improve the

year-round infrastructure for residents of the region. This is true also of services—water, sewerage, refuse disposal, hospitals, rescue services, police, information centres, garages, shops, toilets, roadside rest areas—inadequacy in any one of which may spoil the visitor's holiday and damage the reputation of the area. Such services have to be paid for (sometimes, as with water supply, to an extent much above local needs): but they help to earn the income from tourism, and, if skilfully planned, can form part of the year-round social structure of the area.

IMPACT OF AMENITY AND TOURISM ON THE ECONOMY AND LAND USE OF THE REMOTER AREA

The impact on the economy. I have mentioned that British holiday-makers and foreign visitors together spend at least £800 million in Britain each year. To this should be added a further large expenditure on recreation away from home—and we have the prospect of substantial increases in both these figures in the future.

How much of this expenditure now comes, or could come, to the remote regions? We have no detailed figures, but the gross annual tourist expenditure is estimated to be about £115 million in the South West,[3] £100 million in Scotland,[14] at least £50 million in Wales.[4] For parts of these regions, e.g. the county of Cornwall, the gross income from tourism equals that from manufacturing industry, and is only just less than that from agriculture.[10]

Of this total expenditure, probably 50–60 per cent is spent on accommodation and food, about 15 per cent on travel within the region, and the rest on recreation, shopping, entertainment, eating out, etc.[10] A fairly high proportion is thus paid for labour and for local products or services, rather than in such forms as petrol tax which go straight out of a region. It has been estimated that gross tourist expenditure has a higher multiplier effect within a local economy than the average general expenditure within that economy.[3]

In terms of direct or indirect employment, tourism has been estimated to support at least 9 per cent of the total civilian work force in the South West,[5] 11 per cent in Cornwall,[10] 10 per cent in Pembrokeshire.[2] There is, of course, a seasonal element in this, with some adverse economic effects (such as importing seasonal workers who then take their wages outside the area, some winter unemployment, and some seasonal diversion of labour out of other industries). But the general impression[3, 10, 15] is that the bulk of the 'indirect' labour force (e.g. in garages or transport) is employed year-round on this and other work, and that much of the 'direct' labour force in hotels, restaurants, etc., is either employed year-round or family labour prepared to work hard in the summer and to slacken off and even 'live off their fat' in the winter.

Tourism is thus already a substantial element in the economy of many remoter areas, and can certainly become so for others. But there are clear dangers in making an area too heavily dependent on tourism: 'a planned level of tourism must be integrated with an improved basic economy since there are limits to the attraction to the tourist of a depopulated countryside, and an economy based solely on tourism might find it difficult to provide the labour force which the tourist industry requires.'[16]

Within the accommodation sector, which has the bulk of the gross income, the economic picture varies greatly. Expenditure per visitor can range from £5 or more per day in a luxury hotel to less than £1 per day on a camp site. But this, of course, reflects costs of comfort, service and food provided. The camp-site operator or the bed-and-breakfast lady, self-employed, with low capital outlay and no S.E.T., may have a high percentage of net return and an income which stays wholly in the local community, with a high multiplier effect. It is the higher forms of 'with-catering' accommodation which face the most difficult economic problems, with labour costs, S.E.T. and the need for steady improvement of capital facilities; and which therefore need high occupancy for a longish season. Indeed a new hotel, with full capital cost to be serviced, can seldom be justified without nearly year-round trade.

For this reason, most of the new hotel building has been in London or other centres, the remoter regions having made do largely with hotel extensions.[11] Government assistance under the Industrial Development Act, 1966, through the Highlands and Islands Development Board, and now more widely under the Development of Tourism Act, should make possible a new growth of hotels—but still only in places where they can attract visitors year-round, as in the Aviemore Centre, or where they can supplement visitors with business use, conferences, local events, travelling salesmen and the like, as in a place like Inverness, Invergordon or perhaps Lerwick.[17] Hotels are not, of course, only used for tourism: they are also, in the words of the Hotel and Catering E.D.C., 'a necessary part of the infrastructure needed to sustain economic development' in the remoter regions.[11]

Where new hotels cannot be justified, it may, nevertheless, be possible to extend existing hotels, on the lines of the growing Irish policy of encouraging a steady 'upward change' in accommodation types, with the bed-and-breakfast cottage becoming a guest-house, the guest-house an hotel, and so on—a fruitful way to encourage native enterprise and local income; and also to improve the return on existing accommodation by actions to extend the season, such as festivals, educational activity, low-season or winter sports, and incentives such as the 'Highland Holiday Ticket'.[17]

It has already been mentioned that any form of accommodation enterprise depends for its economic success upon the existence of attractions, and the adequacy of communications and services, in the area. The higher grades of hotel or holiday camp, for whom this dependence is critical, often themselves take the initiative in providing the attractions—from golf courses to fishing rights, swimming pools to skating rinks (witness the Aviemore Centre and the Coylumbridge Hotel)—or in pressing for public or co-operative effort to ensure they are provided. But a substantial part of the cost must fall on public funds, as is well recognised in the longer-established resorts. In the South-West, for example, urban district councils in holiday areas levied 175 shillings and spent 209 shillings on average per head of resident population in 1967–8, against 126 shillings levied and 189 shillings spent by those in non-holiday areas—figures which reflect their extra costs in highways, recreation grounds, lighting, public conveniences, publicity, and, in some cases, new sewerage schemes to prevent fouling of beaches. It should be said that the same holiday towns had an average rateable value per head of £45, against £34 for the non-holiday towns.[3]

The order of magnitude of public costs in servicing tourism and recreation will, of course, vary widely, according to the infrastructure which exists and the size of the 'threshold' which has to be crossed when the numbers of visitors pass a given point. The potential order of magnitude is well illustrated by the proposals in the Cairngorm Area report[12] for £34 million of largely public investment, much of it directly for tourism. It should be emphasised that new infrastructure can usually bring benefits to other parts of the local economy as well as in tourism: and vice versa, that capital development undertaken for other purposes, for example hydroelectricity, can have a strong by-product in tourist activity. But in an increasingly interventionist economy, with limited capital resources, we must weigh carefully the economic arguments for each major investment.

The impact on land use (including farming and forestry). Up to now, farming and forestry have largely stood aloof from tourism and recreation, often more concerned to restrict their negative impacts in litter, fires, vandalism or traffic, than to find positive and mutual benefit in them. But interest in such positive benefit is now growing.

The most obvious link with *agriculture* is, of course, in farm holidays, already an important source of income to many farmers and of holiday enjoyment to town families. A recent report[18] has shown that some 18 per cent of all farmers in Cornwall now take in holiday-makers; that at least a further 20 per cent would do so if they had space or time; and that gross receipts from visitors amount to more than a quarter of their net income for a majority of farmers concerned. Of course, many of the small dairy farms in Cornwall, near to the attractions of the coast, have both the need, the space and the opportunity for this type of trade. The two-room crofter's house in the Hebrides, or the remote hill farm in the Pennines or Wales, may seem less suited to the purpose. But even in such areas growth in farm holidays could be encouraged by extensions and chalet building of the type grant-aided in parts of Ireland; by conversion of farm buildings or layout of caravan and camp sites; by opening of tea-rooms and craft workshops[19]; and also by creating attractions.

Thus the farmers, individually or in groups, could exploit or create opportunities for riding, shooting, fishing, nature study, even for educational use of the farming process and of the countryside. Action of this type, including game management and creation of farm ponds, has converted thousands of American farms into largely recreational enterprises; is the subject of current experiment projects by the Countryside Commission in the Lake District and Snowdonia; and deserves substantial thought here at a time of growing economic uncertainty for much of our marginal agriculture.

In *forestry*, too, we are seeing a swing towards recreation and amenity, not just as secondary aspects but as equal and, in places, dominant factors in forest planning and management. The Forestry Commission is already catering for public use, for example in its

Forest Parks, school forests, and camp sites such as that at Loch Morlich.[20] Now the Countryside Act has given the Commission a specific brief for recreation, including powers to plant new forest for amenity purposes. We are likely to see, in the State sector at least, not the actual multiple use of forest land, but the increasing use of forests as the setting and shelter for recreation, from camping to watching deer, picnicking to orienteering.[21] The likely consequence will be growing adjustment of forestry layout and regimes, some loss of timber output, and, hopefully, much new planting for the specific purpose of recreation and amenity—the sort of swing that has transformed the Dutch Forest Service into a primarily recreational agency.[22] Although the direct income from recreation—in camping and parking fees, shooting licences, game products, photographic safaris and the like—may never be very great, this use may well help to justify switching land from agriculture to forestry, even at times of the high interest rates which have been shown to favour farming.[23]

This leads on, of course, to the wider issue of land use and conservation. As pressures on our limited land surface grow, the public interest in the sound management of our rural land is becoming stronger—not only to produce wholesome food and sound timber and to sustain a social economy, but also to conserve soil and water, to enhance the climate, to provide opportunities for recreation and education, to protect and encourage variety and wealth in wild life and in the scenic and historic heritage. Such management demands a width and unity of understanding, and a humble realism about resources, which it is difficult to achieve today with our fragmented land-ownership, pursuit of single-purpose aims and proud technology. For too long now we have been abusing our land, over-cutting, over-grazing, polluting, eroding, taking out more than we put back, until much of the land is in poor heart, the soil thin, the wild-life depleted, the rivers polluted, the heritage attenuated. None too soon, we may be moving towards an era of better management, for example in the legislation on common land, the East Hampshire Study,[24] the reclamation of derelict land. But the need is far greater than our present effort, in the remote areas as elsewhere, and it may be that the demands of tourism and recreation can not only themselves be sensitive to their effect on resources,[16] but also provide the impetus for wider change.

IMPLICATIONS FOR PLANNING AND ACTION

Finally, what implications do tourism and amenity have for planning and action? I said at the start that amenity includes aspects of development and of conservation. This duality is critical to the future of the remote regions. How in the terms of the National Parks Act, are we to balance 'beauty' and 'access'? How can we attract tourists without over-running the very resources that attract them? How do we reconcile development and conservation?

At the same time, our planning and action face other challenges. How can we assess the real economic impact of what we do? How can we choose between the types of tourist, and of tourist development, open to us? How can we produce firm plans, yet be flexible to changes in circumstances? How, most tricky of all, can we bring together the diverse people involved in the amenity and tourism of a region?

These were the questions which in 1965 faced the advisers to the Irish local authorities on planning for amenity and tourism in a country with a rapid growth in tourism, magnificent but fragile resources, inadequate services, and strong economic need in its remote rural areas.

They tackled the problem of balancing people and resources by adopting the idea of 'capacity'—capacity not only in beds or water supply, but in attractions and natural resources. It was proposed to measure the capacity of each area's resources—for example, its beaches, mountains and fishing waters—to take human use without damage to the resource or to the recreation experience; and of the extent to which these were already taken up by residents of and visitors to the area. The surplus of uncommitted capacity was then the 'product' which the area could use to attract new visitors, and also set the ceiling to the number of those new visitors if the character of the area was not to change.

Beside this were set the capacity and usage of other resources which the visitor would need—accommodation, wet-weather or evening facilities, water and sewerage systems, road capacity, public transport—so that one had a firm basis for judging the demands of new tourists upon these resources and the points at which thresholds would be reached and new capital investment required.

The relevance and likely impact of different sorts of visitor were briefly studied. This was important. In the past, in most tourist-minded regions, there has been a tendency to welcome all kinds of visitor and encourage all types of holiday development. It may seem natural to think that this will continue and that the trends in holiday-making should be accepted in order to get all the benefit in an increasingly competitive field. But this very competition demands a more deliberate approach. It is necessary to *be* competitive; it is equally necessary to build long-term strength into a region's economy, and to obtain maximum benefit from capital resources which will inevitably be scarce. We must, therefore, understand and build upon our strength. The aim must be to attract chiefly those visitors who bring the strongest economic return on the region's resources, i.e. those who most effectively use whatever surplus resources we now have; who cause least costs in new resources or in competition with other basic resource-users such as industry; and who bring the most direct benefits by their expenditure.

Our work in Donegal[25] showed clearly that two small parts of the county had a level of tourism damagingly in excess of their capacity; that the rest had enough surplus natural resources to take a large increase in tourism without damage; that the type of resources was particularly suited to many British and some Continental visitors; that investment would be needed in accommodation, facilities and some services; and that a high gross return on this investment could be expected.

The last seven or eight years have seen substantial planning effort in relation to tourism in many of our remoter areas, as illustrated particularly in the reports on the south-west[3,9,10]; the studies of Pembrokeshire,[2] Snowdonia and other areas in Wales; the county tourism plans in Scotland; the Tourism Development Plan of the Highlands and Islands Development Board[17]; and the almost completed series of nine regional studies commissioned by the Scottish Tourist Board.[14] These reports have given a good impression of the natural resources of each area, but they have varied greatly in their coverage of accommodation, infrastructure and economics and hence in their precision as a basis for action.

It is on the theme of *action* that I want to conclude. I have emphasised the three main needs of tourists—attractions, accommodation, services—and the interdependence of the varied private and public bodies who control them. We must realise, in fact, that tourism is an *industry*—an industry not confined to the hotels and

D

restaurants which come together in the British Hotels and Restaurants Association, the Hotel and Catering Industry Training Board, and the Economic Development Committee for Hotels and Catering; or which are eligible for registration, grant or loan under the Development of Tourism Act. The industry extends to the full range of elements I have mentioned—all types of accommodation, attractions, facilities, communications, infrastructure, services, information, even conservation.

Looking at this range of features, one can see how fragmented they are; how varied in size and sponsorship; how interlocked with other interests in investment and in land; how lacking in machinery for co-ordination of investment and management. Hence the uneven standards of service and of resource management, the lack of information, the absence of key elements, above all the absence of concerted action.

Of course, we are moving towards collation of effort, away from narrow or single-purpose action. We have the excellent work, in exposition and information, of the National Trust for Scotland[26]; the Highlands and Islands Development Board, with its powers to initiate, co-ordinate and assist effort in tourism as in other fields; the Agriculture Act, with its multi-purpose Rural Development Boards; the Countryside Acts, giving wide powers to the two Countryside Commissions and encouraging public support for private enterprise; the Transport Act, bidding the Waterways Board to plan for recreation; the Commons Registration Act, providing a first basis for agreed management; and now the Development of Tourism Act, providing for research and assistance to tourist facilities as well as aid to hotels. We also have the growing liaison between all these and other bodies at national level, through the Countryside in 1970 Conferences and in other ways—liaison which is vital as we multiply the number of public bodies in each region who can influence tourism or amenity.

But it is at the county or area scale that effective, unified action really counts. At this scale we need a new range of bodies, not necessarily of uniform units, not supplanting local government, not necessarily executive in function, but able to bring together the public, commercial, private and voluntary bodies concerned with tourism and related matters; to achieve agreement on a tourist purpose for the area, and on collated investment programmes; to clarify what new elements of information, advice, training and public action are needed; and to initiate these or press regional or national bodies to do so. The council for Wales and Monmouthshire,[4] the Scottish Tourist Board[14] and the Highlands Board[17] have all emphasised the need for area tourism organisations. Recommendations for such a body were made in the Royal Grampian Study[16] and the Galloway Project;[27] and not the least reason why Aviemore is an apt venue for this Conference is that the Cairngorms Sports Development Company is one pioneering example of how such a body might work.

REFERENCES

1. *Digest of tourist statistics*, British Travel Association, 1969.
2. *Present and future demands for holiday facilities in the Pembrokeshire National Park*, Economic Associates Ltd. for National Parks Commission, HMSO, 1967.
3. LEWES, F. M. M. *et al.*, *The holiday industry of Devon and Cornwall*, University of Exeter, 1969.
4. *Report on the Welsh holiday industry*, Council for Wales and Monmouthshire, HMSO, 1963.
5. *A region with a future: a draft strategy for the South West*, South-west Economic Planning Council, HMSO, 1967.
6. *Fourth wave—the challenge of leisure*, Civic Trust, 1965.
7. *Pilot national recreation survey*, British Travel Association, Keele University, 1967.
8. *The Scottish Economy 1965–7*, HMSO, 1967.
9. *A Study of Tourist and Holiday Facilities in South-West England*, Miles-Kelcey Ltd., Consultants for British Travel Association, 1969.
10. *Survey of the Holiday Industry*, Cornwall County Council, 1966.
11. *Investment in Hotels and Catering*, Hotel and Catering Economic Development Committee, N.E.D.C. Office, HMSO, 1968.
12. *Cairngorm Area: Report of the Technical Group on the Cairngorm Area of the Eastern Highlands of Scotland*, Scottish Development Department, HMSO, 1967.
13. *The Week-end Motorist in the Lake District*, Countryside Commission, HMSO, 1969.
14. Report of the Scottish Tourist Board, 1968–9.
15. *Tourism in Northumberland*, Northumberland County Council, 1966.
16. *Royal Grampian County*, Department of Geography, University of Aberdeen for Scottish Tourist Board, 1969.
17. *Third Report of the Highlands and Islands Development Board, 1968*.
18. DAVIES, E. T., *Tourism and The Cornish Farmer*, Department of Economics, University of Exeter, 1969.
19. *Land Use in the Highlands and Islands*, HMSO, 1964.
20. *Public Recreation in National Forests*, W. E. S. Mutch for Forestry Commission, HMSO, 1968.
21. KILPATRICK, C. S., *Public Response to Forest Recreation in Northern Ireland*, Forestry Division, Ministry of Agriculture, Belfast, 1964.
22. *The Task of the State Forest Service of the Netherlands*, State Forest Service, Utrecht, 1966.

23. *Forestry, Agriculture and the Multiple Use of Rural Land*, HMSO, 1966.
24. *East Hampshire A.O.N.B.: A Study in Countryside Conservation*, Hampshire County Council *et al.*, 1968.
25. *Planning for Amenity and Tourism*, A project of the Government of Ireland assisted by the United Nations Special Fund and the United Nations, The National Institute for Physical Planning and Conservation Research, Dublin, 1966.
26. *Seeing Scotland 1969*, National Trust for Scotland, and other publications.
27. *The Galloway Project*, Regional Studies Group, Strathclyde University for Scottish Tourist Board, 1968.

5 | Population Changes and the Provision of Services

J. GARETH THOMAS, M.A.
Registrar,
University of Wales

One of the classic remoter rural areas of these islands is that central part of Wales which in terms of physical geography and topographic features is bounded to the north by Snowdonia and its eastward extensions, and to the south by the Brecon Beacons, the Black Mountains of Carmarthenshire, and the Preseli range in North Pembrokeshire. The western boundary is the Irish Sea, a fact which perhaps gives added significance to the word 'remote' as part of the theme of this Conference, while to the east the river systems of the Dee, Severn, Wye and Usk, opening as they do on to the plains of Cheshire, Shropshire and Herefordshire present, if not a sharp boundary line, then at least a significant boundary zone.

By virtue of its location alone, therefore, Mid-Wales is remote, and this remoteness is intensified by the region's physical characteristics. The existence of the moorland core of Pumlumon (Plynlimmon), with river systems draining west or east from the central watershed, means that natural lines of movement are very restricted so that the region has, as it were, an 'in-built' remoteness and sense of isolation.

These two factors of external and internal remoteness have also operated to establish and maintain Mid-Wales as a predominantly rural area. There are of course small market-towns and there is some industrial development (v. Chapter 4), but neither its raw materials (or lack of them), nor its general location in relation to potential or existing markets, have allowed Mid-Wales to develop any industries, extractive or manufacturing, which could have been the basis of any substantial urban development. Scattered lead mining and small scale woollen manufacturing, using water or imported fuel as a source of power, did not need, could not have maintained, and therefore did not create urban sprawls. The impact of the Industrial Revolution upon this region was small and the essentially rural nature of its economy and landscape was very largely preserved.

It is because Mid-Wales is so obviously remote and rural, and because it has these characteristics in such good measure, that in this chapter it will be treated as a case study for an examination of the problems associated with the provision of services in regions of declining population. Some of these problems may be unique to Mid-Wales, but others will have a general and widespread application.

The total population of this geographical region is *c*. 300,000 and it is administratively divided into five counties, Brecknock, Cardigan, Merioneth, Montgomery and Radnor. It reached its peak population in *c*. 1871 and since that date has lost almost a quarter of the population which was there at that time. From 1901 to the early sixties of this century the loss was about 600 per annum, and this from a region which at best was barely 'normal' in its rural population density. Overall figures are, however, inevitably misleading, and if the pattern of population movement within and from this region were to be analysed in more detail, three specific situations would be recognised, each one with its own areal pattern.

The first of these is to be seen in those areas where the population is decreasing both as a result of predominantly outwards migration and as a result of natural causes. These are the areas which are reaching the final stages of the demographic cycle in which, as a result of migration of the child-bearing age-groups, the residual population is unable to maintain, let alone increase, its own level by means of natural growth. There is no 'in-migration' of younger people, and the whole process becomes one, therefore, of cumulative decline. In Mid-Wales it is the upland core and its fringes which have reached this stage, which might, perhaps, be described as Stage III.

The second situation is that where natural trends and migration trends are at variance, and this is to be found in most of the lower foothill and upper valley lands which surround the upland moorland core. Here the population shows a natural increase which is offset by outwards migration so that the overall result is one of population decline. These are, of course, the critical areas, because this situation will inevitably lead to one of decline unless something can be done to arrest the outwards movement. These two situations are, therefore, very closely linked, and the latter might be described as the intermediate stage, or Stage II of the demographic cycle.

By contrast with these two basically unhealthy situations, the third is one where there is both natural increase and inwards migration, and one which, therefore, presents no real problem. It may be surprising to discover that this situation exists at all in what is obviously a problem region, but the explanation lies in the fact that it is restricted to the market towns and their immediate hinterlands together with certain very limited areas which for economic or physical reasons are particularly attractive in relation to the rest of the region.

This areal differentiation means that not only is there movement out of the region as a whole, but there is appreciable movement within it. Such internal movement, however, takes place according to a definite theme, that of outwards movement from the core to the peripheral areas of the towns, and a similar migration from those peripheral areas to the towns themselves. These last areas also, of course, have a dominant trend of movement out from the region entirely. Although the theme may, therefore, be a common one, the actual pattern has internal variations, with the result that not always can the problems be considered for the region as a whole. The basic problem may be the same, but its actual manifestation and the method of dealing with it must take account of areal variations.

Over-riding the causes of this theme of one-way movement, of which more will be said in the succeeding paragraphs, is the way in which individual persons or groups either wish to, or are able to, react to these causes. Some can and wish to react quickly, thus creating a mobile element in the population, while others form an immobile element which under some circumstances can be regarded as stable, under others as residual. The reasons for these varying reactions to a given set of circumstances are almost as varied as the individuals who provide the reactions. They are sometimes purely personal, deriving from an individual attitude to certain economic and social conditions; they may be sociological in that they are linked to the place which an individual or group with a certain background and education can or cannot find in a particular set of social conditions; they may be purely economic as a stark reflection of lack of employment or inability to make a living. These reasons are important but they are not sufficiently relevant to the subject matter of this chapter to discuss them further here. Two obvious trends which can be recognised as *a priori* and are relevant to it are, first, that the younger element in the population is the more mobile, a fact which was recognised by Ravenstein almost one hundred years ago, and, the second, that in a region of limited economic opportunity such as this, the pull of outwards migration is likely to be strongest upon those people who have developed specialist interests and have received specialist training and education. Apart from these factors which lead to mobility or immobility, and are sometimes difficult to explain, the causes of migration, though complex, can perhaps be summarised as resulting from three main elements, the first of which is purely personal and, therefore operates to a greater or lesser degree in every community.

The second derives from changes in national social habits and requirements. It is linked with the overall increase in the general standard of living and of education which has led to certain social and service conditions being regarded as essential, especially by young people, to the maintenance of what they regard as a 'life worth living'. Young men, and especially young married women are no longer prepared to do without the 'utilities', even though they may have to be privately supplied; they are no longer prepared to live in inconvenient, poorly appointed, and outmoded houses; they are no longer satisfied with having access only to shops with a limited range of goods of whatever type, and they now expect to be able, with ease, to establish social contacts with people of their own age and interests. It, therefore, follows that the remoter rural areas, by virtue of their very location, are unattractive, and when to this are added the conditions deriving from upland physical character- istics the situation is obviously exacerbated.

Only by providing such services as are physically possible can an improvement be effected, and this fact leads on to the third causal factor of migration, namely, the lack of economic opportunity which not only causes migration from these regions, but also prevents the generating of capital and income which could be used to remove the influence of the second factor. In regions such as these, where there is now no extractive or manufacturing industry, where modern agriculture can operate efficiently on a reduced labour force, where much of the agriculture is in any case of the type which never was a heavy employer of labour, and where there is no government capital investment, not only is there an imbalance in the occupational structure, but the level of both personal and public income is below the national average. The latter can be remedied by devices such as rate-deficiency grants, but the former only by migration to a job 'which pays better'. The fact that in these regions there are no such jobs leads inevitably to migration outside the region, either to better one's position, or, as has been mentioned above, in the case of persons with special professional training, to obtain a position of any kind. It is this third element which is the most potent in its influence, and more will be said in later paragraphs of its actual effect. It is perhaps fortunate, however, that it is this very element that at least in some areas within these regions, can be most easily remedied.

Reference has been made above to the pull of migration upon the specialist groups within the population, and this is of vital significance in an area of sparse population since it impinges directly upon the community life of the region in question. The traditional patterns of community life in rural areas are, in any case, being modified and sometimes destroyed by changing social habits, by the development of mass media of communication, and by improved private transport facilities, and these modifications are even more marked in regions such as Mid-Wales which has its own particular background of language and culture. Such changes are obviously not in themselves automatically to be deplored, but unless the disappearance of certain aspects of community life is offset by adaptation and innovation, the whole fabric of that life may be destroyed. To link declining population with declining initiative and intelligence in the area concerned is far too dangerous a generalisation to make, but to query whether persistent decline may not in time rob a community of its reserve of natural leaders and thus lay too much strain on those remaining is merely to be realistic. The catch phrase that 'marginal farms have marginal farmers' is certainly not necessarily true, but it is quite obvious that the more depopulation, when operating selectively, narrows the range of a community, the more restricted and less interesting does the life of that community become unless enormous efforts are made to maintain it.

Before there is any consideration of the problems of providing services for any region whose demographic and economic characteristics are similar to those which have been described, it would be as well to draw attention to the existence of the school of thought which maintains that no such provision should in any case be made, except possibly in very restricted areas within the region. According to this viewpoint, regions such as this are not in themselves economically viable, and unless they can with certainty be made so at relatively low cost, there should be no attempts to maintain or to improve upon their social viability. Such regions should therefore be allowed to 'run-down' and the population encouraged to move thus creating a completely negative or neutral area which would make virtually no contribution to the national economy but which equally would make no demands upon it. Some kind of exploitation of resources would presumably still be undertaken, albeit on a very small scale, and for this purpose the small amount of population necessary could be grouped in one or two areas thus forming a kind of subsidised 'native reserve'.

This kind of economic thinking is of course completely logical and rational, but it suffers from two major weaknesses. The first is that such a 'final solution' would necessitate compulsory movement of population into the 'reserves', since unless this were done, there would inevitably be a scatter of residual population who would choose to remain, and for these people some basic services would have to be provided. Unless this were done, they would of course be being condemned to living at a standard much too far below the national average to be accepted by any government professing to have a social conscience. Any plan or scheme based on this purely rational approach would therefore need to use coercion in order to be successful.

The second weakness is perhaps even more fundamental since economic arguments of this kind do not appear fully to take into account the amount of social and other capital which already exists in regions such as these. This capital would, of course, have to be 'written off', and the cost, together with the social and economic costs of re-settling the bulk of the population outside the region, would have to be set against the cost of maintaining and developing services for the population as it now exists. This latter cost could in any case be reduced by a certain amount of re-distribution internally of the population which would be much less violent and, therefore, more acceptable than the alternative, and by the intro-duction into the region of additional economic opportunity which would itself, of course, produce a return.

It must surely be accepted, therefore, that even in areas which have reached what has been referred to above as Stage II of demo-graphic decline there will be a residual population unless it is forcibly ejected, and that in Stage I areas the population will be much more than residual so that the provision of services will continue to be a necessity. The problem, therefore, is not whether to provide services or not, but how to provide them so that they can best fulfil their primary function and at the same time act as a generating force in the efforts to rehabilitate and revitalise the economic and social life of the regions concerned.

This whole question can only be fully considered and understood in the context of the settlement pattern to which the services are to apply, since different patterns will present different problems, and even where some are common to more than one pattern, different kinds of solution may well be required in each case. It is in terms of these settlement patterns, their origin and their subsequent development, that the provision of social, public utility, and ancillary commercial services will be considered.

The settlement pattern of Mid-Wales has within it the three elements of scattered or disposed farmsteads, nucleated villages and small urban or even sub-urban focii, but each one of these elements, particularly the first two, will have variations within itself, such variations being dependent upon a variety of physical, historical, economic, and locational factors.

In the upland areas of this region, as in other regions similar to it, the landscape is dominated by the scattered or isolated homestead, be it farm, small-holding or croft. Much of this settlement is comparatively recent and derives from the process of enclosure of the uplands, a process which in this region was comparatively late. During the latter part of the eighteenth century, and in some cases the early part of the nineteenth century, the moorlands and foothills which had hitherto been used as common grazing ground for the summer depasturing of stock belonging to valley farms with common rights, were enclosed by means of a number of private Enclosure Acts.

Although some of the rougher country was inevitably left as open sheepwalks, wherever possible the land was carved up, at least on the map, into new farm units, many of them geometric in pattern; roads were constructed, boundaries erected and farm-houses built so that there was virtually a process of colonisation. Not all the land had previously been empty, however, and one significant element which was already in the fringe areas when the Enclosure Acts were passed was that of illegal encroachment with its associated 'squatter' settlement, usually a small, poorly built house, surrounded by its patch of enclosed land. Although there was frequently no absolute legal right of ownership, despite the oft-quoted but never proven traditional right of the 'one-night house', the persons who had made these encroachments were often such as would brook no interference, with the result that many of these settlements were allowed to continue, sometimes by tacit, sometimes by legal, agreement, sometimes by default.

Into this landscape of haphazard scatter of farmstead and croft self-sufficient in economy and, therefore, requiring few, if any, services there came, in the nineteenth century, the influences of lead mining. Because of the nature of this mineral deposit, its exploitation was again predominantly scattered in character relying more on the small isolated mine or adit rather than on large-scale undertakings which would create mining villages. There were, however, a few of these, though still relatively small, so that the effect of lead mining was two-fold. In the first place it introduced a limited number of small nucleations which were uni-functional, consisting almost entirely of one or two rows of miners' cottages and little else. The second effect was that by providing an additional source of income deriving from work in small mines which were, of course, themselves scattered, the economic viability of existing crofts was improved and their number increased.

With these improved economic conditions there came a need for the basic services and there developed a community life, which in this instance derived from and was based on religious nonconformity. These two factors, together with a third, namely, the building of 'elementary schools' under the terms of the Education Act of 1870, affected both the physical and social pattern of what were by now becoming definite communities with their own identity.

In order to provide the basic services there grew up at convenient points, though in this type of country such points are not thick upon the ground, small settlement clusters which are perhaps better described as 'nodes' rather than 'nucleations'. For the major and more sophisticated services it was necessary to utilise the resources of the nearest market town or lowland village or, of course, do without them altogether; but these 'nodes' would include a small but very general store, a smithy, possibly a carpenter's shop, and a few odd-job men who would show a surprising ingenuity and versatility when any additional service might be required,

The building of the chapel (or chapels) at this node, together with, though not invariably, the school, not only increased the nucleation but made it, of course, the social focus of the area. Here also, in the rare instances where it was provided by local effort or generosity, the 'village hall' was built although the usual pattern was for the chapel to be used also as a secular meeting place. In this particular context it must also be remembered that, because of the cultural tradition in this part of Wales, it was normal for much of what may be termed 'public social activity' to be carried on in farmhouses which would in turn act, as it were, as the 'Community Hall'.

It will perhaps have been noted that one element missing from the 'node' is the 'village pub'. This absence would not only be due to the influence of non-conformity but would reflect also the very limited economic functions of these 'nodes' in communities of this kind. A node which could graduate to, or become so dissolute as to support, a 'pub' was really 'a village' which would have functions and services deriving from an economic and social situation different from the one which has just been outlined, and of which more will be said later.

It has been necessary to spend some time describing the evolution of this cultural and physical landscape because unless there is an understanding of the origins of a particular situation there can be no understanding either of the present problems or of the various types of solution which might be applied to it. It is maintained also that these problems can only be understood and solved if there is an appreciation of what has happened to these communities from the time that they became established to the present day, when, through no fault of their own, they have become 'problem communities' in our society.

What has in fact happened has been the result of three separate but closely-linked trends and events. The first of these is the most clearly defined and is derived quite simply from the fact that lead mining has no longer become economic in this region. The reasons for this are not relevant to this discussion, but its two-fold effects impinge directly upon it. In the first place, they have completely removed the economic basis of the existence of the mining village or 'node' settlement which have been described above. Since these settlements were by origin 'uni-functional', and since, because of the nature of the lead deposits, such villages were more often than not sited in locations so isolated as to preclude their assuming any other functions, it follows that once the economic reasons for their existence were removed, they would inevitably disappear as significant nucleations and become purely residual in function and appearance. In the second place, the removal of a subsidiary source of income deriving from lead mine working has a profound effect upon the 'crofting' element in the settlement pattern in that it reduced such establishments from viable into non-viable economic units. The obvious and inevitable result was that many of these were abandoned and became derelict. The third trend is the result of changes which have affected the economics of upland farming in regions such as the one with which we are concerned. This has been dealt with elsewhere and the basic developments are the reduction in the number of separate farm units and the concomitant reduction in the labour force which is necessary to operate the new system. The decline in the sources of subsidiary employment referred to above means that there is now no local outlet for the surplus labour force which has resulted from these changes in farming systems.

The combined result of these three trends is to remove the economic basis for the existence of this type of community and this type of settlement pattern. Such communities and such patterns do not, however, disappear overnight and the idea of residual economies, residual settlements, and residual populations becomes a real problem. The question is, therefore, how to deal with a society or community which is running down but which also needs to be readjusted to a new set of economic conditions. The element which is running down is residual, but the element which remains after readjustment is permanent, and needs to be serviced permanently if these areas are not to be allowed to become completely derelict.

With modern methods of transport there is, of course, no physical problem in making the normal social services available to these areas, provided that the high cost of this provision is accepted. The contribution from these areas to the local and national exchequer is small. Rateable values are so low as to require rate deficiency grants, personal income levels are below the national average, and although the areas are not 'depressed areas', yet by virtue of their limited occupational structure they do little to generate income or capital. A full range of social services is, therefore, provided for a population which does not pay for it, and which because of its scattered distribution requires the organisation of those services to be more complex than elsewhere. The result is that far from being underprivileged in this context, these areas are, in fact, over-privileged since their populations are able to enjoy an element of almost personal service which is denied to those of us who live in the conurbations and large cities.

This situation would seem to be inevitable, since if services are to be provided at all, there is an irreducible minimum provision which must be maintained, and economies of size become impossible when the size involves population numbers which could be adequately serviced by one police officer, or doctor, or teacher but which occupy such a large terrain that such an arrangement becomes physically impossible. In education this problem can fairly easily be solved, though possibly not without damaging effects on the cultural and institutional framework, by closing small village schools and transporting children daily to a centrally located, often purpose-built, 'school campus', but this solution is obviously not applicable to all the social services. Although it can be argued that perhaps not enough has been done to explore the possibilities of rationalisation along these lines, nevertheless in some instances at least the basic problem would still remain.

Precisely the same problems apply, of course, to the development of the public utilities and there is no need to labour the point about the expense of supplying piped water and mains electricity, for example, to individual scattered farmsteads often separated from each other by quite difficult terrain. Here again the economy of the area plays a part since there would, of course, be less of a problem if, for example, a high consumption of electricity which would ensure a good return on capital invested could be anticipated. More often than not, however, for economic and possibly social reasons, the reverse is true and once again, therefore, the dominant theme is that of exceptionally heavy subsidy.

There is one group of services which, by their very nature, will automatically adjust themselves to any subsidy which is needed by the simple expedient of passing it on to the consumer, and this is the group of commercial services. While this group seems well able to adjust itself to changing physical and economic conditions so that it need not occupy much of our time, there are two problems of which we ought perhaps to be aware. In the first place, if the population falls below a certain level, the necessary profit margins of commercial services can only be maintained by price increases which would in the end defeat their own object. Such services would then be withdrawn, or have to be subsidised from public funds, a situation which already obtains in many areas as far as public transport is concerned. The second is that in order to make commercial services economic, it might become necessary to increase prices to the extent that these areas become high-cost areas, a situation which would raise serious problems since the level of private incomes is, in any case, below average.

The problems which have been outlined above apply also to the lowland areas of this and similar regions, but to a much lesser extent. In these areas the population density is greater, the settlement, though still predominantly scattered, is thicker on the ground, not only because there are more farms but also because the type of farming is such as to be able to support an appreciable 'secondary population'. The greater the amount of lowland the greater the amount of this secondary population with the result that definite village nucleations now begin to appear in the landscape. Although these may not be the traditional manorial nucleations of the lowland zone of England, they are nevertheless villages which have grown out of the agricultural economy of the area, sometimes boosted by a particular local factor such as a railway or a quarry or a group of lead mines, and they are therefore relatively much more stable than their counterparts in the uplands. Since they are also nucleations which are chronologically and economically of some standing in the landscape, such villages have, over the years, tended to gather to themselves certain new and varied functions. The traditional village elements of church, chapels, school, surgery and inn were here established, and although there might not be the traditional manor house, there was often a 'residential element' which fulfilled similar functions, for example, as employers of labour. Because of their relative accessibility, such villages were able, moreover, to call more easily on the services, and share in the life, of a near-by market whose own existence would be, of course, a function of the more active economic life of those areas. The overall result was the evolution of a definite economic and social pattern, namely, that of a 'normal rural', though scattered, population tributary to a village which, together with its neighbours, formed a group which was tributary to a small market town. A definite hierarchy of settlement pattern thus emerged.

Although this may appear to have been a satisfactory and stable situation, it must not be assumed that these areas were immune to the effects of population loss, because their stability is really only relative to their neighbours in the uplands. The occupational

POPULATION CHANGES AND THE PROVISION OF SERVICES

structure may be more varied, but it is still not sufficiently so to prevent the outwards migration of persons who are professionally trained or who have had special skills. Farming may be prosperous and efficient, but only at the expense of a reduction in the direct and indirect labour force required. Services, both commercial and social, are needed and can be provided on an economic basis, but with improved transport facilities they can often now be best provided from the neighbouring town. Both the level and the intensity of general activity have, therefore, fallen, but not to the extent that would raise any serious problems as far as service provision is concerned. Such problems do exist, but only as a pale reflection of those which have been described above as existing in the upland areas, and they are in any case further alleviated by the fact that the village settlements in particular are often able to continue adapting themselves to changing circumstances and to continue to develop new functions.

This is particularly true of villages which are tributary to a market town which has itself either been given or has developed new functions, whether they be administrative or industrial. Such villages, provided that they are conveniently located, can and often do become dormitory villages and they establish a commuter relationship with the town. This relationship and this function are completely new to this region, of course, but they neither cut across nor do they destroy the traditional relationships, and what is more important, they introduce into the village a new population which often re-vitalises some of the old village functions. Provided that this kind of development can be strengthened where it now exists, and introduced into areas where it does not, it would appear that since the physical difficulties of providing services are not great, their cost can be balanced against the numbers and type of population which make use of them. Where services are not provided in such areas, there is of course little chance of rehabilitation. Stagnation and decline then set in and the whole process becomes cumulative.

From what has been said above it will be seen that the real problems of the provision of social, public utility, and commercial services in areas of declining population, while obviously linked to the plain fact of decline, are exacerbated to the point of being well-nigh insoluble if the decline is occurring in a particular context of economic conditions and pattern of settlement. It may well be that certain trends of population change in certain communities just cannot be adjusted to modern social and economic conditions without a fundamental reappraisal of the basis of the continued existence of such communities and an acceptance of the social and institutional changes which such a reappraisal would imply. This aspect will be considered in more detail in the final paragraphs of this chapter.

The services which have hitherto been considered may be regarded as essential to the continued existence of any community, but there is an additional group of 'recreational services' which, at least to some people in Britain today are just as essential. Even though there may not be agreement with the view that without a local Bingo Hall, or even cinema, a community cannot be expected to live, and no one should be surprised at this fact, nevertheless it is a responsibility of society to see to it that some recreational facilities are available.

Here again it is necessary to be brutally realistic and to accept the fact that in areas of dispersed and sparse settlement, with no natural physical or social focii, it is today neither economically nor socially possible to introduce an elaborate provision of community centres and sports organisations for the simple reason that the right kind of population would just not be available to support them. There is the additional fact that with the coming of electricity to these areas self-made recreation has been usurped by that made for one by other people on television. It must also be remembered, as has already been mentioned, that many of these communities have a long tradition of self-made recreation within quite clearly defined social, cultural and religious groups, and to apply to them the standard of provision required by some of the more rootless communities of Britain would be both purposeless and unwelcome. Where there is a demand for a particular service, however, and where this can be adapted to the local conditions, as in the case of mobile lending libraries, the success is quite phenomenal, but this example is perhaps an exception. The operative words are 'where there is a demand', and some sociological enquiry would perhaps be necessary to discover precisely what is the nature of the demand before there are any plans for provision. Even where a demand was proven, however, there might have to be acceptance of the fact that it would be physically impossible to satisfy it.

In this context of the provision of recreational facilities, as in so many others, the problems of the lowland areas of these regions are insignificant when compared with the uplands. As has already been explained, the scatter of settlement is less diffuse, and the density of population is greater. These facts, coupled with the existence in the landscape of natural settlement nucleations with relative ease of access from one to another, lead to a situation where supply and demand can be fairly easily matched as a result of the activities of the communities themselves. If outside help is needed, possibly in the provision of physical facilities, it can take the form of an initial capital contribution which can then be managed by the community concerned. There would thus appear here to be no serious problem provided that the continued 'run-down' of these areas can be arrested before both in numbers and in distribution pattern the demographic pattern deteriorates too far.

There is, of course, one other aspect of the provision of recreational facilities which is the reverse of that which has just been described, namely, the facilities which these regions themselves, by their innate physical characteristics, provide for people from elsewhere. This aspect of tourism has been dealt with in Chapter 4, but it is perhaps worth re-emphasising that in regions with individual physical and cultural characteristics, a balance needs to be struck between the advantages derived from the capital and income generating results of tourism, with its broadening of economic opportunity, and the effect of such developments upon the physical and cultural landscape upon which the tourist activities are based.

Enough has been said already to indicate that the whole physical and economic institutional framework of regions such as Mid-Wales needs a fundamental reappraisal if any problems are to be solved or even ameliorated. If this is done, and if changes are made, these will naturally impinge upon the region's cultural characteristics, and upon its associated institutions. Where these are not markedly different from those of surrounding regions few problems may arise, but more often than not, because the 'remoter rural areas' are remote, they have either developed their own particular institutions or have succeeded in preserving some, which formerly were more widespread. The most obvious of these is that of language, but even where this has disappeared, society has often succeeded in retaining certain cultural aspects which were associated with it. Religion, not only in its type, but in the part which it plays in the community, is an example of what may best be described as 'a general outlook or attitude to life'—a phrase which, though vague and imprecise, nevertheless has a definite meaning to anyone who has lived in or studied the regions with which we are concerned.

It is thus apparent that not only from the standpoint of the institutional framework, but from that of almost every facet of the life of these regions there must be an adjustment if they are not on the one hand to become demographic deserts or on the other to be maintained by the state as some kind of 'native reserves'. New capital, new opportunities, and new incentives need to be injected, and new provisions made, if these regions are to have any worth-while existence, worth while both to themselves and to the country at large. It is obvious that this cannot be done without changing their physical, economic and social character, but it surely must be done without destroying that character completely. Some areas may need to be literally evacuated, some economic and social systems changed, some cherished attitudes and methods abandoned, but the object of the whole reappraisal should be to modify the fabric of society, retaining that which is good, rejecting that which is outmoded, thus strengthening the fabric so that it can, while retaining its individuality, adapt itself to modern conditions and in so doing retain its self-respect.

Part 2

THE REGIONAL APPROACH

6 | Problems and Objectives in Rural Development Board Areas

J. MORGAN JONES, C.B., C.B.E., M.A.
Formerly Deputy Chairman Designate,
Wales Rural Development Board

THE AGRICULTURE ACT, 1967—PART III

Part III of the Agriculture Act deals with 'Hill Land' and empowers Ministers to appoint Rural Development Boards for certain areas of Great Britain. The Secretary of State and the Minister of Agriculture, Fisheries and Food are the responsible Ministers for Scotland and England respectively: in Wales the same Minister shares responsibility for certain matters, including the establishment of a Board, with the Secretary of State for Wales.

The Minister of Agriculture has made proposals for a Board to cover about 3,000 square miles in the Northern Pennines and few outstanding procedures remain to be completed.* A proposal to establish a Board for a much smaller area in Wales has encountered opposition and it is understood that some months may elapse before Ministers are in a position to put forward an Order for Parliamentary approval.

Boards are designed to meet the special problems of the development as rural areas of hills and uplands. As set out in Section 45 (2) these 'special problems and needs include the special difficulties in the formation of commercial units of agricultural land in such areas, the need for an overall programme for guidance in making decisions as to the use of land in such areas for agriculture and forestry, so that those two uses are complementary, the need for improved public services in such areas in step with their development for agricultural and forestry purposes, and the need for preserving and taking full advantage of the amenities and scenery in those areas in the course of their development for those purposes.' The Act

* The Order establishing the Northern Pennines Rural Development Board came into effect on 1st August 1969.

109

also emphasises the special economic considerations and the long-term nature of forestry and refers to amenities in the widest sense of the term. Boards have a statutory duty to keep these needs and problems under constant review and, in consultation with the local authorities and other bodies concerned, to draw up a programme for action to meet them. Boards will be able to acquire land by agreement, to 'Manage, improve, farm, sell or let land' and to enter into transactions, some of which may involve loss, in the process of promoting amalgamations and other projects in the interests of the community. Provision by way of grant or loan is made in Section 47 for:

'(a) financial assistance for providing or improving communications and public services in the Board's area;

(b) financial assistance towards expenditure incurred in installing or connecting a supply of electricity, gas or water to a dwelling-house or other premises used in connection with agriculture or forestry or for the improvement of accommodation on such premises for tourists, being expenditure incurred by an owner or occupier of the premises;

(c) financial assistance towards expenditure incurred in providing or improving a site on an agricultural or forestry unit for tourists' caravans or as a tourists' camping-site, being expenditure incurred by the occupier of the agricultural or forestry unit.'

In addition, within a Board's area, persons relinquishing land for afforestation as part of an approved amalgamation scheme will, subject to the Board's agreement, be eligible for the outgoer's grant.

Parliament, conscious no doubt of the difficult and complex tasks which Boards would face, gave them specific powers designed to facilitate their objectives and to prevent the frustration of their programme. These include the need to get the Board's consent to transfers of title (except to members of the family) to agricultural land in private use, and to the afforestation, in any one year, of areas exceeding ten acres in each unit of ownership. In certain circumstances a Board will be able to acquire land compulsorily if that land is essential for a scheme of amalgamation (or boundary adjustment) desired by the large majority (in terms of heads and acres) of the interests concerned. The Act carefully circumscribes these powers and also ensures that the proposals of Ministers are fully ventilated both locally and in Parliament before a Board can be established.

BACKGROUND LEGISLATION

The Agriculture Act, 1967, can be fairly regarded as the culmination of policies aimed at enabling the agricultural industry to adjust itself to an increasingly competitive economic climate. Measures specifically designed to improve fixed equipment on farms generally started with the Hill Farming Act, 1946, which offered 50 per cent grants for the *comprehensive* rehabilitation of farms qualifying for hill sheep subsidy. In 1951 these benefits were extended to the lower ranges of hills capable of rearing cattle as well as sheep, but not suitable for fattening animals and crop production. These Acts have been of immense value to thousands of hill farmers in the United Kingdom, but it must be accepted that in the early stages many promoters of schemes were over-optimistic in their estimates of the capital expenditure their enterprises could carry, and increasingly found that the 'comprehensive' requirement of the Act became a deterrent. This experience, supported by further investigations, influenced the content of the Farm Improvement Scheme made under the Agriculture Act, 1957. Thereby grants of one-third were offered for *individual* improvements on farms generally, provided the unit concerned was capable of yielding a reasonable living, or would do so after the improvements. This Act also cut fresh ground in that some of the costs of farm amalgamation became eligible for grant.

During the following ten years economic pressures, including the rising costs of land, fixed equipment, and labour, focused attention on the economic difficulties of many small-scale producers. Simultaneously, the accumulation and analysis of statistical data proceeded apace and enabled economists to devise an acceptable method—the standard man-day method—of measuring the size of each farm business. Broadly, these studies showed that about two-thirds of the UK's farms were below 'commercial' size (i.e. were not in effect 'two-man' units), and that about half of them should be regarded as part-time units.

These conclusions pointed to the need for a larger measure of agricultural adjustment. A White Paper entitled 'The Development of Agriculture' was published in August 1965. Its philosophy, later incorporated for the most part in the Agriculture Act, 1967, which gave authority for the amalgamators and outgoers grant, was clearly set out in the opening paragraphs:

'1. The Government believe that one of the more important problems facing agriculture today is that of the small farmer trying to win a livelihood from insufficient land. As time passes, his difficulties will increase. He will find it more and more difficult to maintain a standard of living in keeping with modern times.'

'3. Many of them (i.e. the smaller farmers) may be able to increase the size of their businesses through better management under the revised Small Farmer Scheme. But, looking ahead, many others, however hard they work, and however well they manage their businesses, just cannot hope to get a decent living from their farms at prices which the taxpayer and the consumer could afford . . .'

The White Paper, at paragraph 18, outlined the need for specia measures to help readjustment in the hills and uplands where, in addition to improving farm structure, 'there is a need for more coherent planning of the use of land particularly for agriculture and forestry, but also for other purposes, such as recreation and tourism. All those who have studied this problem have emphasised the need for integrating over a reasonably wide area the use of land for agriculture and forestry in the hills so that they are complementary, and not antagonistic, to each other. They also urged that there need be no conflict between recreation and tourism on the one hand, and agriculture and forestry on the other.' Paragraph 19 adds: 'Lastly, the Government recognise that where special steps are necessary in a hill and upland area to secure a reorganisation and improvement of the rural economy, public services may have to be improved to serve the fuller development of the area.'

THE MID-WALES PROBLEM

The legislation described above was, at least to some degree, influenced by a series of official and private reports on Mid-Wales.* The Main Documents are:

(1) 'The Second Memorandum of the Council for Wales and Monmouthshire', July 1953 (Command 8844).
(2) 'The Mid-Wales Investigation Report of the Welsh

* Mid-Wales is not a precise term. The report on 'Depopulation in Mid-Wales', commonly called the Beacham Report, covered the counties of Cardigan, Merioneth, Montgomery, Radnor and the rural areas of Brecon. The other reports dealt with areas within this perimeter.

Agricultural Land Sub-Commission', December 1955 (Command 9631).
(3) 'The Mid-Wales Problem', A report by the Welsh Council of the National Farmers' Union, December 1964.
(4) 'Depopulation in Mid-Wales, HMSO 1964.

Government pronouncements on (1) were published in a White Paper 'Rural Wales' in November 1953 (Command 9014) and on (2), in a paper entitled 'Mid-Wales Investigation Report—Conclusions and Recommendations' in July 1956 (Command 9809).

The official reports varied in their emphasis. The Council for Wales was deeply concerned with public services and communications. The Beacham Report emphasised the interwoven effects of a declining population and an unfavourable age structure, producing a vicious circle unattractive to industry. The report of the Welsh Agricultural Land Sub-Commission dwelt on the poor structure of hill farms and the need for a comprehensive approach to their problems. As this historic document is now out of print, some extracts from it are given in Appendix I. The common elements in these reports may be summarised as follows:
(1) Mid-Wales has suffered severely from depopulation;
(2) the basic reason for this depopulation is the absence of a stable economy;
(3) the area contains too many farms incapable of yielding a satisfactory living on a full-time basis;
(4) there is undoubtedly scope for the development of the basic land-using industries of the area—agriculture and forestry;
(5) there is a need to diversify the economy;
(6) public services must be improved;
(7) the need for a measure of self-help in parallel with greater aid from central Government.

It is significant that in most respects the findings of the NFU Panel were closely in harmony with the official reports. It recalled that 'all examinations of this region have underlined the factors of economic instability, remoteness, inadequacy of public facilities and unsatisfactory communications'. It urged the introduction of light industry. It drew attention to the scope for a larger farm-based tourist industry, for planting more trees and for growing more food. But it did not disregard the fact that the need for these measures stemmed from a chronically bad structure in the agricultural industry. It also declared: 'the fact is that whilst farming as a whole is not unremunerative in Mid-Wales there is a stratum in agriculture whose prospects—judged more by the standards expected by their children than those which they themselves expect—can no longer depend upon income derived from husbandry. For some of these men the finger of amalgamation beckons; for others the hope lies in intensification of production or the means to buy extra land, in more effective co-operation with neighbours to reduce purchasing, production and marketing costs; or in supplementary incomes from industries complementary to farming. . . .'

FEATURES OF THE AREA PROPOSED

The Wales Rural Development Board Area proposed by Ministers after the consultations stipulated in the Agriculture Act, 1967, is shown in Fig. 6.1. It comprises parts of the counties of Cardigan, Montgomery, Radnor, Brecon and Carmarthen. Its choice rested on several considerations. Documentary evidence showed that the area was mainly hill land containing the problems mentioned in Section 45 of the Act. The suggested boundaries broadly complied with the requirement of the Act that Ministers should have regard primarily to natural conformations, features and boundaries. It was also judged that the area proposed was suitable administratively in that it was neither so large as to be unwieldy nor too small to be a worthwhile unit of operations.

The area covers about 1,300 square miles in Central Wales with a boundary running east of Pumlumon (Plynlimmon) to the Severn Valley at Berriew, then south of Newtown to link up with the Ithon Valley; it then runs west of Pumlumon to Cardigan Bay with Aberystwyth as a mid-point on the coast. About 13 per cent of the area is owned by forestry interests. Approximately 85 per cent of the land is normally eligible for the special grants and subsidies available to hill and upland farmers: in addition, there are valley bottom farms which are operated with upland areas of livestock rearing land. Within the area there is quite a wide variation in physical conditions such as:

    (a) part of the Central Wales massif—high plateau between 1700 ft. and 1900 ft. dominated by Pumlumon which rises to 2468 ft.;

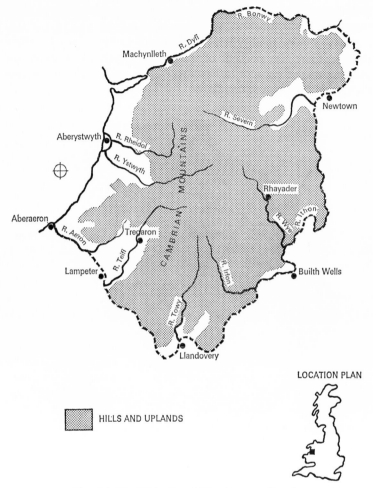

FIG. 6.1. The Wales Rural Development Board.

(b) the surrounding dissected uplands with summit levels between 1100 ft. and 1300 ft.;

(c) the upper parts of the Towy, Teifi, Dovey, Ithon and Severn river systems;

(d) the coastal plateau north and south of Aberystwyth at altitudes of 400 ft. and 600 ft. above sea level.

Rainfall varies between 40 in. at the coast to 80 in. in the central massif and falls to 40 in. (or even below) on the east side of the area.

This range of physical conditions gives rise to wide differences in farming systems. In short, while much the greater part of the area consists of poor quality land suitable only for extensive livestock rearing, there are pockets of good land which are suitable for growing sale crops, and rather larger areas well suited to the production of fat sheep and milk.

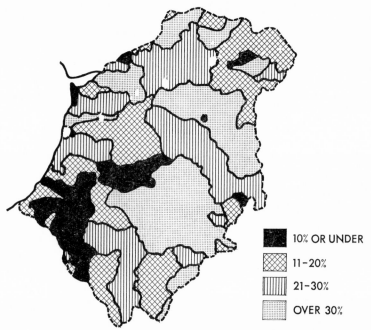

FIG. 6.2. Percentage of agricultural holdings with 600 standard man days and over, Wales Rural Development Boad.

Likewise conditions are not uniform so far as the organisation of the industry is concerned. It was estimated that the area contained 5,560 agricultural holdings and, using the official classification, of these 54 per cent were part-time, 28 per cent were viable but below commercial standard and 18 per cent were commercial. These averages mask wide variations between districts. One or two quite large parishes in the area have 40 per cent of the holdings in the commercial class; by contrast, in 20 out of the 51 parishes in Cardiganshire affected by the Ministers' proposals the proportion of commercial farms is 1 in 10 or less (Fig. 6.2). As was to be expected the area embraces estates and individual properties which are well equipped and expertly managed side by side with others requiring a great deal of planned improvement. By and large the area is well farmed, bearing in mind the physical conditions; and large numbers of owners and occupiers have made good use of the grants and subsidies for which they were eligible.

Turning to more general aspects, the main features of the area are:

the low level of population;

the almost complete absence of industry;

the wide stretches of unspoilt and attractive country.

The total population of the area is estimated to be about 42,000 people, i.e. 1 person per 20 acres; the largest centre of population bordering the area (Aberystwyth M.B.) has about 11,000 people (including students, but excluding people in new housing estates just outside the M.B. boundary). In 1966 only about 4,000 people (2,600 males) were employed in the manufacturing industry in the whole of the Employment Exchange areas within which the Area lies. A great deal of the central massif is virtually uninhabited. The area contains important water undertakings at Nant-y-moch, Elan, Claerwen and Clywedog which, incidentally, have added to the attractions of the wide-open spaces making them more accessible and introducing a wider range of water sports.

In the context of the factors which foster urban development the area is remote. Yet it is well placed in relation to holiday traffic. It is virtually bounded by the main roads running east/west which link the Midlands (ex Shrewsbury and Hereford) with the attractive coast-line between the Dovey and Aeron estuaries.

PUBLIC INQUIRY AND MINISTERS' DECISION

The proposal to designate the area just described as the area of the Wales Rural Development Board was generally welcomed in the summer of 1967; in fact, four out of the five county councils concerned were in agreement with it. Ministers accordingly advertised their proposals, with the map, in September and October 1967 and specified 6th November of that year as the last date for the receipt of objections under the Act.

In the event a large number of objectors exercised their statutory rights and accordingly a Public Inquiry, in which hearings were conducted in Welsh and English, opened in April 1968. It occupied a total of 44 days and was concluded in October 1968.

Broadly the criticisms which emerged before and during the Inquiry can be summarised as follows:

(a) Boards were not necessary for the rural development of the area;

(b) Boards, in any case, should be elected;

(c) amalgamations were proceeding apace and Boards should not be vested with compulsory powers to this end;

(d) farmers were making satisfactory incomes;

(e) in any event the benefits offered for the Board's area were outweighed by the loss of freedom to dispose of land.

In reply to a Parliamentary Question on 2nd April 1969 the Secretary of State for Wales (speaking also for the Minister of Agriculture, Fisheries and Food) stated, *inter alia:*

'The report concludes that the proposed area of the Board, regarded as a whole, contains the problems and needs for which a Rural Development Board is designed and could profit from the operations of a Board. It suggests, however, that there is a case for modifying the area originally proposed so as to exclude certain portions amounting to about one-eighth of it. My Right Honourable Friend and I accept these suggestions and we intend, after completing the statutory processes relating to a modification of the area, to seek the authority of Parliament to establish a Rural Development Board accordingly.'

The area to be excluded by the modification of the advertised proposal is about 32,000 acres in Montgomeryshire and 70,000 acres in Carmarthenshire.

PROBLEMS AND POTENTIALITIES

If current assessments of economic and social trends are to be accepted, the task of the Wales Rural Development Board will be arduous, prolonged and challenging. Thus, it has been estimated that by 1976 the number of holdings under 300 acres in Great Britain will decline by 60,000.[1] There is every prospect that very soon there will be several million more cars in Britain. The expectation is that the high cost of land and labour will necessitate a larger proportion of bigger well-equipped units on the one hand, while, on the other, the holidaymaker will help to fill the income gap for

those farm families who will wish to remain in their native surroundings. The problem of adjustment will have to be solved
mainly on the farm. At the same time, it is recognised that a parallel
process of fostering other forms of employment and of improving
communications is essential. In an article on Co-operation and
the R.D.B. in 'Farmer Business in Wales' the Right Honourable
Cledwyn Hughes, Minister of Agriculture, brought out these basic
points:

'If we want a farm industry that can provide its inhabitants with
a decent livelihood at present-day standards and able to keep its
young people from drifting elsewhere, we must start by getting many
more full-time farms of a size that will enable their occupiers and
their families to run them as efficient and prosperous businesses. . . .
Another aspect of the problem is the need for a better relationship
between agriculture and forestry, so that farmers and foresters may
co-operate in putting our land to the use for which it is best suited. . . .
The Government has also realised that the natural attractions of the
area may also make their contribution to the income of the local
inhabitants. So the Board will try also to ensure that, in the course
of agricultural and forestry development, the amenities of the area
are preserved and made accessible to many more people.'

Although the Board's objectives can be set out in these simple
terms, its task will not be easy. At an early stage in its operations
it will need to break down the hostile attitudes which were ventilated
at the Public Inquiry and to seek means of winning the active co-
operation of the farming community. The Board will always be
confronted with the problem of trying to ensure that its day-to-day
decisions will fit into the long-term plans—which themselves need
to be flexible—for the benefit of the locality concerned. Added to
this is the reluctance of the farm population to change its way of
life, however clear the economic case for so doing. The vital need
for an informed and sympathetic human approach to this very real
problem is reflected in the legal requirement that Rural Development
Boards shall consist mainly of persons with first-hand knowledge of
agriculture and forestry. Ministers have recognised the importance
of local knowledge and contacts—nine out of eleven designated
members live within the Board's area or on its boundaries.

The Board is required by Statute to prepare an overall programme
for guidance on land use, to keep the problems and needs of its
area under constant review and to draw up a plan of action. A full

E

assessment of the Board's task and opportunities will therefore not become apparent until survey work has been carried out to indicate the plan and form of action likely to yield the most fruitful results in a reasonable time. As already indicated, however, much information was available before the Draft Order was advertised and it is significant that the conclusions based on it stood up to the test of the Enquiry. Thus, on the important question of farm structure it was argued that amalgamations were proceeding apace without the Board. But the examples produced by the objectors did not invalidate the conclusions of the Regional Land Commissioner in his Proof of Evidence:

'The circumstances necessary for fully satisfactory results from amalgamations now taking place frequently do not exist. So much depends upon the owner of a suitable holding being willing and able to buy additional land when the vendor wants to sell it. These two separate sets of circumstances frequently do not coincide. It is my experience that amalgamations often take place of two or more farms a considerable distance apart although there are other holdings which could be amalgamated with each to give more satisfactory results. Difficulties then arise of providing adequate fixed equipment as well as of day-to-day management. A Rural Development Board can purchase and hold land until such time as a suitable amalgamation can be made, conducive to the full development of agriculture in the area'.

The formulation and execution of the Board's programme will call for the fullest consultation with, and co-operation from, local authorities and other interested bodies. For example, satisfactory arrangements for ensuring the complementary use of land for agriculture and forestry involve the economists and the custodians of amenity as well as the technical experts responsible for agriculture, silviculture and roads. Again a good deal of field work must be conducted before the scope for transfer of agricultural land to forestry can be quantified. Nevertheless, it is already accepted that more land should be afforested in some parts of the Board's areas that many minor roads need to be improved in the interests of the two industries, and that Mid-Wales contains very few examples of positive agriculture–forestry integration within the boundaries of a single farm or as between a group of farms in an upland valley.

Another problem which looms large in the area—and on which full information for long-term planning is lacking—is the question of flooding land for the construction of reservoirs. All that can be said at the present time is that demands for water are increasing daily; that the economics of desalination are not known with any precision and that any proposal to build more reservoirs in the Mid-Wales uplands will meet fierce opposition.

Fortunately, as already indicated, the Board's area is well placed as regards farm tourist industry. In his evidence at the Public Enquiry, the representative of the Wales Tourist Board stated that: 'Mid-Wales, in particular, stands to benefit from an expansion of tourism. The area possesses a number of significant advantages. In the first place, it has space which means for the visitor uncongested roads, a good network of paths and bridleways leading to open commons and uplands. Secondly, it has considerable unspoilt scenic variety and attractions with lakes, forests, mountains and moorland. Thirdly, the area possesses excellent fishing which is, at present, somewhat under-exploited. Fourthly, it lies in close proximity to an attractive and popular coast-line, nowhere being more than two hours motoring from a bathing beach. Finally, it is easily accessible from the English Midlands and North-West. This time-access factor is of considerable importance in terms of the future when the demand for week-end holidays and 'mini' holidays is likely to increase substantially. For such short holidays it is essential that the destination lies within a comfortable evening drive of the home area, otherwise too much time would be involved in travelling. With the progressive decrease in working hours, longer annual holiday periods with pay, relatively higher and expanding family incomes, better education and the increase in mobility resulting from the great spread of car ownership, more and more people in the English conurbations will want to get away from their industrial environment to a sharply contrasting rural area.

'There is at present an excellent demand for farm-house holidays. Changing patterns in tourism will intensify rather than weaken this demand, and the Wales Tourist Board foresee no risk of over-provision of this form of accommodation. Our surveys have shown that there is a large, untapped reserve of such accommodation in Mid-Wales. Farm-houses in the area are generally substantial, solidly built, clean and well kept. The decreasing size of the family unit residing in most farm-houses has meant that, in many cases, there are one or two unoccupied bedrooms and a little-used 'front parlour', which could be used for accommodating visitors. Farm guest-houses in Mid-Wales could, ironically, attract visitors over a longer season than a sophisticated hotel in a large resort. The main reason for this is that visitors selecting farm-house accommodation are generally less weather-conscious. Spring and autumn, when the countryside is as beautiful as in summer and when interesting farm operations are carried on, can, therefore, be sold more realistically than a coastal resort depending on bathing in the open sea. . . .'

Whether extensive developments on these lines take place depends on a number of factors. Farmers in the area often combine food production with other activities but, as elsewhere, they tend to look askance at visitors who are about the place when the farm folk are busier than usual. Broadly speaking, a farm tourist industry calls for an entirely new attitude to the use of time, of premises and of the farm home—all of which, of course, is of vital concern to the farmer's wife and daughters. Then comes the planning, financing and execution of improvements to the house and homestead involving extensive contacts with local and central government staffs. Finally, proposals for individual properties have to be fitted into the pattern of public services. These inter-locking steps mean that a healthy and expanding farm tourist industry will not come about without conscious effort and close co-operation between the Board and all the bodies responsible for rebuilding the rural economy and safe-guarding amenities. The Board itself will have no powers over planning and highways, but it is hoped that a beneficial two-way traffic of ideas and suggestions will emerge. At the same time the Board will be able to assist highway authorities in planning—and financing—road improvements with an eye to the agricultural, forestry and farm-based tourist industries thus catering for works which were outside the scope of the Agriculture (Improvement of Roads) Act, 1955. As the Board's programme gathers momentum the need for virtually new roads designed mainly for tourist traffic will no doubt demand consideration.

Another important aspect of area planning is the location and timing of industrial and urban development. Agencies such as the Mid-Wales Industrial Development Association and the New Town Development Corporation are already active in this field and will undoubtedly look to the Wales Rural Development Board for guidance on the extent to which special measures will be needed to cater for the occupiers of non-viable units.

Ministers have indicated that a R.D.B. in full swing could expect to draw £500,000 annually from the Exchequer. As this figure could include interest payments on borrowed capital, a Board's business activities by way of grants, loans and such purchases of land as may be necessary could be substantial.

It is difficult to forecast the time it will take to reach such a point. Very soon after its formation a Board will be concerned with the normal land transfers which arise from death, retirements and changes of farm. In a recent year the total number of transfers in the counties affected by the Ministers' original proposals was 152, but no estimate has been made of the proportion of this figure which would fall within the Board's jurisdiction. Again it is not easy to forecast the number of applications for permission to plant trees but in recent years total plantings in the Board's area have not exceeded 2,000 acres annually.

The expectation is that the appointment of a Board will of itself stimulate farmers and owners to a point of decision on their plans for the future. The response to the Amalgamator's and Outgoers' grant scheme has been promising: even so only 30 firm applications for amalgamation grants and 26 outgoers' payments had been approved for the Mid-Wales counties by 6th June 1969.* But many informal enquiries have already been made in the Board's area and it is reasonable to judge that a fair proportion of these will come to a point once it becomes known that the Board is there to help negotiations between neighbours, for example, and empowered to buy the outgoer's farm at a fair price if no other arrangement is consistent with good estate management. Farmers in parts of Mid-Wales should be specially interested in the provision that the outgoer's grant is available for the surrender of land for afforestation. Likewise the applications for grant aid for roads and the farm tourist industry will no doubt begin to flow in when the Board is in a position to announce the rates and conditions of financial assistance.

In the long term, of course, the extent of a Board's activities will depend largely on factors beyond its control. A full discussion of these is not appropriate to this chapter but a few matters need to be mentioned. A large programme of afforestation as part of a timber import-saving programme cannot be ruled out of consideration. Equally, an expansion of the current import-saving programme on

---

* These figures include Carmarthenshire which accounts for 11 and 10 respectively.

the food front could greatly reduce the scope for further afforestation. The position at the moment is that for the immediate future—i.e. as long as subsidies for hill sheep and cattle remain at their present levels—upland farming is reasonably secure. But an industry whose net income, by and large, is no greater than its subsidy receipts is vulnerable. Criticisms that the present rates of subsidy are both too high and are not conducive to efficiency in production could, in time, result in changes which would be crucial to a good many hill farmers. The economic insecurity would be much accentuated if Britain adopted other forms of support for the industry—either unilaterally or as a consequence of entry into the European Economic Community. Hill farmers are notoriously weak sellers, and it is very questionable whether their share of the increase in price to the consumer which other support policies postulate would be sufficient to counterbalance the loss of regular subsidy payments. A well-established and informed Rural Development Board would be invaluable in easing the acute problems of readjustment which would arise from the changes briefly mentioned.

REFERENCES

1. *The Field*, p. 256, 13 February 1969.

Extracts from Report of Welsh Agricultural Land Sub-Commission. Conclusions and Recommendations

(a) *Types of Farming*

In view of the climatic conditions and the quality of the land we consider that the farms in the area can be used most efficiently for the rearing of cattle and sheep with the exception of limited areas in the Teifi, Wye and Teme Valleys, which are suitable for dairying. The dry hill soils of Radnorshire are suitable for poultry-keeping as an enterprise ancillary to the rearing of cattle and sheep.

(b) *Pattern of Ownership*

The ownership and letting of farms, on Welsh upland estates in particular, is not and probably never has been an economic proposition. Consequently, with the break-up of the large estates, owner-occupiership has developed comparatively rapidly. We have found cases where this system results in a shortage of working capital and a low standard of production. However, in the foreseeable circumstances we consider that owner-occupiership is likely to be the more satisfactory future pattern of ownership in the reference area. In reaching this conclusion we have given due weight to the limiting effect of security of tenure on the development of economic holdings and the creation of new tenancies. But the outlook and circumstances of individual owners and occupiers are subject to great variation and any attempt at regimentation would be fatal. We envisage that considerable areas will be offered for sale and acquired by the Government for afforestation and that parts of such areas will be retained in agriculture.

(c) *Pattern of Occupation*

Farms for livestock rearing, which is an extensive system of farming, should generally be larger than they are at present. Larger units are also essential for more economic production, including the maintenance and improvement of fixed equipment, and for providing the occupiers and their workers with up-to-date standards of living. We consider that this last factor will become increasingly evident in view of the likely labour requirements for forestry, hydro-electric schemes and other possible developments. It is difficult to recommend an optimum acreage as there is such a wide variation in the quality of the land within the area. We feel that our recommendations in this respect can best be expressed by stating that a whole-time upland farm unit should be large enough to maintain a minimum flock of about 500 Welsh breeding ewes throughout the year, or an equivalent number of other stock. On the fringe of the Central Moorland Region this would mean a unit with at least 100-150 acres of enclosed land and 500 acres of rough grazing, whilst on medium-quality land in the Western Plateau Region and the Eastern Plateau Region a unit should comprise at least 200 acres of enclosed land though the area required to form a satisfactory unit would be less if there were common grazing rights. These recommendations accord with the views of experienced and progressive farmers whom we met during our visits to the reference area and who, in many cases, are seeking to enlarge their enterprises up to this desirable level by the acquisition of extra land so as to have a unit large enough to justify full mechanisation and to employ at least one regular worker. The pattern of amalgamation emerging by sporadic purchases of vacant holdings is not always ideal but it is difficult to formulate a workable scheme whereby two, three or more uneconomic units can be welded into one stable well-planned holding, since contiguous units do not fall vacant at the same time. Possibly some scheme for compensating occupiers relinquishing small units to this end could be devised. In paragraph 126 (1) we recommend the provision of housing accommodation for retired farmers.

We reckon that, wherever possible, hill land should be farmed with lowland in the proportion of 3-5 acres of hill land to 1 of lowland. For physical reasons, it is clearly not possible for hill land to run continuously with its lowland in all cases and we recommend as an alternative the farming of severed hill and lowland units together. Where the movement of stock takes place on the hoof it would appear that about four miles is the reasonable maximum distance although the system can be effectively worked over greater distances where motor transport is available. It is of paramount importance to the long-term continuance of such a tie-up between upland and lowland that the occupier should have the same regard for the land and stock of the upland unit as of the lowland unit.

With regard to dairy holdings situated in the river valleys, of which there are a few in the area, we consider that a holding of this type should be from 100 to 150 acres in extent in order to comprise a reasonably economic unit.

We do not envisage a uniform pattern of large units. We consider that there should be a number of small-holdings in favourable areas within reasonable reach of centres of community life, in order to diversify the agricultural economy and to provide farming opportunities for young people. There is a very large number of small units in the reference area and we consider that some units up to about 30 acres will continue to be occupied on a part-time basis. Some units up to 50 or 60 acres will also survive if the occupiers are prepared to undertake some part-time work, e.g., haulage for the Forestry Commission with farm horses. Small-holders who are unable to provide machinery for their own holdings are able to co-operate with neighbouring occupiers of large farms on a mutual basis.

(d) —

(e) *Afforestation*

We are in accord with the Government's proposals to develop forestry in the uplands of Wales, as this will assist to remedy the marginality of farming due to the lack of community and public services.

There are remote areas of poor land in the reference area which cannot be developed and equipped economically for agricultural production. Such land, most of it in the Central Moorland Region, should in our view be afforested and we think that the agricultural prospects of much of this land are so poor that most of it will continue to be offered for this purpose. Some of the land on the Cambrian Range is unplantable and this might be fenced and let for summer grazing of cattle and sheep, after experimenting with a pilot scheme.

We recommend the closest co-operation between agricultural and forestry interests which require to be co-ordinated locally as they are on properly managed estates. Furthermore the material advantages to be derived from a happy marriage between the two must be warmly commended and given adequate publicity. Only in this way will existing prejudices be overcome and the partnership welcomed as it deserves to be, as forestry is a long-term policy involving rotations up to 70 years or more. We suggest the following as being some of the specific points to which consideration should be given:

(i) Forestry roads should, wherever reasonably practicable, be planned to provide access to farms and upland sheepwalks.

(ii) In appropriate cases, the pattern of forest planting should have regard for the maximum provision of shelter for homesteads and stock. Owners should be informed that quite small areas are acceptable for planting.

(iii) Areas afforested should be fenced. Fences should continuously be maintained during the whole of the life of the trees.

(iv) Parts of forestry acquisitions suitable for agriculture should be retained for that purpose, particularly where the construction of forest roads will make the land more accessible.

(v) Forestry equipment and labour should be made available to farmers on a contract basis for road-making, bulldozing, drainage and other heavy work.

(vi) Forestry workers should be released for work on farms in increasing numbers during the summer months and transport provided by the Forestry Commission on a repayment basis. There is likely to be a growing demand for seasonal casual agricultural labour.

(vii) In the main, forest workers should be housed in existing villages and hamlets in order to strengthen and diversify the present community life.

(viii) Farmers should be prepared to assist the Forestry Commission by keeping horses for casual haulage work, keeping a lookout for fires, etc.

(f) Basic Services

As a first stage in the development of the reference area, we recommend that encouragement should be given to the improvement of public roads and the extension of public water and electricity supplies by the authorities concerned, in order to provide a firm base for the future development of agriculture and forestry. In view of the changes which are taking place in the agricultural pattern and the tendency towards more compact communities, we consider it is essential that expert advice on trends in agriculture and forestry should be available to authorities concerned with development of public services before minor branch extensions are undertaken. In the first stage, development should be confined to the 'trunk and limbs' of the system of public services, rather than to the 'fingers'.

(g) Co-ordination of Rural Development

Our investigation has shown the need for co-ordination of the development of upland farming, afforestation and the provision of public services in a period of transition. We recommend the setting up of machinery for ensuring that the development of upland areas is guided on economic lines without waste of resources.

7 | Problems and Objectives in the Highlands and Islands

PROFESSOR SIR ROBERT GRIEVE, M.A., M.I.C.E.,
M.R.T.P.I., A.M.I.Mun. E. Hon. A.R.I.A.S.
Chairman, Highlands and Islands Development Board.*

The Highlands and Islands as a geographical region begins on, and extends north and west from, 'the Highland line' on the margin of the Lowlands of Scotland; for administrative purposes, including the domain of the Highlands and Islands Development Board, it begins a little farther north and west and is taken as the seven Highland counties of Argyll, Inverness, Ross and Cromarty, Sutherland, Caithness, Orkney and Shetland. By any interpretation, this is the most distinctive and largest 'remoter rural' group of counties in Britain. By definition it is entirely on the periphery of the continuously settled and urbanised lowlands, its extremities being 100–350 miles away from them, and 500–800 miles from London. In Scotland the contrast is stark between those counties with only 5 per cent of Scotland's population in nearly half its area, and Glasgow and the West Central Counties with half the total population in 5 per cent of the area.

The outstanding characteristic of the region is the narrowness of the inhabited tracts of coast and glen amid a vast expanse of moorland, mountain and sea—a total of 275,000 people, of whom three-fifths are in rural settlements, strung out through 14,000 square miles of territory (47 per cent of Scotland and one-sixth of Britain), for over 400 miles from 'Southend' in the peninsula of Kintyre to the farthest North Isles of Shetland. In land-use terms, under 7 per cent is cultivated crops and grass, 5 per cent is in forest plantations and of the dominating rough grazing nearly a third is high-lying deer forest. (Appendix I). There are some large estates—the Secretary of State for Scotland being the largest single owner through the Forestry Commission and the Department of Agriculture and Fisheries for Scotland—and many smaller, often owned by absentees and run by factors. Crofting is a distinctive form of tenure

* Now Professor of Town Planning, University of Glasgow

130

and way of life, mainly on the west and north coasts and Isles, though it should be emphasised that crofters and their dependants amount to only one-fifth of the total population. The Gaelic language and culture is still lively, though again mainly in the crofting west, where in the Outer Hebrides, 80–90 per cent of the people speak Gaelic as well as English. In the north, in Shetland and Orkney, the historical affinities and dialect, and many current interests, are Norse.

If this and the problems outlined later were all there was to distinguish this region, it would indeed be nothing but 'remotest rural'. But it has other more positive characteristics which the Board is more concerned with. It has high-yielding forest land and produces timber, pulp and paper; it carries ten times as many sheep as people and over 300,000 head of cattle; it has important fisheries all round it, not all exploited by strangers; it produces a great wealth of whisky, aluminium, woollen goods, machine tools and a growing diversity of smaller manufacturers; it has many scientists and technologists among the 2,000 employees of the United Kingdom Atomic Energy Authority in Caithness, half of them immigrants; and it accommodates and gives recreation to a great and growing company of holiday visitors. All this is resource use contributing to exports or import saving and easing the pressures on urban Britain.

Above all, perhaps, it has many long-settled and still stable communities, as well as newer immigrants, who feel pleased enough, or even privileged, to be here, who regard their own way of life as the centre of things, who look not on themselves but on metropolitan Britons as living in a remote area, and who are accustomed to travelling, or hearing from, the world far beyond the congested confines of Glasgow, Birmingham or London.

PROBLEMS

The first Annual Report of the H.I.D.B. notes that '. . . most opinions, as we have studied and listened to them, accept that depopulation of the area is the central problem—indeed it is almost the only common factor' among the diversity of views put forward. This is not now a problem of overall high rates of decline—which have, on average, slowed down—or high rates of migration loss—which are now generally lower than the Scottish average, but of the long-term effects on widely scattered communities of 200 years of emigration, which had its beginnings in the suppression of the Clans after the Risings of 1715 and 1745 and in the later Clearances of subsistence peasantry from the glens in favour of sheep farming and deer and grouse shooting. These effects have been not only an ageing of the population and a lowering of the natural increase to half the Scottish average (and in most of the rural areas to around nil), but also a lack of enterprise and confidence, and a serious thinning out of communities already too small and too isolated.

Unemployment has for some time been at about double the Scottish average rate, which in turn is higher than the Great Britain average. Under-employment in crofting areas and among women, and seasonal unemployment in tourism and fishing are special features. Personal incomes for tax purposes are considerably lower than the Scottish and UK averages—in 1964–65 respectively £265, £330 and £400 per head of population. Here as elsewhere the decline in the need for and, indeed, the supply of agricultural workers proceeds at an alarmingly increasing rate: fortunately this has little effect in crofting and family farming areas but a serious effect in, for example, parts of Orkney, Caithness and around the Moray Firth. At the back of all these problems has been the more general one of lack of alternative job opportunities and of a diversity of jobs in an unbalanced economic structure with, in particular, only a static 10 per cent of the labour force in manufactures.

There has been the further basic deficiency of private and public enterprise to deal with these problems. Since the passing of the first Crofters Act of 1886, a score of specialised agencies for the Highlands has been set up by Government and voluntary bodies, in addition to the wide range of normal Departments and Local Authorities operating in the area. But with a few notable exceptions, and granting the important and costly basic services of roads, air services, electricity, water and housing laid on in recent decades, these agencies' functions have been mainly regulatory, welfare, subsidy paying and the provision of infrastructure on an *ad hoc* or fragmented basis. The total effect has been to support the existing social and economic structure rather than to make radical and co-ordinated changes or stimulate new enterprise; and to confirm the historical sense of failure to cope both among Highlanders and politically conscious Lowlanders.

THE REGIONAL APPROACH

There is nothing new in a regional approach to the solution of these problems in the sense that the Highlands as a whole have been recognised throughout Scottish history as a very different area from the Lowlands and one requiring special military, administrative or economic arrangements. What has been growing in the past decade has been a recognition, for example by the Secretary of State's Advisory Panel on Highland and Island affairs, of the inter-linkages between problems in the same region and of the need for an executive co-ordinating body able to operate over a wide front in the region as a whole and in particular parts of it. At the same time there has been the advance in national economic planning for 'regions' such as Scotland and the work of the Scottish Office culminating in the White Paper[1] on 'The Scottish Economy 1965–70' which enabled the Highlands' opportunities for development to be seen on the same criteria as those of other regions of Scotland, just as Scotland was now seen as a region able to use spare labour and other resources for the growth of the United Kingdom economy and by so doing to mitigate inflation and physical congestion in the South-East.

This was the prelude to the setting up of the H.I.D.B. by Act of Parliament in 1965 as an executive agency of the Secretary of State for Scotland, with the two-fold purpose of 'assisting the people of the Highlands and Islands to improve their economic and social conditions and of enabling the Highlands and Islands to play a more effective part in the economic and social development of the nation.' The Act gives it special powers and finance to make grants and loans to private enterprises, to carry out projects itself, to enter on to and acquire private land and buildings, to concert, promote and assist other activities and to keep the economy and welfare of the area under review. It can have up to seven members, the majority full-time, appointed by the Secretary of State and it is required to have a main office in the Highlands. This is in Inverness, the largest town (population 32,000) and the administrative centre of the region. The Board is so far the only body of its kind in the United Kingdom.

OBJECTIVE

In taking up this challenging task in its first year, the Board had one difficulty—the wide range of views strongly pressed upon it from all quarters about the nature of the Highland Problem and its solution. But it had two advantages—the regional study and policy guide lines set down in the Government's White Paper on the Scottish Economy,[1] and the long experience of Board Members and many of the staff in Highland affairs and their awareness of experiments in the rehabilitation of lagging regions in other countries, notably in Norway. From all these sources, the Board distilled its own objectives and priorities which were discussed in the Foreword to the first Annual Report: this described the Board's aim as adding '. . . another perfectly possible way of life to that in the great cities. In offering that alternative to the important minority in any urbanised country who wished to take it, the Board will also be engendering a greater flow of products for the United Kingdom.' In this dual sense, the Board sees rural development as complementary, not inferior, to urban, and of prime importance nationally.

The Board accepted the White Paper's three main props for development of the economy—forestry, tourism and manufactures. Forestry is a growing industry in the region in terms of acreage (from 180,000 in 1949 to 441,000 in 1967), of timber output from maturing forests, and of employment when ancillary workers are included. Yet the percentage of land in forest plantations is still only 4·9, compared with 8·4 in the rest of Scotland, and surveys suggest that at least 15 per cent is physically plantable. For these reasons and for its wider economic returns to the nation, as well as for its benefits in shelter, amenity, recreation and soil regeneration, the Board is not impressed by any application of rigid commercial criteria to the Forestry Commission's planting programme and believes that increased afforestation will prove a wise long-term investment.

Tourism is also seen by the Board to be a growth industry and has been given special attention in finance and staff to cater for the large present and potential market of urban and overseas visitors who seek to use and pay for an important natural resource in one of Europe's last unspoiled areas. As Fraser Darling has put it 'let it be quite clearly understood, the recreational value of Highland

land is now likely to be its greatest commercial value. This fact is one it took me too long to realise, brought up in the conviction that the agricultural quality of land was its criterion of value.'[2] Greater stress than in the White Paper was and is laid by the Board on the *promotion of manufactures* 'as the most urgent of all relative to the immediate need to stem a substantial proportion of the emigration of talented sons and daughters from the Highlands and Islands . . .'; as the most deficient element in the Highland economy; and as a task suited to the Board's new powers of promotion whereas 'forestry, in the public sector, is the job of a powerful organisation backed by Government policy and finance; and tourism is supported by the unquestionable appearance every year of more visitors'. The policy in this field is three-fold:

(i) to encourage the growth of industrial enterprise wherever a developer shows a personal and specific desire to settle or expand his enterprise;

(ii) to pursue a more methodical programme for building small industrial growth points in scale with the possibilities of the West and the islands (this is regarded as especially important to balance the effects of (iii));

(iii) 'we will do our utmost to generate major growth points, involving substantial increases in population, wherever the natural advantages of the area seem to warrant it; the Moray Firth is unquestionably the most important of these areas'. In this strategic priority, the Board has two other aims in mind—'to move the industrial centre of gravity of Britain farther north' and to see that the bigger centres are planned and designed so that the country would be proud of them.

A further difference in emphasis from the White Paper was the importance attached to the development of inshore and off-shore fisheries and processing as having a special geographical significance in certain islands and other communities. Nor did the Board discount agricultural production, but wished to make it clear that it would not help the depopulation problem—rather would it 'give more food from the Highlands for the rest of the country rather than more people for the Highlands'; and a policy statement in March 1968 set out the measures the Board would take to raise the productivity of land and labour.*[3,4] Crofting was not discounted either, given

* *Occasional Bulletin* No. 2, pp. 56–63—Annual Report for 1968.

its dependence on supplementary income from small industries, forestry and tourism since it 'appears to be a form of living and working which gives deep satisfaction to those who follow it' and 'if one had to look now for a way of life which would keep that number of people in such relatively intractable territory, it would be difficult to contrive a better system'. Services are maintained and communities kept viable '. . . and even on the lowest estimate of its role, i.e. that of maintaining a living countryside in which the rest of the country can move, enjoy and recreate itself, it could claim justification'.

TACTICS

How should such a widely based set of policies and priorities be implemented? The Board's tactics have from the beginning been to move into action as quickly as possible. They set up a grants and loans scheme to encourage and assist any worthwhile enterprises; a management and accountacy service to guide and nurse these and other small businesses in deficient matters such as book-keeping; a young projects staff to investigate and execute practical Board schemes in fisheries, bulb growing in the Hebrides, tourism and small industries; an area development scheme for major industrial growth in the Invergordon–Inverness area of the Moray Firth; and a Counterdrift Register of over 7,000 people willing to move into the Highlands and Islands when jobs and houses are available. Later there have been expanding programmes of staff work in Information Services, Tourism and Transport, Land Development and Regional Planning and Research.

There are four full-time and two part-time Board Members. A gradually increased staff drawn from the public services, commerce, universities and local schools now numbers 160 in 9 Divisions. They have been supplemented by the use of specialist consultants from private firms and universities, notably in the case of the Moray Firth growth area. Also, consultation and negotiation with existing bodies such as the Forestry Commission, the Department of Agriculture and Forestry for Scotland, and transport authorities who are able and willing to implement Board strategy on their own account and with local authorities whose infrastructure powers and plans are directly affected by the Board, have been an integral part of the operations. Liaison with universities and institutes is mainly in the fields of resource 'capability', geography, economics and sociology. It is the Board's hope that the various strands of research for development can be brought together in a distinctive research institute, providing a centre of studies relevant not only to the Highlands and Islands but also to similar regions elsewhere. As a first step, a small research library and study centre is to be set up in the Board's premises.

The Board has been criticised by some economists for not yet working out long-term plans, including employment and investment targets, for each sector of the regional economy and each distinctive sub-region, especially since the White Paper implied concentration of effort on favourable sectors and locations in view of the traditional confusion of aims and diffusion of money and time on the diverse and dispersed communities of the Highlands and Islands. The Board's answer is that this is a long job and to have started by doing it would have delayed any impact in a community long cynical of pigeon-holed surveys and proposals. The first urgent priority is to give confidence and bolster morale by getting some practical and imaginative things done and by seeking out and encouraging local economic enterprise wherever and whatever it might be; plans when they come, will then be credible. In any case, a strategy was set down in the beginning and not objected to in Parliament; detailed plans and programmes for some sectors, such as tourism and transport, and some areas, notably the inner Moray Firth have been made; and with the appointment of professional staff, including a Regional Economist, to the Planning Division and to a Land Development Division, a watching brief on the economy is being built up and its first fruits include a new chapter on statistical indicators of regional change in the third Annual Report.

AREA DEVELOPMENT

It is inherent in our concept or regions and their development that they can be of any size and that any one is an integral part of a larger scheme of things. But it is also made up of a diversity of smaller component 'regions' and this is especially true of the Highlands and Islands which has at least five major sub-divisions and scores of communities, often small and isolated, with different voices and different problems and capabilities. Recognising this

and with a mind to the White Paper guide-line on the need to concentrate efforts at priority locations, the Board has devoted a good
deal of attention to 'area development' i.e. the planning and implementation of schemes of development for priority districts of its
territory with distinctive opportunities and/or problems. In line
with the priority it sees in promotion of manufacturing industry,
the first area development schemes have been for major industrial/
urban growth in areas best suited to this—first, the inner Moray
Firth, a strategically placed lowland of 70,000 population on a
coast with deep-water estuaries; secondly, Wick–Thurso in Caithness,
a detached lowland of 28,000 population with a large technical and
scientific labour force, in the UKAEA's Experimental Reactor and
associated plants; and thirdly, Fort William, a smaller growth point
of 10,000 population in Lochaber with two major industries—the
old established British Aluminium Company and a new pulp and
paper mill.

Moray Firth Development has seen an impressive concentration
of Board effort by Board Members and a small planning staff on
publicity, high level negotiation with industrialists and central
government departments, constant liaison with local authorities
and expenditure of £140,000 on feasibility studies by consultants on
major industrial promotion, power generation, coastal terrain, piers
and ports, foreshore reclamation, and a physical plan for expanded
towns, traffic, and landscape, to provide a potential capacity for
270,000 people. This priority for M.F.D. has certainly paid. In the
first place the government has permitted, and assisted, the British
Aluminium Company to erect a new aluminium reduction works at
Invergordon (Alcan also wished to go there, but are now building in
Northumberland) which is to produce 100,000 tons of aluminium a
year from alumina brought in by sea to a new deep-water pier.
It will produce three times the present output of the two existing
B.A. factories in Lochaber and employ 650. Also, a new Grampian
Chemicals Company proposes to bring in crude oil by ocean tanker,
refine it and establish a series of ancillary chemical industries.

Caithness is a more difficult area and has been given second
priority, through a working party of board, government and local
officials. There is a breathing space of a few years before the run-
down of manpower in UKAEA is added to that in agriculture and
efforts are continuing, for example, to increase livestock production
and to find a suitable electro-intensive industry which would use

local natural and manpower resources. Lochaber, like Caithness, has had a fast growing population in present years but it had also been growing slowly during the previous 50 years. It now cannot absorb all the school leavers and dependants of immigrant families coming on to the labour market and this raises the question of how long and how fast growth should be expected to continue.

A modification of this policy is being worked out for some 25 centres of population with their hinterlands in the west and north. Some of these areas have populations of 6,000–16,000; most have only 500–3,000. Concentration in and around these centres is being considered as offering the most efficient use of labour and services in a dispersed population to meet the needs of small new industries, services for developing tourism, fishing, forestry and agriculture and a greater concentration of costly infrastructure investments. This work is in line with the emphasis of the new Town and Country Planning Bill and consultations to this end, as well as for economic and social development, are proceeding with County Authorities and the Crofters Commission.

Some districts, including small islands, have no such centres—they contain in all only about 8 per cent of the Highland population—and in them as well as in some of those with centres, the emphasis is on *comprehensive rural resource development*. So far, only two such areas have been examined—the Strath of Kildonan in Sutherland, and the island of Mull in Argyll. In both, progress has been slow, as they are problem areas of land use given to the Board to tackle when it was set up, rather than selected for their advantages for development. Efforts are being made to select, within the regional framework of functional priorities and resource feasibility studies, a number of other rural districts, preferably with access to a minor centre, where there are known to be one or two favourable prospects of resource development which can be promoted with the staff and finance available, and where local communities and local authorities can be fully involved. Some of the areas with potential land resources are likely to be in the central Highland zone which is virtually un-inhabited, whereas the existing pockets of population, labour and services—themselves scarce and costly resources—and of the poten-tial for industrial and tourism growth are on the coasts or eastern straths. Nevertheless, where there is a prospect of, say, high-yielding forestry and recreational activities on a trans-Highland route, new settlement may be justified.

PRACTICAL RESULTS

The greatest part of the Board's effort in finance and staff-work is
devoted to its grants and loans scheme, which is a more flexible
version of Board of Trade aid in Development Areas, allowing the
Board to give loan and grant assistance normally up to £50,000 to
any commercially viable enterprises which are likely to maintain or
increase employment. The results in the three and a half years are
summarised below. In addition to the Board expenditure of £5·2

Table 7.1.   *Applications approved for Loans and Grants: to 31st May 1969*

	No.	Loans	Grants	Total	No. to be employed
		£'000s	£'000s	£'000s	
Manufacturing and processing	221	1,220·9	363·8	1,584·7	1345
Tourism, catering and transport	294	931·0	738·6	1,669·6	1081
Fisheries	139	835·2	106·9	942·1	532
Agriculture and horticulture	38	201·9	38·3	240·2	59
Others, mainly services	300	524·5	280·5	805·0	596
Total	992	3,713·4	1,528·1	5,241·5	3613

millions nearly as much was contributed by the developers themselves. New employment of 3,600 is quite significant in a working
population of 100,000 bearing in mind the limited number of
entrepreneurs and the small-scale of most projects in this region.
In relation to population, the greatest impact of the scheme has
been in the crofting and fishing county of Shetland, where a great
variety of enterprises has been encouraged to take advantage of
the scheme; whereas the least impact has been in the neighbouring
island county of Orkney which has tended to rely almost entirely
on its agricultural industry, a relatively prosperous but declining
employer.

In addition to the attraction of major industries, like British
Aluminium to the Moray Firth growth area, which are financed by
the Board of Trade, the Highlands and Islands Development Board's
promotional efforts and grants and loans scheme have been used to
introduce 42 new manufacturing industries into the region employing

a total of 609. The bigger employing firms are mainly around Inverness, Campbeltown and Fort William, but the smaller ones are widely dispersed from precision engraving in Skye, to spectacle frame and perfume making in Barra, and knitwear in Lerwick.

The Board's tourism development plan takes account of marketing, promotion, accommodation, resources, services and research, and a main objective is to lengthen the season by special publicity and reduced terms. As agencies for this, 13 new Area Tourist Organisations have been set up. Over 1,800 extra bedrooms have been provided as a result of grant and loan assistance to hotels and boarding-houses. One of the first Board schemes approved by the Secretary of State was for the building of five large hotels in the Western Isles and mainland at a cost of £1 million and the first of these is now being built in the island of Mull: they will be leased to hotel operators.

The Board's fisheries development scheme provides for the building of 35 new boats by 1971 at a cost of around £900,000. Eighteen boats have been launched and 25 allocated so far and, bearing in mind that the majority of the men are new to fishing, these results are encouraging. Because so many are new to it, practical sea-going training has been made part and parcel of the scheme. A total of 126 new and second-hand fishing boats have been assisted and there have been substantial developments ashore in the shape of new and improved processing and ice plants, lobster storage tanks, boatyards and other facilities. Altogether the Board has invested £1·6 million in the industry leading to some 902 jobs, and with private contributions and grants from the statutory fishing authorities this is an all-round demonstration of faith in the future of this industry.

One of the most striking projects at the Board's own hand in the agricultural field has been an experimental bulb scheme in North Uist in the Outer Hebrides. Following intensive investigations by our own staff and by soil experts from the Netherlands, six acres of bulbs were planted in 1967 on land sub-let from local crofters and they produced bulbs of excellent quality with considerable yield increases. Another 20 acres were planted in 1968, and further land is being selected for planting to bring the total to 50 acres. The results so far encourage the belief that, given expert management, large-scale but concentrated bulb growing in the Hebrides could be a profitable undertaking.

In transport, the Board's role is primarily to advise the Secretary of State and the operators on priorities in the interests of regional development. The importance of the arterial links by air, rail and road with Central Scotland and England have been stressed to some effect, especially for the Moray Firth growth area. For internal services, special attention has been given to reducing sea freight charges and to the types of vehicle, terminals and organisation appropriate to generally light traffic on widespread networks. Progress is being made, for example, in the use of light aircraft and airstrips and roll-on roll-off vehicle ferries.

These and many other effects of the Board's work have, it is generally believed, given growing confidence to the people of the Highlands in their own enterprise, and confidence that the Board can help them in many new ways. The work of the Board has excited a great deal of interest, some opposition, and a large measure of support. It is looked to as the one agency of government which ought to be tackling almost any aspect of life in the region and often seems to be shot at, or got at, from all directions at once. But the fact that the public and even Members of Parliament often look first to the Board rather than to the specific statutory Departments to get things moving is a measure of the confidence placed in a regional, locally based, executive arm of government.

The overall impression of the Highland economy in the 1960s which emerges from our recently completed work on statistical indicators is at best one of apparent stability. Underlying this there is a continuing loss of young people through migration, a tendency for greater concentration of population in the larger towns, and a substantial decline in agricultural employment. The appearance of stability is achieved only through the compensating effects of the growth of tourism and sea-fishing, a slow but progressive build-up in manufacturing industry, a sustained programme of afforestation, and probably by a continuing inflow of elderly people. In many parts of the region, for instance, in Orkney, the position is by no means stable, and even the overall stability is vulnerable on many sides to technological and other outside influences. It has to be remembered, too, that the state of the regional economy is the result of a great variety of private decisions and national or international influences and that whereas the Board's annual expenditure is between £2 million and £3 million, the Departments of the Scottish Office alone spend a total of some £43 million in the

Highlands on agriculture, forestry, fishing, education, health, housing, roads and infrastructure in general.

CONCLUDING QUESTIONS

In the light of its experience, answers to three of the main questions about remoter rural areas are:

(i) *What should be the long-term objective?*
The primary objective is to offer another perfectly possible way of life to that in the cities. The first means to that end should be to encourage greater self-reliance among existing communities by seeking out and assisting all forms of local enterprise and by promoting practical and fairly short-term projects which can give confidence. Morale based on some economic activity is more important than the perfect plan. Remoter areas like the Highlands which already have some remaining cultural identity and social self-sufficiency may be better placed in many ways for future stability than those which are tied by the neck to metropolitan centres. The second longer term target is more people, including immigrants, which means more employment especially in manufactures and the rural growth industries of tourism and forestry. Bold measures, flexibly financed, will be essential, supported by rigorous feasibility studies and co-ordinated so far as possible with central government as well as local authorities and other interests.

(ii) *How are they affected by the changing demands of the rest of the country?*
Some of these demands should be met by the above objectives, for example, for fewer unproductive subsidies to rural industries and population, and for greater opportunities for a minority in the cities to re-settle in rural regions. Demands for recreation in all its forms are growing and so far can be met without serious land use problems in this spacious region, except for some roadside and town congestion. It should be possible to work out proper principle and standards of land use and conservation, as well as to exploit opportunities for commercial development, and the Board is collaborating in this with the local planning authorities, the Countryside Commission for Scotland, the Nature Conservancy and the National Trust for Scotland.

Generally speaking, the same is true of growing demands for certain types of industrial development, which can certainly be accommodated if well-designed and planned to give, *inter alia*, a minimum of disturbance to farmers.

(iii) *Is comprehensive development a desirable and practical means to these objectives?*

Yes, in so far as H.I.D.B. is a comprehensive development authority (excluding infrastructure); yes, in respect of major industrial/urban growth areas. For smaller rural area development schemes, it is also desirable but not always practicable. Since both natural and human resources are scarce and dispersed, no one of them, separately, is likely to suffice and their multiple use should be planned, as it is in good estate management. But the initial selection of such areas is all-important, if only because of the large amount of staff time and consultation with interested bodies which will be involved. Resource capability and economic cost-benefit studies are essential. It is desirable to include a small population centre, existing or planned. There should then be a policy distinction between areas selected because of social need and those which are marked out by their more favourable economic prospects.

REFERENCES

1. *The Scottish Economy, 1965–70.*
2. DARLING, F. *The Future of the Highlands*, p. 52, Thomson and Grimble, 1968.
3. *Agriculture*, Occasional Bulletin No. 2, Highland Development Board, 1969.
4. Highlands and Islands Development Board Third Report, pp. 56–63, Inverness, 1969.

APPENDIX I

Population, Land Use, Numbers of Cattle and Sheep, Highlands and Islands of Scotland, 1968

1968	Highlands and Islands		Scotland	
	Million acres	*per cent*	*Million acres*	*per cent*
Rough grazing (including deer forest)	7·58	84·3	12·17	63·8
Crops and grass	0·59	6·7	4·28	22·4
High Forest (1967)	0·44	4·9	1·27	6·7
Scrub and felled woodland (1967)	0·16	1·8	0·41	2·2
Built-up areas (approximate)	(0·04)	(0·4)	0·62	3·3
Unaccounted for	0·18	2·0	0·32	1·6
Total land area	8·99	100·0	19·07	100·0
	Millions		*Millions*	
Total cattle	0·32		2·1	
Total sheep	2·58		7·8	
Population	0·28		5·2	

8 | Regional Problems and Policies in the European Economic Community

PROFESSOR PAUL ROMUS
Institute of European Studies,
University of Brussels

No approach to European regional structures can now leave out of consideration the vital factor represented by the establishment of the European Economic Community. The Community,* of course, initially inherited the regional problems existing in the Member States, but it adds a new dimension to these problems and provides a new context for the national policies put in hand to resolve them. To the extent that their powers and resources allow, the European Communities have contributed to a better distribution of economic activities in the territory of the member countries. These few points constitute the thread of what I am going to say.

REGIONAL POLICIES AND PROBLEMS OF THE MEMBER COUNTRIES

In the regional sphere, as elsewhere, the structures of the European Community are first and foremost a direct consequence of what exists in its constituent States. Some of these structures go back a long way and can be explained by the combined influence of geography, history and politics. The regional policies pursued by the States are of relatively recent date, having been launched between 1950 and 1962. Taking these policies in the order in which they were introduced, I propose to make a brief analysis of them and of the problems they were designed to clear away.

Italy
The main problem for Italy, whose regional policy goes back to

* Familiarity with the terms used to describe the E.E.C. institutions is promoted by reference to Colman[1] and Broad and Jarrett.[2]

1950, is the underdevelopment of that part of the country south of Rome, the Mezzogiorno, including the islands of Sicily and Sardinia. This area, which has more than 20 million inhabitants (38 per cent of Italy's total population), contributes only 24 per cent to the gross national product, thus reflecting a level of development per capita only 66 per cent of the national average. A great deal has been done since the *Cassa per il Mezzogiorno* was set up in 1950. First planned to last fifteen years, the *Cassa* was extended for a similar period in 1965. Italian regional policy is backed by exceptional financial resources and considerable aids to investment. Until 1957 it was mainly aimed at the modernisation of agriculture, but since then the stress has been on regional industrialisation, by the provision of infrastructures and the creation of industrial areas. Despite a high rate of growth, very close to the Italian national average and well above the European average, the gap between the levels of development in North and South remains. The flow of migrants from the Mezzogiorno is proof that the problems have not been solved: between 1950 and 1967 the area lost more than 2·3 million of its population. Great efforts will still have to be made, therefore, if people are to be discouraged from leaving southern Italy.

Germany

The Federal Republic of Germany introduced its regional policy at much the same time as Italy, but the analogy between the two countries stops there. The origin of Germany's regional problems is essentially political and arises from the division of the country into two. The regions bordering the Eastern zone of Germany, the *Zonenrandgebiete*, had to face two problems in the years immediately following the last war—the loss of their eastern hinterland, and a flood of refugees from Eastern Germany and various countries of Eastern Europe, numbering at present more than 11 million people, or almost a fifth of the West German population. And then there are regions in Germany which have to cope with a structural problem—generally in agriculture or mining—which is tending to get more intractable. In the aggregate, German regional policy affects an area peopled by 14 million inhabitants, or 23 per cent of the population. Financial aids to investment, linked with the dynamism inherent in certain regions and their favourable situation, have greatly contributed to resolving the most serious regional problems.

Those regions which are still greatly dependent on coal-mining are still a cause for concern.

The Netherlands

The beginnings of regional policy in the Netherlands go back to 1952. In a territory which, after all, is small by European standards there is a considerable imbalance in the distribution of population and economic activities. The West, with one fifth of the country's area, contains almost half its population and more than half its economic potential. And a still smaller area, Randstad Holland, formed by the Amsterdam, Rotterdam and Hague conurbations, has 4 million inhabitants, or 37 per cent of the population, in 10 per cent of the total area. By contrast, the north, with its relatively great dependence on agriculture, and the south-east with its declining coal industry, are marking time as regards growth and the level of development. All in all, regional policy is concerned with areas having a population of 2·5 million, or one fifth of the population of the Netherlands. A policy geared to the establishment of industrial centres and the grant of subsidies to industrial investment has yielded remarkable results in this country, where the regional differences in per capita income do not exceed 20 per cent. Town and country planning is nowhere so advanced, in any part of the Community, as in the Netherlands: the reclamation of land from the sea, spectacular though it is, is only one aspect of it.

France

The first decrees introducing regional policy in France date from 1954–55. The regional problems with which France has to cope are the concentration of population and industry in the Paris region, and the relative underdevelopment of certain parts of the country—problems which are linked, at least to some extent. The Paris region constitutes the worst case of centralisation in the European Community: with more than 9 million inhabitants, the region contains nearly 19 per cent of the French population on 2 per cent of the national territory. The west and south-west, on the other hand, which are still preponderantly agricultural and under-industrialised, are much less developed than the national average. These two regional problems are of very long standing, but the decline of the Nord and Lorraine is a recent phenomenon. The targets of French regional policy are decentralisation away from

Paris and the development of regions which are lagging behind or declining. In one way or another, regional policy concerns an area with 30 million inhabitants, or 60 per cent of the population. Incentives to move out of Paris or to develop other regions have made it possible to slow down the growth of the Paris area and to promote regional industrialisation. The creation of regional metropolitan centres and large development projects in certain areas will probably lead to a renaissance of the regions of France.

Belgium
Belgium has had a regional policy since 1959. The essential problem in this country, which was one of the first to be industrialised in continental Europe, is the decline of its old industrial regions based on coalmining, iron and steel, and textiles. Of all Community regions, Wallonia has suffered the biggest drop in coal production and has had the lowest growth rate. By contrast, Flanders is experiencing a remarkable upsurge, the port of Antwerp attracting increasing investment in the growth industries. Belgium's regional policy concerns 3·5 million people, of 36 per cent of the total population, fairly evenly divided between the two language regions. Since the aids are identical in the development regions, most are applied for in the region which has the better infrastructure, i.e. Flanders, which has received nearly two thirds of the country's regional aid. The absence of priorities corresponding to the real regional difficulties is the reflection of a political situation which is outside the province of this chapter.

Luxemburg
Finally, Luxemburg too has been tackling its regional problems since 1962. In quite a small area there exists a fairly substantial imbalance between the iron and steel basin of the south-west, which has more than a third of the population and accounts for the major part of the country's economy, and the Ardennes in the north, with only 7 per cent of the population and a few declining industries. Although the establishment of a few industrial enterprises seems to have sufficed to resolve the difficulties of the north, Luxemburg's dependence on iron and steel is disquieting for the future.

REGIONAL PROBLEMS AT COMMUNITY LEVEL

The regional problems I have outlined concern areas whose size, contents and institutional organisation vary considerably: nineteen Italian regions, eleven German Lander, four different parts of the Netherlands, twenty-one French regions, three Belgian regions and a segment of Luxemburg—just about sixty economic regions in all.

The striking thing when we study regional problems at Community level is their great diversity. The regional approach enables us to understand Europe in its variety and to go beyond stereotyped national images.

The first problem is the uneven spread of development. It would seem that the most highly developed regions in the Community are in close proximity to each other. The east of France, the west of Germany, and the north of Italy, are, very broadly speaking, the most developed parts of these countries. If we add the Netherlands, Belgium and Luxembourg, we find that between the North Sea and the Channel, on the one hand, and the Alps and Mediterranean, on the other, there extends an area centred on the Rhine, the Meuse, the Scheldt and the Rhône covering 35 per cent of the Community's territory. This area accounts for 45 per cent of the Community's population and 60 per cent of its product. It contains the Community's chief resources, best communications and largest ports. Surrounding this region, which might very roughly be called 'central', we have a more or less 'peripheral' region whose level of development (particularly in Southern Italy) is below the Community average. In the Community as a whole there is a disparity in per capita income of the order of 1 to 3 or 1 to 4, and perhaps even more, between the most developed and the most backward regions.

The second problem is regional decline. This, it should be noted, can be partly or totally masked by a certain level of development. Decline is a continuing process, the converse of growth, which can be observed at any given moment. In different degrees, depending on geological conditions and location, decline is affecting all the Community's coalfields and, sometimes, its steelmaking and textile centres. Again very generally speaking, decline is to be found in those parts of the Community which were the first to be industrialised, and it corrects—perhaps it even cancels out—whatever observations may be made about the distribution of development.

The third regional problem is the excessive concentration of population and economic activity in a number of large urban centres. The Paris region, Randstad Holland, the Ruhr and the big cities of North-West Italy are among the conurbations in which the problems of town planning, governed in turn by traffic problems, require ever-more costly public investment in a situation which is becoming increasingly difficult.

Finally, the frontier regions represent a fourth problem. Here, a distinction should be made between the external and internal frontiers of the Community. Certain regions on the Community's outer frontier are contiguous with countries with which economic relations are difficult and precarious. This is especially so with the German regions bordering the Eastern zone and Czechoslovakia and, to a less extent, in Friuli-Venezia Giulia along Italy's border with Yugoslavia. The situation of these areas has not in fact been changed by the establishment of the Common Market, but it is quite another matter with the regions on the Community's internal frontiers. These areas—at the points where two or more Community countries meet—have had their position completely reversed: from having been peripheral in the national context, they have become central in the Community context.

ECONOMIC SIGNIFICANCE OF THE COMMON MARKET FOR REGIONAL POLICY

The primary economic significance of the Common Market is that it puts everything on a larger scale. By substituting for six countries, the most populous of which has 60 million inhabitants, a single entity of 183 million inhabitants, the Common Market provides the opportunity for a fresh distribution of economic activities. This means that from now on the siting of investments will have to be thought of no longer in terms of six national territories but in terms of a single Community. In other words, the Common Market could bring about a concentration of economic activities in the most highly developed and best equipped regions, those most favourably situated for obtaining supplies and dispatching products—that is to say, those with a modern transport infrastructure.

It is doubtless to prevent this happening that the European

F

Treaties contain a few references to regional development, though these by no means amount to regional charters.

In fact the objective of a regional policy in the Community is fully expressed in the idea of equilibrium, of balanced growth in the various regions and, more particularly, of making up the leeway lost by the less fortunate.

As regards responsibility for regional matters, the least that can be said is that it is not chiefly in the hands of the European as opposed to national institutions. The European Institutions at present have no powers of initiative on regional policy. Whatever action has to be undertaken, the Treaties specify that it is put in hand either at the request of the Governments concerned or proposed by them to the Commission of the European Communities. It would seem that the European institutions can play only a complementary role and that the main responsibilities are vested in the Member States.

In this matter, as in many others, we come up against the political question (which has to be answered first) whether or not there is a resolve to build a Europe which would be more than a mere aggregate of national sovereignties.

And yet, whatever areas of power the States would be prepared to surrender to the Commission, there are few fields in which co-ordination of national policies will be so necessary as in regional matters.

The member countries' regional policies are essentially embodied in aids of a financial or fiscal nature—bonuses, interest rebates, low-interest loans, accelerated depreciation, tax relief, etc.—all of which amount to a subsidy ranging, according to region, from 10 per cent to nearly 50 per cent of the total cost of a given investment. Where they help in solving serious regional difficulties, these aids are authorised under the Rome Treaty as exceptions to the principle of free competition, which would normally exclude them. The States have realised how profitable these exceptions could be and are now vying with each other in calling for aid for regional difficulties; their arguments do not always carry conviction.

It would seem, then, that national regional policies should be co-ordinated and that no other body is better fitted to do this than the Common Market Commission.

CONTRIBUTION OF THE EUROPEAN COMMUNITIES TO REGIONAL DEVELOPMENT

The contributions which the European Communities can make to regional development fall under the heads of financing, transport infrastructure, and regional studies.

Economic conversion

Under the terms of the Treaty of Paris, the European Coal and Steel Community High Authority (E.C.S.C.) can finance programmes for 'the creation . . . of new and economically sound activities capable of assuring productive employment to . . . workers made redundant in the coal and steel industries where the re-employment of these workers is giving rise to regional difficulties.

E.C.S.C. action in this field began in 1961. It has continued to grow as more and more pits have been closed down. E.C.S.C. loans are granted at the request of the Governments concerned. They are medium-term credits bearing interest at 4·5 per cent. They never cover the total financing need but help to carry out the particular scheme. The most positive aspect of Community action lies in the stimulating and guiding effects it is intended to have.

Between 1961 and 1968, the E.C.S.C. granted about 100 loans totalling 142 million units of account.* All these loans went, of course, to the coalmining and steelmaking regions. Those benefiting most are Wallonia (with 22 per cent of the total), North Rhine-Westphalia (with 15 per cent), Dutch Limburg (13 per cent), Nord/pas-de-Calais (11 per cent), and the Sulcis area in Sardinia (10 per cent). The essential purpose of the loans has been to bring in new industries and in some cases to set up 'industrial areas'.

Regional development

The task of the European Investment Bank (E.I.B.) set up under the Rome Treaty, is 'to contribute, by calling on the capital markets and its own resources, to the balanced and smooth development of the common market in the interest of the Community. For this purpose, the Bank shall by granting loans and guarantees on a non-profit-making basis facilitate the financing of . . . projects in all sectors of the economy. . . .'

* 1 unit of account is equivalent to $1 U.S.

The kind of project which can be financed by the Bank is specified in the Treaty:

(*a*) projects for developing less developed regions;

(*b*) projects for modernising or converting enterprises . . . called for by the gradual establishment of the Common Market;

(*c*) projects of common interest.

European Investment Bank credits are generally medium-term. They are intended to supplement others and never cover the entire financing requirement. Interest is at the capital market rate.

Between 1958 and 1968 the E.I.B. granted 160 loans totalling 892 million units of account. These figures relate to projects on Community territory and do not include loans to associated countries (which amounted to 242 million units of account). Of this total, 67 per cent (117 loans totalling 595 million units of account) went to Italy. France followed up with 17 per cent of the total, then Germany with 12 per cent, Belgium with 3 per cent and Luxemburg with 1 per cent. The Netherlands had not applied for any loan up to the end of 1968.

By sector, 39 per cent of the loans were for industry, 33 per cent for transport infrastructure, 6 per cent for telecommunications, 11 per cent for energy and 11 per cent for agriculture.

Italy's overwhelming share in E.I.B. credits is due to two factors. First, a Protocol concerning Italy, annexed to the Rome Treaty, recognises the existence of less-developed areas in southern Italy and recommends that in helping Italy to implement its development programme the Community institutions should employ all the ways and means available under the Treaty, in particular by making adequate use of E.I.B. resources. Second, from the outset of the Bank's activity, its Board of Governors laid down directives giving an order of priority for projects submitted: projects for developing less-developed regions, followed by projects of common interest and, finally, conversion projects, which in fact have no priority.

Reorganisation of agricultural structure

A leading objective of the E.E.C.'s common agricultural policy is 'to increase agricultural productivity by developing technical progress and by ensuring the rational development of agricultural production and the optimum utilisation of the factors of production, particularly labour'. In working out this policy, account is to be taken of 'the

particular character of agricultural activities arising from the social
structure of agriculture and from structural and natural disparities
between the various agricultural regions'.

By virtue of these provisions a European Agricultural Guidance
and Guarantee Fund (F.E.O.G.A.) was set up comprising two
sections. The Guarantee Section covers expenditure relating to
refunds on exports to non-member countries and buying-in on the
internal market, and the Guidance Section helps to meet expenditure
on structural changes made necessary by the development of the
Common Market.

Thus from the point of view of regional development it is the
Guidance Section of the F.E.O.G.A. which is called upon to play
an important part by subsidising up to between 25 and 30 per cent
of the cost of projects concerned with the improvement of production
structures in the strict sense (such as soil improvement schemes) or
the structure of agricultural markets (marketing of produce, development of outlets). The Guidance Section helped to finance 729
projects totalling 131 million units of account between 1965 and the
first instalment of the 1968 projects.

The chief beneficiaries have been Italy (34 per cent), Germany
(27 per cent) and France (22 per cent). The figures are not broken
down by region, but it is obvious that action is in the agricultural
areas which are structurally weak.

Redeployment of workers
The redeployment of workers paid off by their firms and wishing to
acquire new occupational skills can be helped by Community aid—
from the E.C.S.C. High Authority when those concerned are miners
or steelworkers, and from the European Social Fund in the case of
any other worker.

(a) *E.C.S.C. aids.* On the same grounds that it can act in the
financing of industrial conversion, the E.C.S.C. High
authority can contribute to the readaptation of workers in
coal and steel industries. But whereas it makes loans in the
case of industrial conversion, subsidies are granted for help
in the social field. These subsidies can help to pay for allowances to tide over workers between jobs, resettlement
allowances, and expenditure on retraining workers who have
to change jobs. The High Authority makes the payment of

grants conditional upon the State concerned making a special contribution of at least the same amount. This action is always undertaken at the request of the Governments concerned.

Between March 1954 and the end of December 1968 the High Authority contributed a little over 106 million units of account to readaptation operations which affected 377,000 workers throughout the Community. It should be emphasised that these figures represent the applications which were accepted by the E.C.S.C. In practice, a certain number of workers succeeded in changing jobs before having to make a claim on redeployment aids, and the real figures— although unknown—are lower than these. No regional breakdown of redeployment aids is available. The lion's share obviously went to workers dismissed by collieries (308,000 workers and 84 million units of account). Of the general total, a little more than half was in respect of workers in Germany.

(b) *The European Social Fund.* To a very large extent the European Social Fund is to the E.E.C. what the redeployment aids are to the E.C.S.C. The responsibility of the European Social Fund is to cover, at the request of a Member State, 50 per cent of the cost of occupational retraining and resettlement allowances for workers who have been unemployed for at least six months or whose employment is reduced or suspended as a result of their firm going over to other products.

Up to the present, action by the Social Fund has been solely for the benefit of unemployed workers.

Between 1960 and the end of 1968 the Fund granted assistance to 959,000 workers for a total amount of over 80 million units of account.

Most of this went to Italy (34 per cent), followed by Germany (27 per cent) and France (26 per cent). Like those of the E.C.S.C., the statistics of the Social Fund are not broken down by region.

Of the general total, 74 million units of account were granted for retraining 311,000 workers and 6 million units of account for resettling 648,000 workers.

Transport infrastructure

The Treaty establishing the European Economic Community instructs the Commission to work out a common policy for transport rates and infrastructure.

As far back as 1960, the Commission began to concern itself with setting up a transport infrastructure network responding not only to the requirements of the main Community through routes, but also to those of regional policy and in particular the links between the chief industrial areas for their raw material supplies and the marketing of their products. Recommendations were drawn up to this effect, but it cannot be said that they have been followed equally expeditiously in all the Community countries.

In order to encourage the Member States to harmonise their transport networks (in terms of where and when to invest), a consultation procedure for infrastructure investments was instituted in 1966. The Member States were asked to notify the Commission of any investment projects of interest to the Community as a whole— whether on the railways, the roads, or inland waterways. The 'Community interest' of a project is appraised by taking account of its effect not only on the growth of trade between member countries but also on the development of one or more regions of the Community.

Regional studies

The European Communities can contribute to regional development by special studies.

The Paris Treaty formally requires the E.C.S.C. High Authority to participate 'at the request of the interested governments, . . . in the study of the possibilities of re-employing, either in existing industries or through the creation of new activities, workers unemployed by reason of the development of the market or technical changes'. The E.C.S.C. has thus financed several studies which deal either with specific regions or with various aspects of the industrial conversion of the mining regions.

The E.E.C. has also financed regional studies in various Community countries. The major study so far related to the establishment of an industrial development centre in southern Italy (Bari-Taranto), with particular reference to the manufacturing activities which could be put in hand in the area, the optimum scale of production for each plant, what goods and services would be needed for each activity, what market there would be for each plant, and what infrastructure would be required to develop the area. Other studies covered the Eifel–Hunsrück region, eastern Bavaria and Schleswig-Holstein in Germany and the area comprising the southern part of the Belgian Province of Luxemburg and the northern part of Lorraine in France. Studies are currently in progress on the Liege–Maastricht–Aachen frontier region, tourism in Calabria and the development of the Nantes–St. Nazaire area. Quite recently, a study on Wallonia was launched.

TOWARDS A COMMUNITY REGIONAL POLICY?

Although the contributions of the European Communities to regional development are not negligible, their main value is as an example. It is no exaggeration to say that the European Treaties and the machinery employed by the European institutions have left their mark on the member countries' legislation and conduct.

But the few regional provisions in the European Treaties do not add up to a Community regional policy, and the European Economic Community was very conscious of this when, in May 1965, it published a document.[3] This document, which was in fact a follow-up to the reports of three working parties on regional policy completed in 1964, proposed an action programme for the Commission in this sphere. As ill luck would have it, the Memorandum was no sooner published than the Community entered into its crisis of July 1965–January 1966, which was not calculated to encourage Community initiatives.

Meanwhile, a Medium-term Economic Policy Committee had been set up, part of whose work carried on through this crisis and was completed in 1967. The Medium-term Economic Policy Programme (1966–70) which the Committee framed contains a chapter on regional policy which is very largely a summary of the First Memorandum of May 1965, but also represents a step backward the 'confrontation' of policies and is silent as regards the regional from the proposals then made. For example, where the Memorandum spoke of co-ordination of national regional policies and regional programmes, the Medium-term Programme proposes programmes.

Since then the three European Executives have merged into a

single Commission of the European Communities, within which a Directorate-General for Regional Policy has been set up.

A memorandum has just been drafted on the general lines of Community regional policy. The memorandum will shortly be submitted to the Council of the Community, and perhaps this is an appropriate place to summarise its conclusions. It should first of all be emphasised that the problems of regional policy are immense and of great urgency. The Member States must take the most direct interest in them; regional policy is an indispensable approach to economic policy, and particularly to structures policy. In view of its importance to the structural organisation of the Common Market, it is important that the national administrations should combine their efforts with those of the Commission by appropriate contacts and co-operation.

The work to be done in conjunction can be outlined as follows:

(1) Improvement of sources of information concerning regional structures in the Community and problems associated with future developments. This involves:

(a) systematic information, as homogeneous as possible, on the structure of the different regions of the Community and the siting conditions they offer;

(b) a joint examination of the long- and medium-term outlook for regional structures, taking into consideration the effects of the likely trend in the various sectors (primary, secondary, tertiary and quaternary) and the factors determining the location of industry;

(c) a study of the main approaches open to the Community in the framework of international competition.

(2) Confrontation of the regional policies of the Member States with the regional structures referred to in 1 (b). This involves:

(a) confrontation of the objectives pursued by national regional policies and the priorities they entail with the general prospects at Community level;

(b) confrontation of the resources employed by national policies (government assistance, for example) and the means which the Treaties make available to the Community institutions, taking into account:

(i) the special problems which the existing structures pose for the different regions, and

(ii) the adjustments which these regions must carry out.

Some of these problems call for very special attention in view of their importance in the framing and implementing of regional policy.

We are here dealing with problems created by the sociological trend towards an urban way of life and with the ways in which the make-up, size, and geographical distribution of tertiary and quaternary development centres would make their solution possible, while at the same time establishing better regional balance.

It is also a matter of the problems arising from the principal means of communication which govern the establishment and development of activities in the different regions of the Community. This concerns the main internal routes, particularly when they ave an impact in an area extending beyond national frontiers, and also the ports, which can play a decisive part both in directly stimulating regional development and in assuring a balance between the regions of the Community.

In addition there are the problems of equipping, preserving and exploiting natural sites and resources, and, more particularly, the problems associated with the water economy, woodland and tourism.

All these problems of general interest should be studied by the national administrations in conjunction with Commission departments.

The Commission believes that all these approaches should help the elaboration, within a reasonable time, of a common design on which to base adequate co-ordination of regional action programmes.

By this joint approach to the fundamental problems of the regions making up the member countries, the Community should be more rapidly and more fully in a position to respond not only to the objectives which the Treaties lay down in the regional sphere but also more generally to those of co-ordination of economic policies and improvement in living standards.

The Commission is convinced that energetic action in this field is likely to promote better-balanced joint growth because it will be qualitatively better based and better distributed, aiming to make all regions participate directly in the development of the Comunity.

REFERENCES

1. COLEMAN, J. (Editor) *The Common Market—The Treaty of Rome Explained*, Anthony Blond, London, 1967.
2. BROAD, R. AND JARRETT, R., *Community Europe: a Short Guide to the Common Market*, Oswald Wolff, London, 1967.
3. First memorandum of the Commission on Regional Policy in the European Community (*Community Topics* No. 24), European Community Service, London, 1966.

Part 3

9 | The Remoter Rural Areas in the National Context

PROFESSOR MAXWELL GASKIN, D.F.C., M.A.
Department of Political Economy
University of Aberdeen.

To place the remoter rural areas in the context of the national economy requires us to examine three questions. The first is the nature of the structural relation between these areas and the rest of the national economy, together with the conditions which determine it. The second asks about the place of the remoter rural areas within the context of policy, national and local: the discussion of this will occupy the greater part of this chapter and will emphasise the broader aspects of the matter. Thirdly, the future prospects and possibilities of the remoter regions will be examined. It will be apparent that in distinguishing these three areas of discussion I am dividing up what is only imperfectly divisible, and some issues will have to be considered in more than one place. Also, I shall be looking at the question almost wholly in economic terms, and in some directions this may produce an unbalanced or distorted view of the position and possibilities of the remoter rural areas.

THE ECONOMIC POSITION OF THE REMOTER RURAL AREAS

The word 'remote' implies distance, or separation; and in the present application these words should be interpreted as distance or separation not from some presumed economic or social centre of gravity of the country as a whole, but from major concentrations of population wherever they are. In this sense the Scottish Borders are remote from the large populations to the north and south, and the most westerly parts of the West Midlands region from the conurbation to the east. In other words 'remoteness' is not a synonym for 'peripherality', although obviously some major examples of the areas we are considering are peripheral in the usual meaning of the word.

165

With this qualification, the word 'remote' implies that we are concerned with areas that are distant both from major markets for their outputs and from the sources of some of the inputs that industries in them might need. The most obvious economic consequence of this condition is its effect, through necessary transport, on costs; and it is usual to regard this as placing an important constraint on the economic activities conducted within the remoter areas. Clearly there is a measure of truth here, but it cannot be accepted without reserve. It has, for example, been shown by more than one study[1,2] that over a wide range of manufacturing industry, transport is a comparatively small item of total costs. On the other hand the factor of distance as it bears on delivery times and personal communities is of increasing significance. The trend in industry and commerce of running on lower inventories, and relying on more hand-to-mouth supply arrangements, puts a premium on speedy and reliable, as much as on cheap, transport. Again, the increasing integration of ownership of industry and the growing number of branch plants and subsidiaries are enhancing the importance of easy personal communications. In one way or another, distance is an appreciable influence on the economic structure and development of the areas we are considering, but its significance will clearly vary between the regions. In the really peripheral areas, such as the Western Isles and far north of Scotland, Cornwall and West Central Wales, and perhaps in some parts of all the remoter rural areas, distance must exert a considerable influence either through costs or time or both. But it is arguable that in parts of regions like North-East Scotland or the rural North of England, distance is not the all-powerful determinant of structure that it is frequently supposed to be; in these areas other conditions must be accorded their due weight.

The most important of these conditions are the size and skills of the labour force. Rural areas which are distant from the industrial conurbations are sparsely populated; with very few exceptions—Aberdeen in North-East Scotland and Plymouth in South-West England are conspicuous ones—they lack sizeable urban centres. Such conditions place narrow limits on the labour force that can be mustered at particular points within them; while the labour that can be obtained in such areas usually lacks the skills more readily usable in manufacturing industry. But there are, of course, other important concomitants of sparse populations, such as restricted local markets and an absence of major infrastructure and some services: these, too, have a deterrent effect on industrial development in the remoter rural areas.

The upshot of the argument so far is that while in the case of some of the remoter rural areas one hardly needs to look beyond the distance factor for the determinant of their economic situation, for others this is far from being the whole story. In these areas the size and distribution of population, with all their consequences, are conditioning influences of at least equal importance. But the size of the population and the character of the labour force it supports cannot be explained without reference to the existing economic structures of these regions and their historical development. In a sense, one could as well define the remoter rural areas as regions which have *not* become industrialised.

Economic structure of the remoter regions
The direct consequence of the conditioning factors noted here is that economic activities in these areas tend to be resource-based, interpreting 'resources' as 'natural resources' and using it in the wide sense; or they consist of supplying services mainly to the populations resident in the regions. Agriculture and forestry are the most widespread industries, with inshore fishing important in some limited areas. Here and there mineral extraction provides a basis for economic life; while we can obviously assimilate to this category of resource-based activities those industries which require access to water, either for processing or power, those which depend on natural features such as deep water anchorages, or those which involve the processing of such primary products as fish or vegetables. And last but not least, the provision of facilities for tourists and sportsmen depends on the exploitation of another order of the natural features of these area

Of course, in a society with high standards of living the remoter rural areas show, along with the others, a high proportion of service activities. The service sector, as normally defined, is a very heterogeneous assembly of activities, but everywhere it is dependent, in some measure, on other activities within a region. This dependence is expressed in the distinction drawn by some regional analysts between the 'economic base' activities, meaning those that depend on expenditures from outside the region—'export' activities, in fact —and 'dependent' or 'non-basic' activities, which depend on internal expenditures. This distinction undoubtedly has value in *understanding* the structure of a regional economy.* However, the identification of 'basic' activities with the primary and manufacturing sectors and 'non-basic' with service activities (possibly including construction), an identification which is sometimes made, is quite unacceptable. A region may contain manufactures that are largely dependent on internal spending, while an advanced economy normally includes service activities—frequently, though not invariably, in the public sector—which are supported by expenditures from outside the region. In the remote rural areas a considerable proportion of services will be of the latter type, though there will also be a strong dependent component in this sector; on the other hand some primary and manufacturing activities will serve local markets.

To sum up at this point, one can view the remoter rural areas as internal 'colonial' areas. Their economies are based on supplying the regions of large populations with goods and services which depend essentially on the use of immovable natural resources rather than on the acquired advantages of skilled labour and management or of a developed industrial environment. Such areas are heavily dependent on their external economic relations, with comparatively high propensities to export and import; and like other 'colonial' areas they tend to depend on external initiative for activities that go beyond the traditional primary industries or the provision of simple services. Within the national context, in Britain as elsewhere, they usually fall into the class of 'lagging' regions. Their economies are heavily weighted with industries which in employment terms are declining or only slowly growing. This results in remoter rural areas exhibiting some, frequently all, of the classic features of 'depressed' regions: relatively high rates of unemployment, low activity or participation rates, high levels of net outward migration, and low levels of productivity and of income per head. There, are, however, certain features which significantly distinguish the rural areas from the other lagging regions of Britain: they have smaller and sparser populations, and they are generally light on manufacturing industry; but on the other hand they are almost wholly unmarked by the depressing inheritance of industrial dereliction.

* For predictive purposes its usefulness is much more open to question. On the use of the 'economic base' concept see reference 2, Appendix E, pp. 159–60.

THE REMOTER RURAL AREAS AND POLICY

In examining the way in which policy bears on the remoter rural areas I shall make a broad distinction between national and local policy. But it must be remarked that this does some violence to the facts since both the 'local' and 'national' planes really resolve themselves into a number of levels at which policy is formulated or promoted, or is in some way constrained. It seems natural to look first and longest at the national level of policy as this sets important limits within which local policy must operate. Also, I shall interpret 'policy' in a broad sense which embraces not only explicit measures with statutory force, but also what one might call 'objective's or 'considerations' of a much less explicit, even vague, character, since some of these are unquestionably relevant.

Three broad types of explicit policies are of paramount importance to the remoter rural areas: the first, the group of policies aimed at sustaining or improving particular industries; the second, financial policy, in the sense of all the objectives which inform, and the measures which implement, the Government's plan for its revenue and expenditure; and the third, the range of measures which we designate as 'regional policy'.

The first of these will not detain us long, not because it is unimportant—quite the reverse—but because these policies are the concern of other contributors to this symposium. The three primary industries of agriculture, fishing and forestry all receive subsidies, or enjoy some form of favourable treatment, which are vital to their economic viability. These are nation-wide policies, of course, but they have an obvious special importance to the remoter rural areas because of the economic structure of these areas. Furthermore, within these national policies there are particular measures of support which in practice operate selectively to the benefit of some of the remoter rural areas—for example, the hill farm subsidies and the various types of financial assistance to inshore fishing. In sum, these policies provide much the greatest volume of overt financial assistance to these regions. How they compare in amount with the less obvious subsidisation of public services through exchequer grants, and the concealed subsidies implicit in the policies of level-pricing followed by private as well as public sector enterprises, it is impossible to say; at a guess, I would say that these latter forms of assistance are the greater.

Secondly, the Government's financial policy must be mentioned, again with brevity incommensurate with its importance since this is one of the major constraints on local action and initiative. I shall confine my remarks to expenditure policy, though recognising that the impact of financial policy on various parts of the country through the taxes it employs is not a negligible matter, particularly since the introduction of the Selective Employment Tax. At the local, as at the national level, finance is always a constraint, tighter at some times than other. For local government the sources of finance are the local rate, exchequer grants of various kinds, and borrowings. Local ambitions, so far as they depend on Central Government finance or the raising of loans—and most projects of a development kind, involving new or improved infrastructure, do depend on these sources—must be limited by the availability of funds. This varies not only according to pressures on financial and fiscal sources, but also with those on the real resources of the national economy as a whole. It is a commonplace that in its management of the economy the Central Government is no longer guided by the older orthodoxy of 'living within income plus appropriate borrowings'; the criterion now is the general pressure of national expenditure on national resources, and the detectable consequences of this in prices, the balance of payments and—to a lesser degree—economic growth.

The present is not a good time for public spending, and financial stringency is biting into many locally desired forms of expenditure. But one can be deceived by the present problem into a mistaken emphasis on the temporary nature of the current concern with public expenditure. The demands of public expenditure on national resources are growing absolutely and relatively: this has already resulted in a steady climb of the share of public sector expenditure within gross national expenditure—from 40 per cent in 1956 to 46 per cent in 1966.* The demands of an increasing population with rising expectations in education, housing and personal mobility, superimposed on the need to rehabilitate or rebuild vast amounts of obsolete structures, services and communications, are imposing,

---

* In calculating these percentages, public expenditure is taken as current expenditure of Central and Local Government (less current surplus and excluding central grants to local authorities) plus gross capital formation of Central and Local Government and public corporations.

and will continue to impose, strains on the public financial system as such, as well as on the 'real' capacity of the economy. These are felt with particular force during periods when national income itself is stagnant or only slowly rising; they would be eased, but by no means eliminated, were a steady annual growth rate of, say, 3 per cent to be achieved.

This pressure on resources will affect the remoter rural areas, along with all other parts of the country; but there are reasons why it may go further in their case. With the growing pressure on national resources generally, and those available to the public sector in particular, there is coming an increasing emphasis on the use of explicitly economic criteria in deciding their allocation, and on attempts to base decisions on quantitative assessments of costs and returns. Few would claim that the present state of applied quantitative analysis allows one to come up with anything more than extremely rough orderings of national priorities in answer to allocation problems. But the regions we are concerned with here tend to present the kind of rather extreme instances where the quantifiable elements within such appraisals seem to offer a com-paratively secure basis for decisions. And whether or not the basis really is secure, I think that we may expect a more confident use of such quantitative approaches to scale down or prevent expenditures in the remoter rural areas than in other types of regions.

This growing emphasis on what the economist calls 'allocative efficiency', in public as well as in private expenditure, coupled with a greater appeal to quantitative or 'commercial' criteria in the definition of it, seems certain to increase the financial pressures on the populations living in the remoter areas, or to whittle away some of the advantages which they have enjoyed in the past. It may, for example, lead to a continuing erosion of the cross-subsidisation of services and goods supplied to these areas, though the pace at which this can proceed in the public sector is subject to the strongly retarding influences of political factors, and it may proceed faster and farther in the private sector.

The policies designed to meet the economic and social problems created by the decline of particular industries are clearly not achiev-ing any major alteration of the trend to depopulation, at least in the inland rural areas. The conclusion I draw from this is that a halting, let alone a positive reversal, of the present trends—assuming either of these objectives to be desirable—must depend on the importation

of new non-primary activities into these regions. This brings us to
the third type of policy, regional policy, and its relation to the
remoter rural areas.

Regional policy and the remoter rural areas
Regional policy in Britain has a history going back to the 1930s. It
began very much as a salvage operation designed to alleviate the heavy
unemployment in the older industrial areas, the economies of which
were heavily weighted with industries that were stagnant or declining,
or that were particularly susceptible to cyclical instability. In the post-
war period average rates of unemployment have continued to run
higher in the 'depressed' or 'lagging' regions than in the economically
buoyant areas of the English South-East and Midlands; but in no
regions have these rates been anywhere near the pre-war levels,
and the amount of energy put into regional policy has fluctuated.
After a burst of effort and achievement in the immediate post-war
years there was a lapse during the 1950s. But since the late fifties
concern about regional problems and disparities has revived, and
the structure of remedial measures has been much modified and
extended.

Regional policy in this country continues to rest, as ever, on a
mixture of social, political and economic grounds, and it is arguable
that the relative weights accorded these considerations have remained
fundamentally unchanged.[3] Be that as it may, it is undeniable that
in comment and exposition, official and non-official, there has been
a shift towards emphasising the more purely economic considerations,
both in justification of regional policy and in prescribing the shape
it should take. There are two strands in the current discussion which
we should notice here since, in different ways, they have a bearing
on the position of the remoter rural areas within the context of
regional policy.

The first is the greater recognition of the importance of labour
supply as a factor in the growth of the economy. An inelastic supply
of labour is seen as a constraint on the achievable rate of growth,
and indeed as one element in the explanation of the comparatively
poor growth performance of the British economy. A policy of
achieving a more even distribution of the rapidly growing sectors
of the economy can lead to a more effective use of the potential
supply of labour, by drawing into employment some of the unemployed labour in the lagging regions, and by raising activity rates

and providing higher productivity occupations in these areas. A somewhat different line of argument, which also holds out the prospect of a faster rate of growth, stresses the importance of a more even regional distribution of demand in relation to industrial capacity and the part this can play in checking the inflation attendant on running the economy at high levels of activity.

The other important development in recent discussions of regional problems has been the emphasis on 'growth points' as instruments of location policy. In the 1960s regional policy has been increasingly, if haltingly, harnessed to the idea of channelling development to those places or zones within the regions of difficulty where there appear to be the best chances of eventually creating self-sustaining growth through concentration and the external economies and industrial linkages that this can generate. Economies of scale in the provision of infrastructure also reinforce the argument for the growth point approach.

The measures which today collectively constitute British regional policy are a mixture of financial inducements, such as the Regional Employment Premiums and the various loans, grants and allowances provided for by the Local Employment and Industrial Expansion Acts; of restrictions on the location of new plants or large extensions, through the Industrial Development Commission system of control; of such direct measures of public investment at the establishment of new towns; and of the favourable treatment of certain regions, including certain zones within such regions, in the matter of infrastructural expenditure. The Industrial Development Act of 1966 created the present 'development areas' as the areas within which the explicit and discriminatory financial inducements are applied. The development areas are widely drawn: they cover 55 per cent of the area of Great Britain and contain about 20 per cent of the total of employed persons. They were selected by various criteria, though high unemployment rates and persistent loss of population through net outward migration were undoubtedly the main considerations. The substitution of these wide areas in the place of the numerous and much smaller development districts—chosen strictly on unemployment rates—of the Local Employment Acts was held to mark a step forward towards a more growth-orientated approach to regional problems, and away from a purely salvage-type policy.

Since 1966 the clearness of the distinction between the development areas and other areas has been somewhat moderated by two subsequent steps. The first was the creation in 1967 of 'special development areas'—zones within the development areas, chiefly in coalfields badly hit by pit closures, for which even more favourable inducements have been provided. The second followed the very limited acceptance of the Hunt Committee's[4] recommendation that 'intermediate' areas be designated with a lower level of stimulative measures than those applying to the development areas.

However, in spite of this blurring of the line, the broad distinction between development areas and the rest remains the significant one for most of the remoter rural areas; for though they do not all fall within the present development areas, some considerable tracts of them do. According to one recent commentator on the 1966 Act, 'The new boundaries (were got) by consolidating the previous development districts and adding to them, . . . without discrimination, the areas of rural depopulation which had previously been recognised only by the special treatment accorded to the Highlands and Islands and in spots elsewhere (notably mid-Wales) to which the Development Commission's small funds have been applied.'[5] Not that all the areas of rural depopulation were so included: some of the 'grey' areas examined by the Hunt Committee fall very clearly into this category and two limited zones have now been included in the intermediate areas. Whether or not a rural area is part of a development area is by no means a negligible fact, especially to the existing manufacturers within it; and, clearly, where a firm on the move is looking for a rural site and other things are equal it will prefer one in a development area. But the very extent of the development areas, and the fact that they include regions of large populations and labour supply, well-developed infrastructure and good communications, inevitably limits very considerably the significance of this status to many remote rural areas. Thus, although some of the remoter areas offer powerful advantages of space and amenity, it is clear that the rural parts of the development areas are in difficulty in competing with the populous regions for the manufacturing industry on which any reversal of their population trends must be founded.

There is a detectable variation in the attitude of Central Government towards individual rural areas. Exceptionally, some remote areas get special treatment, usually for political or related reasons: the Scottish Highlands and Islands region with its Development Board is a prime example. But also within Scotland, the development

needs and possibilities of some of the other areas that lie outside
the populous central belt have received recognition, and an attempt
made to suggest an ordered sequence of development effort in them.
A White Paper,[6] *The Scottish Economy, 1965–1970*, (command 2864),
taking a forward look at the 1970s, sketched a programme which
would include a rapid build-up of population and industry in Central
Scotland, a stabilisation of population in the Western Borders, and
some enlargement of both Dundee and Dumfries. Then, according
to the White Paper (para. 244), 'Future major improvements in
communications will permit the exploitation of the more promising
areas safeguarded by the earlier holding and consolidation operation
—notably the Aberdeen area and the Beauly/Cromarty Firth
area'.

However, the fact that choices have to be made points to certain
difficulties that constrain regional policy. The main one is the rate
at which major redeployment of economic activity can be achieved.
Quite regardless of the effectiveness of the policy implements
themselves—and the very newness of some of these makes this an
uncertain matter—the number of new developments which at any
one time are capable of being located in the development areas is
limited. But more than that, it is possible that even if the expectations of the present measures are fulfilled, the eventual supply of
mobile industry will prove insufficient to meet the ends of regional
policy. In such a situation choices have to be exercised and it is
apparent that regional policy in this country sees as its main task
the restructuring and reinvigoration of the economies of the older
industrial regions. It is there, in Central Scotland, South Wales,
North-East England and similar areas, that the great concentrations
of declining male-employing industries are located; and there that,
quantitatively speaking, the major regional problem is to be found.
Furthermore it is in these areas, or near them, that the more attractive locations within the development areas are situated. And,
compared with the rural areas, the arguments from labour supply
and from social cost and advantage reinforce their claims.

This digression on regional policy prompts a number of observations on the position of the remoter rural areas. First, there is the
clear fact that they come a long way down the queue for the basically
insufficient amount of foot-loose industry. Secondly, this ordering
of their claims is reinforced by a certain scepticism about the
development potential of at least some of the remoter rural areas.

But, thirdly, this view in turn has to be confronted with the consideration that there are dangers in the present position of the rural areas which should be heeded, at least in the case of some of them. In some rural regions the decline of population is approaching (in parts of the Scottish Highlands it has passed) the point where the age structure is gravely affected and the cumulatively debilitating effects of an ageing population set in; in others, for example in North-East Scotland, this situation lies in the future, but not the very distant future if current trends persist. Furthermore, this is not simply a problem of support and social salvage. If there is the possibility of such areas being required for more extensive development and absorption of population later in this century, the case for attempting to stave off severe economic and demographic deterioration in the intervening period is reinforced. Finally, however, to the extent that such aims or concerns produce action to encourage development (as in the Scottish Borders), or lead to pressure on the planning authorities of rural regions to shape their policies so as to attract more development, there will inevitably be a concentration of effort on certain zones within those of the remoter rural areas for which such a role is feasible. This means that, even if this treatment is successful, the problems of the remoter areas not so selected, and of the 'deep' countryside in all of them, will remain.

The recreational role
The other major aspect of the remoter areas in what I would define as the policy context, is the one frequently given most prominence—their recreational role. This relates very closely to, although it is not entirely coincident with, the growth of tourism which is dealt with in another chapter of this volume. The complex and difficult question of predicting the future development of tourism in the remoter rural areas will not be attempted here: it will simply be assumed that in Britain, with its high degree of urbanisation and its particular social habits and culture, access to open spaces in the countryside is of major social importance. Furthermore, the ever-increasing mobility of the population means that advantage can be taken of these areas by rising numbers of the population. Two sorts of need have to be served: on the one hand, there is the need for people from the conurbations for quick access to the nearest 'remote' areas, for short periods; and on the other, there must be provision for the longer forays of the tourist or holidaymaker able to

go farther afield and requiring more extensive facilities. For both these types of user there are the twin basic needs of conservation and access, needs which will pose problems of varying incidence.

In areas that are really remote from major population centres, conservation in the general sense of the preservation of rural aspect and openness is only threatened sporadically at particular points. There is undoubtedly mounting pressure on estuarine areas, even in the remote regions, and this will pose specific problems of amenity and conservation. Again, conflicts will no doubt arise among urban users of particular areas—for example, between visitors to, and would-be residents in, rural areas near large conurbations. Clearly, the nearer one approaches the centres of population the more frequently are genuine and difficult problems of conservation posed. But there seems to be no prospective threat to the existence of considerable tracts of open country in the really remote parts of Britain.

In the more distant regions access can prevent problems. There is first the need to ensure rapid and effective communications between such areas and the places where the bulk of the population live: this is a matter of infrastructure and the extension of it is subject to the usual constraints on public expenditure and the competing claims on public resources. Secondly, there is a problem of access in the sense of ensuring reasonable entry into, and adequate facilities within, much of the land in the remote areas. In some of the rural regions this is likely to call for a more positive policy than we have hitherto had—a policy such as the Countryside Commission was created to promote. There will, of course, be conflicts, in these areas as elsewhere, between the needs of visitors and the interests of farmers, foresters and estate owners. A *modus vivendi* will have to be reached, one that recognises both the national interest in offering wider facilities for large numbers of people to move around in the remoter regions, and the need for greater responsibility in the exercise of this freedom so that the least damage is done to the interests of the other users of these areas.

Local policy objectives and their constraints
So far, in this section of the chapter, we have been concerned with broad aspects of national policy which determine the important limits within which local policy must work. At the local level in rural areas

there is, predictably, a mixture of objectives for policy, but one important underlying aspiration is the retention of population. In practice the strength with which this is held as an aim of policy varies with the degree of recognition of the constraints inherent in the situation of these areas. At one extreme there is the largely emotional attitude that deplores all departures from the *status quo* and would attempt to preserve every community within an area regardless of the costs and the social possibilities. As a proclaimed policy this has great political appeal. But among administrators any attitude of this kind is usually tempered by a consciousness of the financial constraints on local policy; though even here there is often a general desire to retain population, if only to maintain taxable capacity and so avert the erosion of local finance. Among other groups the retention of population excites varying degrees of concern. Employers, for example, may see depopulation as removing their labour force, and consequently deplore it on these grounds; and where they provide services locally they are obviously concerned at the consequent diminution of their markets.

If an objective is urged which looks beyond the simple retention of population, or a modest restoration of past losses, and calls for a substantial increase, reactions are likely to be mixed. Ambitious programmes of repopulation, indeed any planned major developments, come up against an assortment of vested interests opposed to large-scale changes in rural areas. Conservationists of all kinds are concerned to prevent major intrusions into rural environments. Farmers and estate owners may regard large-scale developments in particular places as conflicting directly with their own interests: they frequently oppose them on the simple grounds that such developments deprive them of land. Even such manufacturing and other non-primary industries as there are in a sparsely populated area may look with misgiving on the intrusion of new employing units, which they tend to view not as means of retaining or increasing population, but as competitors for the existing exiguous supply of labour.

But, of course, attitudes vary. The desire for development on a comparatively ambitious scale is to be found in parts of some, perhaps of all, rural areas. For instance, in North-East Scotland there are conspicuous examples of small burghs with considerable ambitions for development; and some of them have had a measure of success in attracting new manufacturing industry. But even here, among the more development-minded authorities, one often meets reservations about the ultimate scale of growth, and about the types of activities that it is hoped to attract. Preferences, frequently expressed, for 'light' industry are sometimes based on the feeling that this type of activity will be physically unobtrusive and offer least disturbance to the existing character of the area.

All policy at the local level is subject to important contraints. The more important of these in the present context are the curbs on local action, but it is worth remembering that the goad is also present and in some cases is the operative 'constraint'. An authority which by inclination is sluggish and backward in providing public services, including those of the developmental kind, is subject to the stimuli of statutory policy and national standards of provision. At the other end of the spectrum, however, the progressive authority, while by no means lacking a measure of freedom, is limited in what it can do to influence the character and level of economic activity within its boundaries. It is constrained, for example, both by finance and by its statutory powers, in what it can do in the way of positive assistance or inducements to industry; in this field very much depends on the central government's regional policy, and whether or not the area concerned lies within a development area.

But a go-ahead authority of this kind is by no means without resource. It can, for example, construct advance factories, though so far very few authorities have taken advantage of this power. It can engage in the mixture of activities roughly describable as 'public relations'. The obvious one here is straight publicity, but it is not necessarily the most important. There is evidence that firms on the move are influenced to some degree by a co-operative attitude on the part of a local authority, such as shows itself, for example, in the speedy laying on of services and a flexible attitude in allocating houses for key workers. Thirdly, a rural region can do much to improve the attractiveness of the area as a whole by additions and improvements to infrastructure and by planning measures conceived on a regional scale. I would argue that measures designed to bring about a greater degree of concentration of population, and consequently of labour supply, will improve the attractiveness of sparsely populated areas to industry, and should form part of any development policy. Such a policy must obviously work within the overall financial limits set by the local rate and by Central Government support; it is also subject to the limitation imposed by the present structure of local government, the boundaries of which are frequently drawn too narrowly to permit a properly regional approach to development with the encouragement of concentrated growth in the most promising areas. But within all these limits it is possible to exercise a degree of useful selection in infrastructural expenditure and in the location of new housing. It is particularly through its control over housing development that a rural planning authority has power to influence the movement of population, channelling existing flows in certain directions rather than others.

Forward-looking policies of this kind are only sporadically present in the remoter rural areas. But, paradoxically, the usually negative influence of finance is tending to urge many rural authorities along paths which more positive aims would cause them to take. For example, financial considerations are partly responsible for the movement towards the concentration of population and services in many rural areas of the country. Some county authorities are pursuing policies of moving rural population from smaller to larger settlements; and while the stimulus here is partly social—people's wishes are increasingly running in this direction—in part it rests on a recognition, however unquantified, that there are economies of scale in the provision of local services. Also, while the important policy of concentrating educational facilities derives most of its present impetus from educational considerations, it is likely that increasing emphasis on allocative efficiency will cause the Central Government to press local authorities to pay more regard to the economy factor in educational planning, as in other directions.

THE ROLE AND FUTURE PROSPECTS OF THE REMOTE RURAL AREAS

Many of the topics which we have so far considered pose problems for the remoter rural areas here and now; they will also continue to do so in the years immediately ahead. The one that, in a sense, serves as a focus for them all is the population question. This requires us to ask what population objective is appropriate for the remoter rural areas. Population is a central concern for regional policy in the remoter rural areas as in any other regions. Of course, almost all policies affecting the remoter rural areas, and especially the support policies of specific industries, have some bearing on demographic trends. And while these non-regionally orientated policies are of lesser importance for increasing, or even stabilising, population over large regions, they do affect one option which in some cases is not to be dismissed out of hand and about which I shall say something shortly. This is 'evacuation'.

Objectives formulated in terms of population levels are, as has been said, central to regional policy. We have seen that at the local level there is a general desire at least to stabilise the number of people living in an area. Nationally, stabilisation of population also appears as a frequent objective for broad regions, though in practice it often commands little more than verbal support. Of course, where one draws the boundaries of areas or regions is all-important. Ignoring, as we surely may, the out-and-out preservationist case, there is a wide recognition that whatever the outcome for the populations of regions as a whole, there is bound to be a considerable redistribution of population within the rural regions, and that this will involve further depopulation of the deep countryside. The effective question, it appears to me, is how much policy is prepared to do, at the national level, to retain population by the encouragement of new manufacturing and other non-primary activities in the remoter rural areas—population which would be relocated and concentrated in comparatively limited zones. The answer appears to be 'not much at this stage' and for the reasons discussed earlier. The problems are admitted; practical recognition is given by the development area status of some rural regions; and there is encouragement to them to do all they can for themselves to halt the present trends. But, as a question of priorities, the claims of the older industrial areas are pressing and it is difficult to argue that they should be even minimally sacrificed to the interests of the rural regions.

Certain other possibilities offer themselves. Some resource-based industries, other than the traditional ones, will continue to hold population in some places. Also, new ones will arise: the possibility of discovering sizeable new mineral deposits is at best uncertain, but cannot be entirely excluded. Processing developments on sites with access to deep water anchorages, or to large supplies of fresh water, are very real prospects, though one drawback with almost all of these possibilities is that they tend to be capital- rather than labour-intensive. A morsel of hope that is invariably thrown before the remoter rural areas is tourism.[7] In the national context this is most important as we have seen; it will certainly grow, with beneficial effects on the incomes if not so much on the employment of the remoter areas. But tourism, with its highly seasonal demands on labour, is no easy answer. It is possible, as one commentator suggests,[8] that this difficulty could be overcome by the development of suitable rural industries; this does not, *prima facie*, seem a promising prospect, though it certainly demands investigation. But quite apart from this problem, it must be remarked that the effective development of tourism in some rural areas would require considerable investment in facilities of all kinds, though no doubt much could be done by a scattering of small schemes.

To take up a point mentioned earlier, there is a type of extremely remote region for which a policy of evacuation, in the sense of withdrawal of all public services and of all but minimal administration, might well be considered. (This has already happened on a very limited scale with some small islands). There would be no need to prohibit the entry of people into such 'empty' areas, as recommended by Noble,[9] so long as they were aware that in doing so they would cut themselves off from public services and official succour. Such areas would amount to no more than the 'bush' of many overseas countries. There would be practical problems arising from the ownership, and no doubt continued occupation, of land in these areas. But there would certainly be no conflict with the recreational function which we have seen is likely to become more important in the future. Indeed, areas of this kind could provide an attractive element of variety for at least some members of Britain's extremely urbanised population.

For regions not nearly so remotely placed, and with an existing stock of sound infrastructure, the stabilisation of their populations at levels not so much lower than at present is necessary if they are not to be condemned to the debilitating process of demographic decline. Some reinforcement of their claim to this comes from their possible future role as locations for part of the expected growth in the national population. The population of Britain is increasing and will go on doing so. Combined with rising standards of living this will lead—is already leading—to explosively rising demands for living space which it will be difficult to provide in or near many of the present populous regions. Only five years ago, a population increase of 20 millions was forecast by the year 2000; this figure has now been revised downwards very much, and the scaling-down process is still going on. But no one doubts that there will be substantially more people—probably not less than 10 millions more than the present number—to be accommodated in Britain by that year. And there is even less doubt about the high income elasticity of demand for living space.

At least one remote region has already staked a claim for the establishment of a large block of population in a part of its area at some future time. The proposals of the Highlands and Islands Development Board for promoting industry and population growth in the Beauly/Cromarty Firth area would, if realised, be a major development of this kind. Other regions, which at the moment fall clearly into the class of the remoter rural areas, are at least as well placed for a role of this kind: North-East and South-West Scotland, as well as a number of areas in England, spring to mind. At the moment studies are in progress, or have recently been completed, of Severnside, Tayside and Humberside as reception areas for size-able blocks of population; and it is likely that in the immediate future, any substantial deployment of population will be to zones such as these, as well as to the new towns already in existence or planned. But depending on the size of the increase which eventually takes place, it may be necessary to look beyond these particular areas to provide a more evenly spread, less congested disposition of population.

But, of course, even if it were decided, as firmly as any long-range plans in this uncertain field can be determined, that some at least of the remoter rural areas should be earmarked as reception areas for increased population, would it really alter the shape of their present problems and future prospects? One thing is clear: any future injections of population into these areas are bound to be in comparatively concentrated units. The attractiveness of the growth point concept with its implications for the concentration of labour markets, and the compelling pressure on public resources with the consequent emphasis on cost-effectiveness in the attainment of public objectives, will dictate this; and though it is hardly to be expected that planning policy will be able to contain all development within limited zones, the physical impact of such increases in population is not likely to be widespread. The economic impact may be somewhat wider: larger and more concentrated units of popula-tion will create demands for goods and services which will afford quite widely spread opportunities for the existing industries of these regions. The higher provision of some services made possible by the increased population will enhance the attractiveness of such remote regions as a whole, and do something to moderate the disparities between them and the more populous regions. But the significance of developments such as these for the problems of the 'deep' countryside and of the areas of naturally sparse population, for example upland areas, will be small. Given that some population will continue to live in areas such as these to exploit their resources, including their recreational resources, the problem of deciding the optimum patterns of service provision and of settlement will remain.

In trying to discern the future pattern which settlement in these *remoter* remote zones might take, I see two questions on which light needs to be thrown. The first is the size of the ultimate population of these areas—'ultimate' in the sense of a position which one can expect to be reached when the pace of current changes, particularly in agriculture, has slowed down. Secondly, we need to know more about the economics of service centres and service provision in such remote and sparsely populated areas. For example, how far should the day-to-day services, which a modern population needs, be provided at fixed, but not over-concentrated, sites relatively near the places where the people live; or, alternatively, should we plan for a greater mobility, either of the services themselves or of their consumers, with the provision based in more concentrated settlements at greater distances apart as discussed by Thurnock.[10] Of course, these questions are not independent of one another, and they interact with other variable factors in the economy. But it would be useful at least to attempt some appraisal of the two issues in themselves. My own guess is that the areas which we now have in view are moving towards a position where, outside the zones of concentrated industrial development and settlement, we shall have a much more thinly populated countryside than at present. Services will be provided at concentrated, widely separated, centres, with the population of the 'deep' countryside leading a highly mobile existence, moving over quite long distances to obtain its normal goods and services. This population may well indeed become less 'rooted' in these areas, may regard itself as no more than temporary users or exploiters of resources. The cultural as well as the economic implications of such a development would be considerable: the 'colonial' analogy may become even more apt in the future than it is now.

REFERENCES

1. *Inquiry into the Scottish Economy. 1960–61*, (Tootill Report), p. 75.
2. *North East Scotland: A Survey of its Development Potential*, p. 103, HMSO, 1969.
3. TRESS, R. C., 'The next stage in regional policy,' *The Three Banks Review*, March, 1969.
4. *Committee on the Intermediate Areas* (Report of the Hunt Committee), Command 3998, April, 1969.
5. TRESS, R. C. *op. cit.* p. 12.
6. *The Scottish Economy, 1965–1970*, Command 2864, 1966.
7. *The Development Areas: A Proposal for a Regional Employment Premium*, para. 51, p. 17; see also reference 4, para. 305, p. 90, HMSO, 1967.
8. ROBERTSON, D. J., 'A Nation of Regions', *Urban Studies*, p. 126, November, 1965.
9. NOBLE, T. A. F., 'The future of crofting', *Scottish Journal of Political Economy 1*, June 1954.
10. TURNOCK, D., 'Depopulation in North East Scotland with reference to the countryside', *Scottish Geographical Magazine*, pp. 266–9, December 1968; see also reference 2, pp. 22–3.

10 | Policy Formulation and the Planner

PROFESSOR A. S. TRAVIS, B.A., M.T.P.I.
Department of Town and Country Planning,
Heriot-Watt University and Edinburgh College of Art

It is often said that the 1947 Town and Country Planning Act[1] gave Britain a unique tool for the comprehensive planning of its land resources. Whilst this may be largely true of the urban context, the rural planning situation has till recently left much to be desired. Nowhere are the deficiencies of the system so marked as in the remoter rural regions. This chapter discusses the planning of the extensive rural and natural resource regions of the United Kingdom, outlining the situation as it developed from the 1947 Act through to and beyond the 1968 Town and Country Planning Act.[2] It includes matters of jurisdiction, means and attitudes, as these have played a major part in shaping the policies, goals and objectives of the local planning authorities.

The subject is both significant and timely: concepts of remoteness are changing—travel time is diminishing, though travel costs may be rising sharply; the meaning and use of the word 'rural' takes on ever-more meanings, and the Maud Report suggests an administrative interpretation of the currently favoured idea of the urban–rural continuum. The situation is one of fluidity and change—a spate of legislation in the last five years has finally reflected a radical change of emphasis in the countryside, acknowledging the desire for positive planning in rural areas in order to satisfy there the urban-generated demands for recreation in its many forms. The idea of regional planning is accepted, but formal administrative machinery, which reflects democratic government at all levels, is yet to be initiated. Rationalisation of boundaries and the co-incidence of boundaries for a range of functions has yet to be achieved, so local government and its planning arm must struggle to reconcile inappropriate boundaries with functions which refuse to stop at some illogical boundary. The findings of the Wheatley Report[3] will be as vital to the improved formulation of future planning policies in rural Scotland as any planning legislation enacted to date.

Tidy hierarchies of policy-making from national to regional and to local scales and the converse—the feedback system—remain simple but acceptable theoretical notions despite the current jungle of administrative boundaries. . . . Central Wales has component county authorities, but no regional authority below the level of the Welsh Office; the Highlands and Islands have county authorities for physical planning, a regional authority for economic (but *not* physical planning) below the level of the Scottish Office, and so on. The regions which are surveyed in these pages are among the most extensive land areas in Britain, containing small residual populations, but possessing considerable natural resources or resource potential. They are some of the most remote in the country and their inhabitants in general have lower incomes than those elsewhere: central government subsidies are thus considerable. In regions like these the physical planner must start by questioning his role and function, and he must assess which are the critical relationships between them and other regions.

RURAL PLANNING UNDER THE 1947 PLANNING ACT

The emphasis in the 1947 Act was urban, even where the planning of counties was concerned. For instance, village planning was seen as town planning writ small, and other policies, such as for green belts, scenic conservation, screening of mineral workings, etc., siting of pylons, were all part of an urban-based fitting of amenity and conservation into the countryside. It is significant that the use of land for agriculture and forestry was not deemed 'development' for purposes of the Act and, therefore, the vast majority of the land resources in the rural counties was not subject to planning control. The 1950 General Development Order[4] scheduled as 'permitted development' certain building and engineering works related to agriculture and forestry use, a situation which was to be changed later. The Order also required formal consultation with the Ministry of Agriculture before any adverse development control decisions could be made regarding siting of development on agricultural land. Even when, later, certain rural building activities became subject to planning control the emphasis was often on choice of materials and their colour, and to a lesser extent the shaping and siting of new buildings.

The emphasis and attitudes of the 1947 approach to rural planning generally is well indicated in official Circular No. 40 on Survey for Development Plans.[5] Here local planning authorities are advised to carry out necessary official consultations in order to minimise the impact of development on good agricultural and forestry land and to cause minimal damage to farm units and to amenity. There was no suggestion of any positive initiative to introduce or to explore with private interests ways of improving the comprehensive pattern of land management. It appears to have been assumed that the 1947 Agriculture Act and government control by subsidies, incentives, etc., could achieve both the best economic and spatial arrangements for the countryside.

Publications which evaluate the planning work done generally during this period reflected the priorities of the time; for instance, the Central Office of Information book on 'Town and Country Planning'[6] gives no recognition to rural, let alone remoter-rural, problems as a major facet of planning. When the 'less prosperous regions' are referred to, this inevitably refers to the declining industrial areas on the old coalfields and is not a reference to the even lower-income remote rural regions which are less populous. National parks, forest parks, nature reserves, are given their due recognition but the planning of agriculture, forestry, water resources, energy, land resource and their inter-relationships are not seen as physical planning. In the context of economic land use it was not until the 1960s that planners began to show interest in the coast, tourism and recreation, and concern with rural blight. An example of the policies and priorities in the planning of rural counties is given in a document[7] by West Suffolk County Council where a sequence of rural planning policies is set out as follows:

concern with safety;
conservation of agricultural land and trees;
general amenity conservation;
control of building development—its location, form and arrangement;
landscape control;
control of mineral workings, etc.;
conservation of villages of national architectural significance, and caravan sites.

PLANNING IN THE REMOTER RURAL REGIONS UNDER THE 1947
PLANNING SYSTEM

The counties which comprise the more extensive and remoter rural areas are generally poorer and far less populous than the rural areas which comprise the hinterlands of the city regions. A key problem, therefore, following on from the 1947 Planning Act was the problem of finance and personnel relating to the setting up of planning offices. Authorities could not necessarily afford either the salaries or the numbers of staff necessary to cover the range of statutory obligations. In some cases the incentives to encourage good staff to come to the areas were inadequate. Furthermore, rural counties were not always well disposed towards the idea of planning and the system, therefore, developed hesitantly. In many cases existing chief officers took on the planning role in addition to their present responsibilities. In other cases adjacent counties would share the services of one County Planning Officer or call in a private consultant to prepare their development plan for them. In a number of cases where separate county planning offices were set up these literally comprised a man and a boy and one cannot but admire the energy and staying power of many of these individuals.

It is difficult to generalise about the staff in these regions as they are as diverse in character and ability as the regions are diverse in tradition, patterns of land tenure, inheritance, age, sex composition, and attitudes. However, it would be fair to state that the majority of those concerned with policy-making, came from urban backgrounds and had had an urban-orientated planning education. The problem of adaptation and adjustment to these new areas, with different conditions, was, therefore, important.

If one examines the coverage of planning work by a typical rural county, for instance Merioneth, then the official work undertaken can be seen to range over: County Maps, Programme Maps, Town Maps, Village Plans and Village Development Plans. The relationship of policies to extensive land use is well brought out in the first review of this County Development Plan where the following statement is made:

'*Agriculture and Forestry*
    It is intended to safeguard, by means of general planning powers, the interests of agriculture and to secure that as far as practicable

future development proposals cause the minimum interference with farm holdings.

It is intended, in the interests of amenity, to exercise careful control over the design of agricultural buildings within the Snowdonia National Park.

It is anticipated that the Forestry Commission will continue with proposals to acquire and plant further extensive areas of land within the County of Merioneth. The agreement on non-afforestation areas drawn up with a view to safeguarding areas of special amenity value and approved by the Forestry Commission and by the County Council will form the basis for consultations on all afforestation proposals, whether with the Commission or with private interests.'

If one looks at the planning system as it developed under the 1947 Act in relation to the remoter rural regions, then at worst it can be said that the counties concerned were obliged to satisfy the minimal requirements laid down by the Ministry, the Scottish Office or the Welsh Office. At best, however, the interpretive role of the county planner, and the range of non-statutory activities initiated through careful liaison with organisations and individuals, represent an impressive record despite the limited numbers of personnel, limited finance and, often, local opposition.

WORK TECHNIQUES AND POLICY FORMULATION AFTER 1947

(a) Growth Points

If one examines a large number of the published reports of authorities in the remoter rural parts of Scotland, Wales, and England it is found that a limited number of general policies have been used. The first and possibly the most common of these is the use of the 'growth-point' concept, though the word 'growth-point' may mean anything from a town to a village, or even a cluster of hamlets. It is difficult, however, to find examples in these areas of the sort of policy formulated in County Durham where certain villages have been formally planned out of existence or planned for contraction, as opposed to those which are planned for containment or growth. The more typical county plan has defined a settlement-hierarchy with towns, small towns, 'key-villages' or 'king-villages' to function as key service points and places of growth relating to a rural catchment area. The term 'growth-point' tends to be used rather than 'holding point' though this is really the intention often underlying the policy. There are political and social objections, it would seem, to recognising the strong trend of decline in certain areas, and the possibility of stretches of countryside depopulating as small towns grow, sometimes has been resisted. Generally, the settlement pattern has been related to the system of routes, but not to assumptions as to the likely support-population based on the extensive areas of rural land use, e.g. agriculture, forestry, etc. The proposed National Park in Central Wales is a break-through in terms of the extent of relationship of land use proposals to settlement change. Assumptions on the support given by tourism, water resource development, and forestry development, have been indicated in a number of studies; together with new industry they are at the basis of the Rhayader Town Expansion Scheme.

The advantages in such policies and the economic justification for nucleating facilities and improvement in a limited number of locations are obvious, judged from examples, notably in the North of England and in Scotland. The post-war forestry villages of Kielder and Bryness are examples of new growth points which are being created on the basis of resource development. Elsewhere, policies of single resource-based growth points (such as the aforementioned) have given way to the consolidation of existing settlements with a wider range of economic, cultural and other opportunities. The most ambitious studies to date in this context have been undertaken by the Highlands and Islands Development Board which has looked at major growth areas on the one hand, and on the other has started to survey development-points in order to define which rural centres would have the catchment and suitable potentials for economic growth.

(b) New Central Places

A major policy stand emerging in the remoter rural areas as an answer to rural depopulation, megalopolitan overpopulation, and the drift to these major metropolitan areas, has been the introduction of the idea of creating new central urban places within these regions themselves. The Moray Firth Urbanisation Programme of the Highland Board, linking port, industry, housing and power development programmes, is a good example. Similarly, the proposed new town in Central Wales, which now appears to have given way to some major town-expansion schemes, is another example of this counter attack on regional depopulation. Current proposals in the Scottish Central Borders and in the Irish Republic and informal proposals for the Solway Region are further indicators of this growing movement, but with the escalation in the size of new towns, and the apparent advantages of the 100,000 to 250,000 population urban complex, national priorities must be invoked if the costs of creating such infrastructure are to be met. The simple alternatives, therefore, to deal with rural depopulation are limited, either:

(1) to concentrate sizeable numbers of people in or within reach of newly centralised economic, cultural and social facilities in the region, or

(2) to make facilities mobile and move these around to service smaller clusters of rural population, covering a more extensive area at a lower density.

(c) Rural Thresholds

The work which has been done in the urban field of cost thresholds of schools, provision of sewerage systems, fire, police, electricity, etc., has tended to be interpreted more simply in the rural context. Target populations for rural settlements have generally used the magical 500, 2,500, 5,000 and 10,000 figures which relate more to school-intake than to any correlation of a series of cost thresholds. The problem is not only one of meeting the costs of providing services but of creating an infrastructure for an economic model suitable for several generations and not just one. Labour is captive if there is one work place per man, or if there are jobs for adults but none for school-leavers who must migrate because of the absence of work vacancies. A work-threshold theory is evolving but this does not yet have sufficient application in rural context to counterbalance the image and the pull of the metropolitan area. 'The Way Ahead'[8] reflects this problem. . . . 'Schools are liable to be closed, so that children are obliged to travel long distances, or, especially in the case of further education, it is grossly uneconomic to establish them in the area at all. Similar economic difficulties affect the provision of health services and public transport. Electricity, gas, water and drainage facilities are difficult to provide and maintain without heavy subsidies. About four-fifths of the cost of local authority services has to be met from the Exchequer. Urban centres are small and have limited service and entertainment facilities.'

The situation in Scotland in many respects is worse than in Wales. The rate of depopulation, for instance, in the Island of

Arran is higher than in Central Wales. The barrier of sea crossings and more difficult topography put up threshold costs, particularly those of freight, transport and all such factors. The extent of travel subsidies in countries such as Norway and Canada are important matters to study in relation to the cost accessibility threshold.

(d) Quality of Life
The balance of migration continues to be overwhelmingly weighted in favour of depopulation. The young, confronted with the limited work opportunities, limited incomes, limited social and cultural opportunities, and possibly the more restrictive cultural and religious norms of these areas, continue to move out in search of the 'better life', which they hope to find in Birmingham or London, and do not believe possible in their home region. The problems of loss of confidence, attitudes, and the need to re-establish hope, are relevant in this context. The Highlands and Islands Development Board is a significant break-through in British terms, and its work makes an interesting comparison with that of the North Norway Fund and the South Italy Fund. However, the prospect of integrated regional development bodies in each of the remoter areas, giving meaning to regional objectives and regional priorities in terms of the quality of life, may still seem distant.

1968 TOWN AND COUNTRY PLANNING ACTS (ENGLAND AND WALES; SCOTLAND)

In evaluating the 1947 planning system, the Report of the Planning Advisory Group[9] admitted that . . . 'the general impression that the county planning, outside town map areas, has tended to become a neglected aspect of planning work and the present development plan system tends to discourage a more positive approach'. The Report and the subsequent legislation which has arisen from it assumes that the need for country-wide land policies is accepted. It assumes that 'firstly the county plan is a crucial link between regional planning and local land use planning'. One may ask which regional body is concerned with regional physical plan preparation for Central Wales, Highland Scotland, the Borders? Perhaps the assumption is an extravagant one, until the findings of the Maud and Wheatley Commissions have been followed through in legislative form. The Planning Advisory Group approach assumes that physical and

economic policies would be defined where they are not yet defined,
e.g. for the remoter rural regions; and it is

'Against this background that the main purposes of the new county
plan would be:

(1) to set out the local planning authority's main objectives and
policies for the county, and to bring these before the public and
the Minister;

(2) to work out the relationship of regional policies to the physical
planning of the county and to show how these policies are to be
implemented at the county level;

(3) to develop physical planning policies that affect the county as a
whole, or large areas of the county, but which are not within the
scope of regional planning—e.g. county communications network
and relationship to the regional network; recreational facilities;
landscape policy; derelict land; mineral resources;

(4) to set the policy framework for development in towns and
villages;

(5) to provide the basis for development control in rural areas where
there is no other form of plan;

(6) to provide, in the preparatory stages, a basis for consultation
and negotiation with county district councils, neighbouring
planning authorities, regional authorities and central government
on matters of common interest.'   (PAG Report, 3.6, p. 22).

THE COUNTRYSIDE ACTS (ENGLAND AND WALES: SCOTLAND)

The new Planning Acts[10, 11] must be seen in the context of a broad
pattern of change . . . the creation of Countryside Commissions,
the pending reform of local government, the Transport Acts and
changes relating to financing of industry, and the administration of
energy and water planning. These are all part of a shift of emphasis
which will have a very strong bearing upon the future of planning
in the remote rural regions. The Countryside Acts have given rise
to the initiation of a much more positive approach to the creation of
recreational facilities and amenity for coast and countryside, and the
related modifications to the powers of bodies such as the Forestry
Commission, Electricity Board, etc., in this respect is a major
step ahead. However, initiation of spatial policies in relation to
agriculture, forestry, and their general integration with recreation-
culture, forestry, and their general integration with recreation-
planning is something which still lies ahead of us, and the recon-
ciliation of the criteria of the War Department, the water and power

authorities, with those of multi-use planning has yet to be achieved
on a general basis.

EAST HAMPSHIRE . . .
A STUDY IN COUNTRYSIDE CONSERVATION (1968)

The techniques of comprehensive rural planning for the remoter
rural areas under the new Planning Act are at an early stage of
evolution. There is a need to pool and feed back knowledge of many
techniques, collected from many sources, if patterns of practice and
policy-making are to be notably improved. The East Hampshire
Study[12] is the first of what it must be hoped will be a series of modern
studies; here a progressive county planning authority has set up a
test study for the planning of one type of rural area. It has relevance
to the planning of remote rural areas, but is not in any way pro-
posing to satisfy the planning needs of these other areas. The
stages of the Study are interesting. They are:

  (1) study of resources;
  (2) study of activities;
  (3) study of interaction and compatibility of resources and
      activities;
  (4) future demands and their appropriate locational and spatial
      satisfactions.

The Study goes on to propose a hierarchy of rural plans similar to
the hierarchy for urban planning, but the classification defined would
not appear appropriate to the needs of the areas with which we are
concerned. Possibly in this context the work of the resource-
planning agencies in the United States and New Zealand would be
more relevant to the desirable type of integrated multi-use land
planning than the East Hampshire proposals, where conservation in
a high-quality farm landscape is one of the major concerns.

PLANNING BULLETIN NO. 8. SETTLEMENT IN THE COUNTRY
SIDE—A PLANNING METHOD

This new planning Bulletin[13] again has limited value for planners
concerned with the extensive resource-regions. It does, however,
accept the need for comprehensive planning and states that planners
'should have regard to other component policies of the plan, for
example, recreation, communications, agriculture, landscaping and
derelict land restoration'. The powers for planning of agricultural

land are not indicated and no reference is made to water-planning, power-planning, forestry-planning and many other fields. Yet, in its conclusions, the report not only backs comprehensive planning but endorses the need for more thorough analysis for rural studies and a far more positive approach in the tackling of rural planning. Each of these studies is a step ahead and is part of an evolutionary process. However, the techniques of planning remoter rural areas may need at this point in time a more dramatic leap in development of method if the scale of problems confronting the professional men in this field is to be tackled effectively.

NEW POLICIES AND TECHNIQUES

There is British precedent for the comprehensive-development approach in the extensive rural areas. The work of the Highlands and Islands Development Board in the Strath of Kildonan and the Isle of Mull, and the comprehensive area management scheme of the Electricity Board in Merioneth, are the beginnings of a new rural comprehensiveness. Already some rural development work in Holland, and in the Tatrys Mountains of Poland, and soil inter-resource based studies in New Zealand and Israel, indicate some of the suitable techniques which are available. As long ago as 1941, Sir Daniel Hall[14] was pleading for the active co-operation of soils advisers, agricultural colleges and many rural management specialists in carrying out of resource surveys and plans. Openshaw[15] in the 1960s is reiterating Hall's pleas when he says we should try 'to determine the potential of each area to find the optimum economic use of any given area to eliminate waste land and determine the potential'.

A national resource survey series in New Zealand,[16] employing staff largely educated in Wales and Scotland, has covered studies on geology, soils, soil potential, water resources, soil and water conservation, climate and weather, population, agriculture, mineral extraction, forestry, and forestry industries, power resources, employment, transport, recreation and tourism, local government and prospects. If rural management is to become meaningful, this view of the comprehensive planning of land, water and human resources has to be accepted, with private and public owners and interests working in close co-operation, while a much wider range of management agreements must be arranged.

The range and character of the problem is such that the use of a systems approach should be helpful in laying a reasonable foundation for decision-making in the complex management of resources both for development and conservation. Given more rational boundaries and a suitable resource classification system, both for mono-use and multi-use, then the planner as an agent of society may be able to help satisfy both the needs of majority interests and of minority interests in the planning of his regions.

A hierarchy of plans in the remote rural regions from the national via the regional down to the local scale will pose the problem of the relationship and conflicts between regional and national priorities and here the feedback system from the local to the regional body will be critical in determining land-planning policies which are viable and economic, as well as being sensitive to the views and needs of the local as well as of the national population.

POLICIES AND PARTICIPATION

The Skeffington Report,[17] like most official planning documents, reflects an urban emphasis, because only a tiny percentage of our population lives on the land. However, the sensitivity of the planner to personalities and local responses in the remoter rural regions is of great importance. The elaborate concepts of decision-making models now defined in studies of Coventry and other major cities, give way to the sensitivity of the planner in dealing with a range of individuals who may well be the critical-decision makers in an extensive rural region.

Goals for programmes which may be elaborate for urban regions and cities are infinitely more difficult to define, let alone achieve, in these highly sensitive areas remote from the big cities. Therefore preparation for participation and change must have considerable bearing on the training of those planners who are to become involved in rural and natural resource region planning. Their understanding must not only be of the physical pattern concerned, but one of sensitivity to delicate local social, political, cultural and linguistic factors. Equally, physical planners will have to come together with a growing range of related specialists in fields such as forestry, agriculture, ecology, hydrology, etc., if the sort of decisions which are made are to be authoritative and not superficial. The restoration of local self-confidence is equally important, if participation in the process of creative change is to be achieved. In this context, links with Universities, Research Institutes, Agricultural Institutes and a great range of other bodies might well be strengthened.

REMOVAL OF BARRIERS

Many people in the remoter parts of Scotland, Wales and even England feel that they have been placed in an under-privileged position whereby they are at the mercy of decisions which are made in places remote from them, and that politicians may have little understanding of the impact and ripple effect of major investment decisions which are made, particularly by the public sector. An ageing population, often seeing its children forced to travel a considerable distance for education and initial work opportunities, becomes resentful of government, and the planner may sometimes be seen as the embodiment of these outside agencies rather than part of a pattern of local or regional self-determination. Attitude is, therefore, a major problem both for the planner and for the planned and the professional and educational barriers which currently place physical planners, agronomists, foresters, and others in watertight compartments act as a major stumbling block towards achieving the sort of system of rural planning which is required. We need:

> 'to think of our physical environment as a dynamic system, whose elements are adapted to changing demands. The environment is conditioned by the variable life cycles of its component parts; on the one hand the *inert* systems of physical development, and on the other hand its *living* elements; people, plants, animals and landscape—the ecological system . . . arbitration will not suffice for the planner; for the practical task of controlling our surroundings, including land and water resources, has to be both positive and creative.' [18]

If resource-planning in the proper sense is now to be initiated in the remoter rural regions, then in fact many of the sensible conclusions of the Land Use Study Group[19] need to be given effect in the near future. Integration of land use is still a primary national requirement, but in this context integration means co-ordination of multiple use of land and associated activities within a given area of land. We do not yet have true rural land development authorities. The long-awaited Ministry of Land and Natural Resources has come and gone, and a close link between agricultural planning, natural-resource planning and conservation, and general physical planning has yet to be achieved. The Study Group recommended that 'a new executive body such as a regional development authority should be created which would operate regionally and be responsible for local interpretation of Central Government policy. It should have the necessary power to co-ordinate effectively *all forms of rural land use.*'

The new Planning Acts, Countryside Acts, creations of new development powers, etc., still do not satisfy this basic recommendation and if good management of our physical resources is justified, then nowhere does this need to be as fully thought out as in relation to our extensive land and water resources. The remoter rural regions are a rich reserve of such resources.

CONCLUSIONS AND RECOMMENDATIONS

(1) There is an outstanding need to educate people specifically for the task of rural and natural resource region planning—people who will understand and be able to play a positive role in the development and conservation of these areas which are remote from the major urban concentrations and centres of political power in the United Kingdom. Such planners will need to develop the sensitivity to personal, social and cultural peculiarities that the best of the existing planners in the field have developed.

> 'The planner, equipped with a more hybrid training in natural and social science, will become less the referee blowing the whistle (i.e. in resolving land use conflicts) and more the conductor of a tolerably well rehearsed orchestra, which will tend to be on a regional rather than a local pattern. Landowners, land-users, and the land-linked professions, including forestry, agriculture, estate management and land agency, and landscape design (now called landscape architecture) will be in continuous liaison with land planning through flexible codes, frequently revised as new knowledge can be built into them, from a greatly increased programme of environmental research.'[20]

(2) There is an urgent need to set up effective and continuing regional and local work groups and liaison groups of physical planners, ecologists, estate managers, agronomists, economists, foresters, water engineers, etc., if soundly based land and water planning policies are to be defined for these regions.

(3) In order to achieve the objective of stabilisation and habiability in these regions, a close look may need to be taken at rural education to see whether it suffers from either rural or urban bias. Even if one accepts the concept of urban and rural continuity, the

roles of future rural universities and research institutes, and the special role and influence of extra-mural university activities—especially 'the Open University'—will be important. Field education and experiments, e.g. test farm work of the Tennessee Valley Authority, the rural Co-operatives of Donegal, are the start of a new pattern of rural change.

(4) There is need to create an interim code of practice for deep rural planning as the East Hampshire AONB Study and other studies to date are not fitted to the planning of such areas. Legislative change may be needed to achieve comprehensive rural planning and this would have to go hand in hand with the establishment of a new resource classification system for positive planning purposes.

(5) The establishment of comprehensive rural regional planning machinery could link its responsibility to a Department of Rural and Natural Resource Planning which might form one of three arms of a new Planning Ministry whose other arms could be concerned with urban-regional and city planning on the one hand, and a Department of Regional Economics (replacing the D.E.A.) on the other.

(6) This assumes that regional bodies as such would be created for each of the definable resource regions,* namely Central Wales, the Borders and the Highlands and Islands. It is assumed, furthermore, that these would combine both economic and physical planning functions and might be responsible to elected regional assemblies. The regional body could have a regional development budget partly drawn from local revenue and partly as an allocation by the central government to the regional government. In such circumstances, the central Government would have to establish guide lines for the inter-regional roles, and relationships between the regions.

(7) As implied in the work of the Land Use Study Group, there is a need for a more formal linkage of the functions of physical-planning agencies with the bodies and individuals concerned with the planning and management of agriculture, forestry and water planning, and a need for close links on power-planning.

(8) The general goals for these regions might be fourfold, viz:

    (*a*) to stabilise the pattern of life and achieve 'habitability' for a rural population with reasonable economic, physical, social, cultural and recreational opportunities in the region;

* Ireland has been excluded from this breakdown.

(b) to survey the resource potentials of land, soils, water, minerals, and do capacity-carrying studies of the areas, establishing suitability for planting, food production, industrial development, port development, etc., with a view to determining the relationship of activities in the region to national objectives for development and for conservation;

(c) to study the recreational potential of the region in the context of economic multi-use of its land and water resources;

(d) to explore means of restoring self-confidence, hope, and belief in the feasibility of positive change and (good) development, in the hope of thereby arresting the loss by migration of the young and energetic members of the community who are its potential leaders, and confirm that it is possible to live a full and satisfactory life in the rural regions as well as in the cities.

REFERENCES

1. Town and Country Planning Act, 1947, HMSO.
2. Town and Country Planning Act, 1968, HMSO.
3. Subsequently published *Report of the Royal Commission on Local Government in Scotland*, 1966–9 (Cmnd. 4150) Edinburgh, HMSO, 1969.
4. 1950 No. 728 Statutory Instrument, Town and Country Planning General Development Order, 1950.
5. *Survey for Development Plans*, Circular No. 40, Ministry of Town and Country Planning, HMSO, 1948.
6. *Town and Country Planning in Britain*, C.O.I. Ref. Pamphlet 9, HMSO, 1968.
7. *Principles of Rural Planning*, County of West Suffolk, 1965.
8. *Wales: the Way Ahead*, HMSO, 1967.
9. *The Future of Development Plans*. A Report of the Planning Advisory Group, London, HMSO, 1965.
10. Countryside (Scotland) Act, HMSO, 1967.
11. Countryside Act, HMSO, 1968.
12. East Hampshire, Area of Outstanding Natural Beauty—A study in Countryside Conservation, 1968. Five Sponsoring Bodies.
13. Settlement in the Countryside—A planning method, *Bulletin* 8, HMSO, 1967.
14. HALL, SIR DANIEL, *Reconstruction of the Land*, Macmillan, 1941.
15. OPENSHAW, KEITH, The Remoter Rural Areas, *Fabian Research Series*, 253, 1966.
16. Planning of Resource Regions (6) in New Zealand, New Zealand Ministry of Works, Department of Town and Country Planning.
17. Paper and Planning Report of the Skeffington Committee on Public Participation in Planning, HMSO, 1969.
18. TRAVIS, A. S., 'Ends and Means—Planning for a Changing Society', *T.P. Review*, July 1969.
19. Report of the Land Use Study Group: Forestry, Agriculture and the Multiple Use of Rural Land, O.E.S., London, HMSO, 1966.
20. NICHOLSON, E. M. in *The World in 1984*, Penguin, 1965.

11 | *Sociological Criteria for Assessing Policies*

PROFESSOR W. M. WILLIAMS, M.A.
Department of Sociology and Anthropology,
University College of Swansea

Nowadays the mere mention of sociology is likely to arouse strong emotions in certain quarters, but this relatively recent phenomenon is of less interest and significance to us than the much older controversy concerning the sociologist's role in planning—using this term in its widest sense. We have to recognise at the outset that the nature of sociology—what it sets out to do, and by what methods— is much misunderstood and that this has in turn produced an exaggerated response to its application, either by expecting too much of it or by dismissing its value in advance. It is true that rural sociology and its relevance to planning the countryside have not been in the forefront of discussion, but this is simply because both activities have, regretfully, been seriously neglected in most parts of the world.

It is, therefore, necessary to begin with a brief definition of rural sociology, together with an equally brief examination of certain basic assumptions that are commonly made concerning the social structure and institutions of rural areas. Sociology is the systematic study of social relations, as distinct from personal relations, which are the concern of the psychologist, or economic relations, which are the field of the economist. It is the essence of sociology that social relations are seen to exhibit regularities which persist and are, therefore, predictable, and which enable us to think in terms of social systems. Not all social relations are systematic and all the parts of a social system are not necessarily articulated into a single functional whole. There may be conflict between one part of a system and another, or there may be discontinuities within the system. There are always forces at work to change a social system or sometimes even to destroy it.

This compressed definition of sociology is not new nor is it particularly controversial: when, however, we introduce the word

202

rural before it, we find ourselves faced with a wide range of conflicting views. There is considerable disagreement over the definition of rural: there are many who object to the notion of dividing sociology in this fashion: there are others who claim that the subject matter of rural sociology is disappearing fast, or no longer exists: there are divisions of opinion on how far it is an applied field of study. For our purposes it is sufficient to note these disagreements and to define rural sociology as concerned with the social relationships of people living in areas where farming and forestry are significant and substantial, since this provides a sufficient criterion to distinguish rural life from other fields of sociological enquiry. One consequence of using this definition is that ecological relationships become important, since it is hardly profitable to consider farming and forestry apart from the complex physical entity 'land'; man–land relationships are more explicit, more clearly articulated in rural areas than they are in our towns and cities.

Two assumptions of major importance are commonly made about rural life: first, that it is simple in structure and limited in content; second that it changes very slowly. Both assumptions are usually related, implicitly or explicitly, to further comparative statements regarding urban life—which is seen as complex and subject to rapid change. The difficulties that result from using such ideas do not depend on their truth or falsity but rather on their operational value, which is extremely limited. There are, moreover, further problems that arise from perceiving rural and urban as parts of a simple whole, or as points arranged on a scale. Last, but by no means least, there are many value judgements associated with these ways of regarding rural life, which in general terms amount to seeing it as desirable, healthy, lacking in stress and conflict, stable and so forth, in contrast to the tensions and evils of life in the city. There has been remarkably little change in this respect since the *Introduction* to the 'Scott' Report[1] quoted G. M. Trevelyan with considerable approval:

'Without vision the people perish and without natural beauty the English people will perish in the spiritual sense. In the old days the English lived in the midst of Nature, subject to its influence at every hour. Thus inspired, our ancestors produced their great creations in religion, in song, and in the arts and crafts—common products of a whole people spiritually alive. Today most of us are banished to the cities, not without deleterious effects on imagination, inspiration and creative power. But some still live in the country and drink in with the zest of a thirsty man the delights of natural beauty and return to the town re-invigorated in soul.'

The significance of the fact that this quotation epitomises the general perspective of one of the most important and influential public statements on rural planning in the post-war period will be examined later: here it is sufficient to note that value judgements of whatever kind are one of the factors to be taken into account by the sociologist in his contribution to the planning process.

It need hardly be said that the remoter rural areas are the most likely to be associated with extreme forms of the assumptions discussed above, since their very remoteness is seen as protecting them from urban influences. To avoid the difficulties inherent in such an approach I propose to examine the *social functions* of the countryside and the ways in which they are inter-related and changing.

In economically developed countries such as Britain the rural areas have four major functions: to serve (i) as the area in which agriculture, forestry, pastoralism and certain other kinds of primary economic activity, for example quarrying, take place; (ii) as the area in which manufacturing industries ancillary to these primary activities, together with other industries removed from congested urban locations, may be found; (iii) as the area where recreational and tourist activities of certain kinds may be developed; and (iv) as the area in which the population maintaining all these activities, together with others who have no direct connection with the economy of the countryside, for example retired persons from towns and cities and commuters, live. These four functions have in common the exploitation of a large area of land in relation to the population dependent upon it, in comparison with characteristically urban uses of space, although the use of the countryside as a place to live in is more and more constituting an important exception. In general, it seems as if the relatively empty areas are becoming emptier while the more densely populated areas are becoming more congested.

The balance between these functions varies for many reasons over a great range from one country to another, but it is arguable that in developed countries broad trends may be observed. The primary production function is declining in importance as the other three increase their significance. Now it will be clear that the framing of policy objectives for rural areas can be seen as making choices which affect the balance of major functions, and from this point of view the sociologist's task is to examine the social consequences of such functional changes. To illustrate this, let us consider the characteristic pattern of social relations that one might expect in our remote rural areas. They are, first and foremost, face-to-face relations, direct exchanges among people who know each other. Such relations may be informal or formal and contractual, but the distinction between these two is by no means clear cut. In a situation where 'everyone knows everybody else', the ways in which people behave towards each other, the ways in which they perceive the actions of others, and the fact that each individual is likely to occupy a number of different roles in local life simultaneously—friend, neighbour, kinsman, etc.—are all to be understood in terms of a highly localised and cohesive social structure. Moreover, these countryfolk look largely within their own *milieu* for the satisfaction of their social and economic aspirations—at least in the first instance. Here then the social order is largely conceived as 'us'—that is, country folk in general, and the people of our locality in particular—and 'them'—townsfolk, strangers, outsiders, all those persons who can be clearly defined as 'different'.

This traditional way of life is associated for the most part with farming or other kinds of primary economic activity and has not been much affected by the other major functions described earlier. What are the likely consequences of a large-scale change in functions upon it? The most significant and far-reaching effects seem to follow a growth of the residential function. Much of rural Western Europe has experienced a significant increase in the numbers of people who are urban by birth and background, who work in towns but who choose to live in the countryside because rural life, as they perceive it, satisfies many of their aspirations. Their numbers are added to materially by other townspeople who choose a rural area for retirement. These newcomers bring their own ideas, habits and styles of life with them and in initiating social relations with the countryfolk 'proper' they not only confront them with a completely new pattern of living, but simultaneously disrupt the rural view of the world as divided into 'us' and 'them'. It is now necessary to have a third category, 'them among us', which allows for the permanent displacement of part of the town and its people and grants it a somewhat uneasy quasi-rural status. We still know very little about the sociology of this development, since apart from R. E. Pahl's study of three Hertfordshire villages,[2] it is still a neglected field of research.

The growth of tourism and recreation is, perhaps, even more rapid and striking and is, of course, directly related to the building of new roads—sometimes specifically for tourists—and the general improvement in communications and services. The growth in private car ownership deserves a chapter to itself. Changes in this function may appear less continuous, in so far as it is usually seasonal in character, but it is no less significant in its effects on rural social life. Tourists and holidaymakers are quite certainly 'them' not 'us' and because of the circumstances of their visit they represent an incomplete and specialised picture of the good life, urban style. They have money to spend, they are determined to enjoy themselves, be friendly, forget their problems and so forth. Those who can afford to buy second homes, country cottages, or abandoned farms for week-ends and summer holidays, who stand between the commuter or retired couple and the day-tripper, are found among the most prosperous sections of the population and are likely to convey a misleadingly affluent impression of town living.

These two major changes in function reinforce each other in their effects on the traditional pattern of rural life. Informal face-to-face relationships between persons who have known each other for a considerable period, if not all their lives, become accompanied more and more by secondary relationships which do not require personal knowledge or familiarity. The social horizon is drastically extended as individuals look increasingly outside the community for the satisfaction of their needs and aspirations. Mass media of communication, particularly television, play a significant role in this regard.

There are further social developments which result from changes *within* particular functions as distinct from changes in the balance of functions. For example, the modernisation of agriculture, the effects of technological advance on farm practice, the trend towards 'agribusiness', bring their own series of changes in the social relations between groups and between individuals. As I have suggested elsewhere, technological change in farming has reduced the authority of the family farmer over his sons and transformed relationships within the family.[3] Economic and financial measures emanating from central government have affected the relationship between employer and employee and between farmers as entrepreneurs. Such instances can be multiplied without difficulty.

This brief discussion has been designed to indicate the ways in which the sociologist can play a part in the formulation of policy objectives through an analysis of the social and economic functions of the countryside. This is, of course, only one aspect of the sociologist's task: another, perhaps more central, certainly more contentious, is concerned with the concept of the community. No one word has created more difficulty and confusion. In 1955 Hillery listed no less than ninety-four definitions of community,[4] while König, commenting on Hillery's article in 1968, suggests that at least as many different definitions can be found without difficulty.[5] Having reviewed the literature exhaustively, both authors provide us with minimal definitions that have some resemblance:

Hillery: 'a social group inhabiting a common territory and having one or more additional common ties.'

König: 'a more or less large local and social unit in which men co-operate in order to live their economic, social and cultural life together.'

Both stress local unity, social interaction and common bonds: both emphasise that the community is the most important intermediary social grouping between the family and such larger social formations as the nation or state: both recognise the possibility of conflict but say relatively little about it.

There are, as we shall see later, considerable difficulties even with these skeletal definitions, but we may for the time being accept this kind of statement in order to produce a paradigm of the rural community which can in turn be used to examine the significance of the concept of community in planning. First, we recall that in rural life man–land relations are explicit and clearly articulated so that in placing the community in a rural context we need to stress its territorial aspect. The settlement pattern commonly found in rural areas—market towns, villages, hamlets, scattered farmsteads and cottages—appears to lend itself readily to the identification of individual communities in a way that is clearly much more difficult in large towns. The 'village community' is thus a social and physical entity which can be explicitly delineated on a map.

Within the boundaries of the rural community, social and economic relations are primary, based on personal knowledge and a sense of belonging to a more or less clearly defined grouping.

Neighbourliness and co-operation, together with a close-knit kinship system, produce a highly cohesive way of life with a marked sense of indentity, allowing each individual to distinguish clearly between fellow members and 'outsiders'.

The picture is a familiar one and it requires only a small addition to invest it with an ideological overtone of one kind or another. If we hold a romantic view of country life, the rural community then becomes 'highly integrated', 'balanced', 'stable'; or it may have less tangible characteristics that are certainly not amenable to scientific investigation. This is clearly seen in a very recent book on a Suffolk village:

> 'In Akenfield, evidence of the good life, a tall old church on the hillside, a pub selling the local brew, a pretty stream, a football pitch, a handsome square vicarage with a cedar of Lebanon shading it, a school with jars of tadpoles in the window, three shops with door bells, a Tudor mansion, half a dozen farms and a lot of quaint cottages, is there for all to recognise. Akenfield, on the face of it, is the kind of place in which an Englishman has always felt it his right and duty to live. It is patently the real country, untouched and genuine. A holy place, when you have spent half your life abroad in the services. Its very sounds are formal, hieratic: larks, clocks, bees, tractor hummings. Rarely the sound of the human voice. So powerful is this traditional view that many people are able to live in the centre of it for years and see nothing more. . . . Perhaps it would be fairer to say that the two contrasting conceptions of . . . happiness, the new—i.e. the literate and informed—and the old i.e. the mysterious and intuitive—are now existing side by side in Akenfield, and with scarcely any awareness of each other.'

Such a perspective frequently goes hand-in-hand with the idea that larger and more powerful communities, that is towns and cities, have replaced the smaller rural communities and that this process is generally undesirable.

In contrast we find the much less fashionable ideological stance which holds that towns and cities are alone capable of technological, intellectual, economic and social progress and that small communities are, correspondingly, provincial, backward, traditionalist and so forth.[7]

Whatever the ideology—and sometimes elements of contrasting ideologies may be found in an uneasy marriage—there can be no doubt that the notion of a balanced and/or integrated rural community is very well established as an ideal in much British country planning. It is also certain that this notion is very closely related to the 'pastoral myth' which has been a persistent feature of English thought since the Romantic poets of the nineteenth century. There is, unfortunately, little, if any, justification for accepting this ideal from a sociological view-point. The notion of a balanced community is at best an ideal type, not found in the real world and, indeed, not so far shown to be of practical value as a blue-print. 'Unbalanced' or 'unintegrated' communities are common enough and many sociologists argue that *all* communities are characterised by lack of integration, by discontinuity, by conflict. Others go further and argue that many of the features of our social life that are most frequently explained in terms of the local community can, in fact, be just as readily understood by reference to associations or groupings of a more comprehensive kind. Even more extreme still are those sociologists who, like Gans, hold that ways of life are not necessarily related to particular types of settlement and that, therefore, using such units of study as the village or rural community may have little or no value.[8]

There are other difficulties of a technical or methodological kind. How does one establish the boundaries of a given community? For example, Littlejohn in his study of the Border parish of Westrigg concluded that the local community had become 'less an area of common life' than an area within which the individual chooses his associations subject to such barriers as are imposed by social class or physical distance.'[9] Other community studies have emphasised the same problem.[10] Does the particular pattern of settlement affect the quality and content of social life? The work of Alwyn Rees and his students in Wales shows that the social life of country-folk may be as close-knit when they live in widely scattered farm-steads and cottages as that found in the compact village.[11] Does the existence of a flourishing associational life indicate a high level of well-being within the community? Frankenberg in his study of Glyn Ceiriog argues that such associations are arenas for conflict and dispute between opposed factions within the community.[12]

In short, sociology does not provide anything like firm evidence for the use of the community as a model unit for planning purposes; still less does it furnish general prescriptions for the most desirable kind of community. Now it does not, of course, follow from this that the community may not be the most useful and appropriate unit for planning purposes in particular circumstances or in a particular region. What does follow is that great care must always be taken to ensure that the ideologies, initial assumptions, and ultimate aims are clearly identified and that terms such as community and integration are clearly defined at the outset. This might appear self-evident and would, indeed, be unnecessary to state were it not for the confusion outlined above.

Moreover, this confusion frequently leads to questions concerning the planner's responsibility to the community, particularly in those circumstances where it appears as if a planning decision or a failure to initiate action lead to adverse effects on a particular settlement or locality. Examples that come to mind are the 'D Category' villages of County Durham and protests that are made regularly in many of our more remote rural areas against the failure to halt rural depopulation. The appropriate question here is, surely, whether the planner is responsible to the community or to society, or possibly to both at the same time. If one sees the community as a microcosm of society, or society as a collection of communities, then presumably some kind of joint responsibility may be possible. Some social scientists do take this standpoint.[13] If, on the other hand, one sees society as much more than a simple aggregate of communities, or as made up of a number of different kinds of social formations including the community, then at least it may be said that the planner has a much more complex and comprehensive task than that of dealing with local territorially based groupings.

Two factors are of particular significance here. The first is that concentration on community planning issues and problems may lead to solutions that are inconsistent with, or even possibly in conflict with, the ultimate well-being of society at large. Secondly, the town or country planner, engaged at either the local or the regional level, is essentially concerned with an activity that manifests itself in buildings and structures which may have a life of up to eighty years and in forms of land use that may last a great deal longer. It follows that the planner must, as far as possible, anticipate social and economic changes in order that the physical results of his policies will not become obsolete or redundant before they have come to the end of their economic life. To do this it is obviously necessary to consider likely future developments at the level of society as a whole and not merely at the local community level. To give a simple example, a major change in government subsidies to agriculture might well have profound effects upon the economic viability of large numbers of farming communities.

This brings us conveniently to the role of the sociologist in assessing policies for the future. It must be said at once that the social scientist has no greater armoury of devices for prediction than the planner: but whereas the planner is required by the logic of the decisions he makes to undertake some form of social and economic forecasting, most sociologists have been extremely reluctant to make predictions of any kind. What follows is, therefore, essentially speculative, is not based on well-tried techniques, and is intended solely to provide an example of the way in which the sociologist can play a part in the formulation of planning policies.

The present social structure of the remoter rural areas must be seen in the context of being part of one of the world's most urbanised countries, which is also highly industrialised and technologically advanced. Other broad background conditions to be taken into account are, *first*, that in agriculture the crucial factors affecting prosperity appear more and more to be size and good management. The trend towards larger farms, fewer farmers and workers, greater mechanisation, continuing technological advance and higher capital investment all militate against the small farmer and the hill farmer. There are perhaps as many as 35,000 small farmers in Britain, the majority of whom are poor;[14] moreover, since the decline in the agricultural labour force never appears to be rapid enough to keep pace with the proportionate fall in demand, earnings invariably compare unfavourably with industry and services.[15] The remoter rural areas are in the main more likely to be adversely placed in this situation than those near our towns and cities. *Second*, that the remoter rural areas have experienced more or less continuous net loss of population since the middle of the nineteenth century. *Third*, that social provision in the widest sense has developed only slowly in comparison with urban areas, so that it is realistic to think in terms of significant relative deprivation. *Fourth*, that the major changes which have taken place in our occupational structure during the century, e.g. a shift from manual to clerical work, particularly among men, and the entry of women into the labour force on a large scale, have been felt less in the isolated areas of the countryside than anywhere else.

In short, the remoter rural areas are in a relatively disadvantageous position and social trends pointing to the future can hardly give rise to optimism. Thus, despite the gloomy economic circumstances of the present, we are likely to become steadily more prosperous so that by the end of the century the average standard of living may be doubled, or even trebled.[16] At the same time, the proportions of wealth and income are likely to remain unequally distributed and the inequality may even increase. Meade, for example, argues forcefully that there is a basic conflict between economic efficiency and 'distributional justice'[17] a state of affairs that would not work to the benefit of rural areas.

Even more ominous are the ways in which these increased earnings are likely to be spent. The largest increases in consumer spending during this century have been in transport and entertainment, with significant increases also in domestic goods such as washing machines, refrigerators, etc., and in house-ownership. (These can be regarded as essentially characteristic of a middle-class style of life, although it would be mistaken to conclude from this that the class structure is changing in any significant way). These changes in the patterns of expenditure have coincided with an increasing concentration on the home—we are all familiar now with the idea of the 'home-centred' society, with each family gathered around the twenty-one-inch shrine in the living-room—and with a marked growth in leisure time. The 'standard working week' has fallen from sixty hours in the nineteenth century to forty-eight hours after the First World War, forty-four after the Second World War, forty-two in 1960 and forty today.[18] Predictions for the future envisage a four-day week of thirty hours, with longer annual holidays.

The transformations in living habits described above reinforce each other in a way that indicates clearly a series of external pressures upon all rural areas. As the home becomes more and more a centre of activity, so too does it become more likely that activities outside the home will tend to become more widespread geographically. Increased car ownership makes this possible and shorter working hours provide the time for it. The family car is in many ways a mobile home, to be followed by the caravan and finally the 'second home'. The latter are as yet relatively few in numbers, but increasing prosperity seems likely to bring marked growth. Moreover, this leisure time is being used very largely in recreational activities that require large areas of land or water—golf, sailing, riding, pony-trekking, walking, etc. With the expected increase in population, such areas will become increasingly scarce, particularly near towns and cities, so that open space, privacy, and quiet will be much sought after, even in the most remote rural localities. Relevant here is the role of mass media of communication, particularly television, and the growth in mass education. Together they have created new interests, widened social horizons and initiated a national culture which many see as a distinct threat to local and regional cultural groupings. A song of the First World War asked:

> 'How're you goin' to keep 'em down on the farm,
> After they've seen Paree?'

a city which is, so to speak, now available by turning a knob in one's own home. Again, the site of this conference is a clear reminder of this spread of interests.

Thus we arrive at the dilemma, complete with horns of a very pointed kind, which may face the 'truly rural' areas of Britain. If, on the one hand, they share in the increasing prosperity by providing for the leisure needs of a mass urban market, their traditional social structure and the locally based community as we now understand it seems certain to be transformed beyond recognition. If, on the other hand, they successfully resist such pressures, their agricultural base is such that they preserve their cultural and social identity in relative poverty and accept virtual isolation from the society at large.

This is, of course, to state the problem in its starkest form, and no account has been taken of a number of relevant factors—for example, the spread of industry into rural areas, the role of development agencies, etc. My purpose has been to show how the sociologist may play a part in indicating likely outcomes, to be taken into account in formulating policies. Sociology does not, in my view, provide the means of choosing one course of action, one horn of the dilemma, with confidence. Such means are provided by an ideology, not a sociology of rural life.

REFERENCES

1. *Report of the Committee on Land Utilisation in Rural Areas*, Command 6378, p. v, HMSO, 1942.
2. *Urbs in Rure*, L.S.E. Geographical Papers, No. 2, 1964.
3. 'Some Social Aspects of Recent Changes in Agriculture in West Cumberland', *Sociological Review, 1*, 1953.
4. HILLERY, GEORGE H., 'Definitions of Community: Areas of Agreement', *Rural Sociology, 20*, 1950.
5. KÖNIG, RENE, *The Community*, Routledge and Kegan Paul, p. 25, 1968.
6. BLYTHE, RONALD, *Akenfield, Portrait of an English Village*, Penguin Press, pp. 16–17, 1969.

7. See, for example, REISS, ALBERT J., 'A Review and Evaluation of Research on Community. A Working Memorandum prepared for the Committee on Social Behaviour of the Social Science Research Council', Nashville, Tenn., 1945, mimeographed.
8. GANS, H. J., 'Urbanism and Suburbanism as Ways of Life' in R. E. Pahl (Ed.), *Readings in Urban Sociology*, Pergamon, 1968.
9. LITTLEJOHN, JAMES, *Westrigg*, Routledge and Kegan Paul, p. 155, 1963.
10. See, for example, WILLIAMS, W. M., *A West Country Village: Ashworthy*, Routledge and Kegan Paul, 1963.
11. REES, ALWYN D., *Life in a Welsh Countryside*, University of Wales Press, 1951 and JENKINS, DAVID *et al.*, *Welsh Rural Communities*, University of Wales Press, 1960.
12. FRANKENBERG, RONALD, *Village on the Border*, Cohen and West, 1957.
13. See, for example, ARENSBERG, C. M. and KIMBALL, S. T., *Culture and Community*, Harcourt, Brace and World, Inc., 1965.
14. DONALDSON, J. G. S. and F. with BARBER, D., *Farming in Britain Today*, Penguin Press, p. 118, 1969.
15. McCRONE, GAVIN, *The Economics of Subsidising Agriculture*, Allen and Unwin, p. 26, 1962.
16. ABRAMS, MARK, 'Consumption in the Year 2000' in M. Young (Ed.), *Forecasting and the Social Sciences*, Heinemann, p. 37, 1968.
17. MEADE, J. E., *Efficiency, Equality and the Ownership of Property*, Allen and Unwin, 1964.
18. WILLMOTT, PETER, 'Some Social Trends' (forthcoming), p. 19, I am much indebted to this paper for its analyses of likely future changes.

12 | *Comprehensive Development*

PROFESSOR D. G. ROBINSON, B.A., M.T.P.I.
Department of Town and Country Planning,
University of Manchester

Comprehensive development as a policy approach in remoter rural areas implies an accent on change rather than preservation. It involves study of the capacity of these areas to meet the needs of both their own inhabitants and external urban populations. This assessment of the vocation (a term coined by Czechoslovakian planners) of the various parts of a remote area presupposes a real attempt to enable its land and people to play an effective part in national life.

Narrow traditionalism and the perpetuation of anachronistic features of the economy and settlement pattern are inimical to a development approach. But adjustment to capacity and vocation will involve a conservation background to policy formation. Policies should look to the best long-term use and management of resources. New approaches should not ride roughshod over the culture and human characteristics of an area but rather enlist and encourage regional consciousness so that it becomes a dynamic and distinctive force for self-help, growth and development, and yet also provides a safeguard for sympathetic treatment of the area's human and land resources. The Greeks called a man who did not participate in the affairs of the community an 'idiot'. It would be idiotic for the inhabitants of our remoter districts to contract out of national life. I am sure they have no desire to do so if opportunities for effective involvement are seen to exist. We must recognise that tensions will arise from the conflict between the desire to accept change because it will lead to an increase in prosperity, and the inclination to resist it because of disruption to long-established patterns of rural life. Whilst the first mood provides the life force, the second should not be regarded as being wholly negative. Metropolitan influences reach to some degree to the farthest parts of our remoter areas. Although it is both desirable and inevitable that countrymen become more metropolitan, sophisticated, and even cosmopolitan in outlook, one would hope that they will retain an innate sense of conservation. We cannot safeguard all the best features of natural and semi-natural environment on a reserve basis. Much will depend on wise management by countryside users. The lion's share of responsibility for protecting the character of the countryside will rest with countrymen, although their effort must be complemented by a better education in environmental matters for the townspeople who will visit the remote areas in increasing numbers.

Comprehensive development is a difficult term. It is a description which alienates as much as it attracts. To some ears it may have an authoritarian ring, raising fears about the degree of control implied by such an apparently all-pervasive activity. Comprehensive development appears to claim the obviously unattainable. No development programme can be completely comprehensive and it would be an unrewarding exercise to try and make it so. What is required, in my view, in all areas, remote or otherwise, is a much greater degree of integration in the preparation and implementation of key social, economic, and land-use policies. Such policies ought to be serving a common objective, politically agreed and socially supported. The agreement on overall goals to which all planned development in a remoter area should relate should be made explicit in a broad strategic policy or plan. Without such guidelines the various public agencies and major private organisations concerned with different aspects of change tend to remain separate in their thinking and their work lacks a concerted impact.

Interrelationship appears to me to be the most important concept underlying comprehensive development. This applies not only to the activities and programmes within the remoter area but also to the area's connections with metropolitan and urbanised parts of the country. We should not lose sight of the interdependence in reality of matters which we presently choose to treat separately for ease of organisation. Rural problems are not separable from urban. This view is summarised neatly in the concept of the rural–urban continuum, developed in sociological literature but capable of a more general application.

Within the rural area we need to give greater organisational recognition to the fact that all activities form part of an area system. They interact, supporting and serving each other, complementing and conflicting. The combined effect provides the quality and quantity of life in the rural area. One of the strategic goals for a backward area will surely be to ensure that plans have a concerted impact which produces as wide a range of opportunities and as good a standard of living as possible for the inhabitants. A growth of understanding of the importance of relationships between sectoral development programmes is shown by the number of recent regional and sub-regional studies in Britain which have been organised as multi-disciplinary efforts. The results of these collaborations have often been less successful than might have been hoped. Their shortcomings can often be traced to a lack of agreement on common strategic goals. Without such agreement it is difficult for the participants to develop a sense of common purpose, a feeling of collective responsibility, and a concern for relationships.

Comprehensive development is an approach which emphasises combined effects and tries to ensure that activities are planned with interaction in mind, so that they work together to further overall objectives. This goes beyond *post facto* co-ordination of sectoral plans—plans to which agencies are already largely committed and which have been prepared separately within a strictly limited outlook. Many such plans are incapable of co-ordination and attempts in this direction can rarely achieve comprehensive development. At present the various planning initiatives in the areas with which we are concerned do tend to concentrate in isolation on appropriate levels of investment for particular development programmes (e.g. more beef production, more fishing, more tourism, more industry, more concentration of settlement). The programmes often work on different time cycles, moving to different target dates. Some programmes are undertaken simply because external funds are available and may be largely superfluous to the area's real needs. Other vitally needed programmes may be missing. There is a tendency to 'discover' problems whose existence has been known for years, and to deal with them *ad hoc*, as if they were completely new and immediately solvable. Often the results of 'blitz' programmes of this type are predictably disappointing, because they lack an understanding based on adequate research and are unrelated to a wider planning context. It is evident that in many cases better groundwork in the past would have enabled better programmes now. By the same token, better groundwork now, with a wide based investigation of resources and study of related possibilities of action, will enable better programmes in the future. There is need for more attention to where sectoral developments should occur in a rural area, so that they can be planned to interact with each other in servicing the local community and the other persons using the area. The level of attack that I am advocating is strategic. If cognizance of interaction and contribution to overall development aims is an integral part of a major sectoral policy, sympathetic interpretation in detailed policy and management can remain the prime responsibility of the sectoral agency concerned. Thus far we have stuck to the term 'comprehensive development'; perhaps the process could be described equally well, and less provocatively, as 'regional planning'.

A look at the number of agencies which may be concerned with remoter areas highlights the need or a strategic overview and purpose. They can be categorised broadly according to their responsibilities as follows, although the list is by no means exhaustive:

1. strategic economic development planning—practised at present by such bodies as the Highlands and Islands Development Board (executive powers) and the Regional Economic Planning Councils (no executive powers);
2. planning of public investment programme for rural areas (different bodies responsible for different sectors, e.g. Ministry of Agriculture, Forestry Commission, Ministry of Transport, British Rail, British Waterways Board, Local Authorities, Tourist Boards, Water Boards, Electricity Boards, Development Commission, etc.);
3. planning for social, economic and land use adjustment for a limited range of production sectors (Rural Development Boards, Crofters Commission);
4. physical planning (Local Planning Authorities, including National Park Boards; Countryside Commissions);
5. Nature Conservation (Nature Conservancy);
6. Major private investment programmes (e.g. country land owners; tourism, industrial, or mineral working entrepreneurs, etc.).

At present no single agency can take the responsibility for a combined attack—planning for production, settlement, and amenity as one operation. The Highlands and Islands Development Board has powers which enable it to go some of the way towards meeting this deficiency and it has become a catalyst for comprehensive development. It is able to represent Highland needs in discussions on national development and to bridge some of the gaps which are left between the activities of existing agencies. The Board is empowered to advise the Secretary of State on questions of Government, investment in the Highlands and to undertake resource investigations.[1] But it operates alongside the existing organisations, neither replacing them nor directly controlling their activities and planning.

Other remoter areas of the country have no machinery comparable with that established by the Highlands and Islands Development Act. It might be argued that it is unnecessary to extend the overall development agency approach to other areas because regulative legislation can give an adequate degree of direction to the processes of countryside change. We can use legislation to give incentives to individuals or existing agencies to adopt a wider approach (e.g. the recent addition of recreational aspects to the Forestry Commission's role, or the suggestion of financial incentives to encourage farmers and landowners to allow multiple use of their land under management agreements).[2] We can alter the legislation under which sectoral agencies work to allow them to take into account the social costs and benefits of their actions. Penalties and constraints can be imposed on land users if side effects of their activities damage other interests. Legislation could be used to require specialist agencies to employ a wider range of technical assistance and thereby broaden the scope of their programmes. It would be possible to require the various agencies to advertise all their major development proposals and give a right of appeal to the public. These regulatory devices and incentives would be worthwhile, but they would not go to the heart of the problem. It would still be difficult for individual organisations to establish what their wider objectives should be. In cases of conflict, the agency with the best staffing and best-researched case would still have a big advantage. *Ad hoc* legislative initiatives would not ensure concerted rural development programmes and the best use of area resources.

The appropriate form for the *overall development agency* will vary according to the needs of particular areas. Some of the problems which the Highlands and Islands Development Board is tackling are peculiar to their region, as are some of the agencies with which they collaborate. The Board does not necessarily provide a precedent which could be followed in all the remoter parts of Britain. It is possible, however, to specify certain characteristics which any *rural comprehensive development agency* should possess:

 1. it should operate over an area of *regional* scale. Rural systems now function over wide areas. This is true whether one looks at the functioning of rural settlement patterns; recreation,

with its scenic-driving 'circuits' and the use of widely spaced attractions during a single recreational visit; agriculture with its linkage of upland and lowland systems; industries with their requirements for large catchment areas for labour and rural raw materials; or forestry, with the economies of scale to be derived from 'forest regions'. Demands and resources can be better equated over a larger area. The region's variety of habitats can be conserved and developed: different parts of the area can be planned for multiple use or single use as necessary according to basic resources. All parts of the region must be carefully articulated, both one to another and to surrounding urbanised systems. Parochial views may dominate if comprehensive planning is attempted only for small areas to the neglect of the regional level of attack. This could lead to over-use of the natural resources of the region in some areas and under-use in others. This is not to deny the need for the strengthening of local government in the countryside with a new pattern based on *town-country units*. But it is difficult to judge the validity of local claims on scarce land, landscape, and public capital investment resources without a regional overview. It is doubtful, too, whether the appropriate technical and financial support could be mustered for a large number of comprehensive development projects covering only small areas. Such an approach would make it difficult to marshal an effective regional case in inter-regional negotiations at national level. The remoter region always stands in danger of neglect from the centre: it must speak with one voice if its claims are to be heard.

2. its concern should be to see that the *economic, social and physical planning* of the region is treated as a combined operation. Strategic guide-lines correlating this wide range of values should be formulated for political adoption. The strategy should demonstrate how the policy for the broad pattern of future settlement and land use is to be buttressed by related programmes of major public and private investment. Other aspects of economic and social development policy should also be aligned to the major strategy, e.g. financial inducements for industrial location, re-training grants, agricultural adjustment measures. The keynote of

the agency's work will be integration rather than co-ordination.

3. the agency should be *innovative* in outlook. Its research and intelligence role will enable it to become the focus for new initiatives. Its concern should be with what *should happen*, rather than with trend indications of what is likely to happen if no intervention is made. Research efforts would seek to identify critical areas of policy where small changes could be expected to produce desirable adjustments in many other parts of the system.

4. it should have the power to *intervene*. Its status in the political system should be such that it has an effective influence over the disposition of major public and private investments, both within the region and in closely connected peripheral areas. It should have its own executive powers and budget. These would be available to bridge gaps in the pattern of existing agency services, and could be used to augment existing programmes where necessary.

5. its role should be continuing and *long term*. Time is needed for consensus to emerge. Programmes of the sort we are discussing must be sustained over a long period to achieve significant results. Patience will be needed to overcome resistance to new initiatives and demonstrate the validity of new ideas.

6. an *indigenous* agency is required. Planning at a distance is not likely to be successful—the possibilities of alienation, misinformation and misinterpretation are too great. The *Tennessee Valley Authority* was the first regional development project for a resource area. One of its aims was to achieve a better relationship of the work of federal agencies by bringing their representatives together 'nearer the ground' than Washington. The results of T.V.A. intelligence work are available to the region in the region. Their experience is that if the planning centre is in the region rather than outside, there are greater possibilities of integrating national and local planning and stimulating local private initiative.

Other chapters of this book discuss the work of regional develop-ment agencies in Britain and abroad on the type of organisation which best fits the needs of comprehensive development. In time our present regional machinery may be given more substance, either in

the form of a Minister in each region, serviced by a regional economic and physical planning office and administering a regional
budget or with regional governments having wide responsibilities
for physical and transport planning, economic development, and
social services. In either event comprehensive planning for remoter
areas would be a regional responsibility, probably best discharged
by locating special sub-units of the regional planning office in the
areas concerned.

I have mentioned some of the technical and professional problems
inherent in a comprehensive approach. They deserve a little more
exploration. A multitude of agencies, organisations, individuals,
and technical and professional disciplines are involved in countryside
planning and development. At present the training and education
programmes of the separate disciplines do not give sufficient attention to the possibilities of comprehensive planning, nor to the way
in which the work of one discipline can relate to the work of others
to mutual advantage. Greater awareness of the possibilities in
comprehensive planning is as important a prerequisite for comprehensive development as any modification of present administrative
arrangements. Physical planners can play an important part in the
work of a comprehensive development agency because their type of
training emphasises an integrative approach. They will make an
even more effective contribution to comprehensive projects as
planning education develops and places greater emphasis on the
practical problems faced by the countryside interests and on the
principles of resource conservation and economic development.
Many of the other disciplines and sectoral specialists who would
work in the agency, or in collaboration with it, in devising strategic
policies have been castigated thus far in this chapter for their
limited, single sector outlook. In fairness it should be stated that
they are not always blind to other considerations, but are usually
encouraged by their training and required by their brief to concentrate on their main purpose. In comprehensive planning work a
broader approach is necessary, enabling all the specialists to gain
a common understanding of the main problems of the area. The
specialists need to be able to communicate effectively with their
fellows and to know how they can contribute their own skills to the
combined planning effort. At certain points of the planning process
it is likely that several agencies will be collaborating. For this
collaboration to be effective it is necessary for the participants to

have a sense of corporate responsibility for the affairs of the region as a whole, as well as retaining their interest in the affairs of their own agency.

Convening a multi-disciplinary group does not of itself guarantee a reasoned consideration of all aspects of regional policy. Working arrangements are needed which prevent the opinion of an expert on his field from being suppressed. Sensible policy decisions will not always emerge from a majority vote.[3] It is a real problem to ensure that the strategic policy which does emerge represents something more positive than the weary outcome of horse trading and bargaining. The sectoral participants must be willing to accept restraints on the unfettered development of their future activities in the knowledge that other sectors are being planned to support and complement their work, and that no one is being forced to go 'out on a limb'. They must be prepared to consider modifying their management aims and practices and be willing to plan for the multiple use of land where this is appropriate in the wider interest. Balanced-decision making will depend on a sympathetic attitude of mind from all the interested parties.

The details of policies required in remoter areas are dealt with in other chapters. It remains for me to touch on some of the base-work which must underlie a comprehensive approach. Important requirements would include:

1. a comprehensive inventory of the resources of the area concerned, the utility of each resource being classified with a wide variety of purposes in mind. Attention would be paid to the capacity of land resources to sustain particular levels of use and population in an evolving technological situation. Adjustment of population levels to the capacity of the resources may involve the encouragement of outward migration or the regrouping of settlement;

2. information on the demands on land and human resources in the area; on social pressures and trends; and on minimum threshold levels for the successful operation of services and activities. Detailed studies of potential supply and demand relations are of crucial importance in determining the 'vocation' and potential specialised function of each part of the area. The demands on the resources of rural areas are largely externally generated and demand studies must therefore extend to the adjoining urban areas, and sometimes to

the national market as a whole. It may follow that it is desirable to concentrate some of the investment effort outside the region in adjoining urban areas in order to increase the demand for the rural area's products and enlarge the work and cultural opportunities for its inhabitants;

3. a continuing research and intelligence programme and a wide diffusion of information on the resources, potential, present uses and demands on the area;

4. a mechanism for monitoring and reviewing the achievement of comprehensive development aims;

5. public access to at least one centre in the area at which up-to-date strategic and detailed plans are displayed and policies explained. Such a centre will provide information to the public on which they may react and participate constructively, and private individuals may see the broad pattern into which their own development proposals and management plans can fit.

No development effort will succeed unless it is able to generate popular support. To do this it must be able to show the people that there are going to be new opportunities and that the area is no longer to be allowed to stagnate or sink into decline. There must be evidence of action as well as of planning. It is not so much the explanation of a blue-print which is required at the regional 'ops room' as some indication of how the local people can take part in the process of getting things done. This is the best way to educate them to be future-orientated. The American planner Edmund Bacon remarked that 'we are in danger of losing one of the most important concepts of mankind, that the future is what we make it'.[4] He said this of the design of cities, but the sentiment is equally applicable to our remoter rural areas.

REFERENCES

1. Highlands and Islands Development (Scotland) Acts, 1965 and 1968.
2. HOOKWAY, R. J. S., *The Management of Britain's Rural Land*, Report of Proceedings, Town and Country Planning Summer School, 1967.
3. BASART, A. H. M., *Approche universelle et multi-disciplinaire des problèmes de santé physique, mentale et sociale en relation avec le logement et l'aménagement urbain et rural*, Paper presented to International Congress of the International Federation for Housing and Planning, Dublin, 1969.
4. BACON, E. N., *Design of Cities*, Thames and Hudson, 1967.

13 | Policy Objectives: An Administrator's Point of View

A. A. HUGHES
Under Secretary,
Scottish Development Department*

An administrator might be expected to look at policy problems from a point of view rather different from those of professional experts. It may be useful, therefore, to outline the role of the administrator in a Government Department concerned with development and to go on to describe the machinery of Government for which he has some responsibility. These subjects are outlined in the earlier parts of this chapter which then proceeds to deal with the basic problems confronting an administrator and his methods for attempting to solve them.

The role of the administrator might be described as implying a duty to secure the effective implementation of Government policy in a particular area of activity within the climate of opinion of the time and within the financial resources available for the purpose. The administrator's colleagues and advisers, whether official or unofficial, and the groups of people who are interested, are together concerned to identify the problems and to ensure that all facets receive proper consideration. The function of the administrator in the last analysis is to reconcile the emerging conflicts and, within the general policy of his Minister, to get such action taken as is possible —action which is not the lowest common denominator of compromise but is capable of reasonable acceptance by the people most affected.

This could sound like a bloodless function. It is not, least of all when the subject is the future of the remoter areas. It is the function of the administrator to resolve the problems in his area of responsibility with sympathy and understanding of the interests which are being subjected to change. The difficulty of the remoter areas may be to stop short of emotional involvement.

* Now Managing Director, Crudens Ltd.

225

It is the continuous paradox for the administrator that, although the strongest voices are heard demanding action for change in general, these same voices are also frequently heard resisting action in particular. The acceptance of real change is more difficult for most people than the recognition of the need for action, and action is frequently interpreted simply as more activity of the kind that already exists and is, therefore, acceptable. The reality is different. The major problems can frequently only be solved by radical change.

MACHINERY OF GOVERNMENT

It may be useful to recollect some of the machinery which exists to enable the general planning in the remoter areas to be co-ordinated.

(a) Planning rests for the moment substantially on the Town and Country Planning Acts of 1946 and 1947. A chain of responsibility from Ministers to the local planning authorities enables positive action to be taken to create the framework and the climate in which community, industrial, and recreational development can take place. The planning resources have always been stronger in town than country, partly because the financial resources of the towns are better and partly, one might think, because the ambitious rural authorities have not seen their limited developments as a cause for concern—requiring the same kind of long-term analysis and preparation. To this extent they are often not ready for the dramatic arrival of major industry and have not sufficiently prepared their citizens for what is involved by way of change.

(b) The Development Commission has the statutory duty to consider and to report to the Treasury upon all applications for advances from the Development Fund established by Part 1 of the Development and Road Improvement Funds Act, 1909. The Commission's main interest is now in rural development and its assistance is directed in two main directions. It grant-aids the Small Industries Council for Rural Areas of Scotland and the Council for Small Industries in the Rural Areas, in England and Wales. It assists local authorities by providing some finance for joint Development Committees. It also seeks to maintain cohesion and the community spirit of the countryside by grant-aiding Councils of Social Service.

(c) The Countryside Commissions have the duty to develop and improve the facilities for the enjoyment of the countryside and to conserve and enhance its natural beauty. These Commissions have been fairly recently established and they have a wide ranging remit to foster opportunities for recreational opportunities in the countryside. At the same time they have a kind of watchdog role in relation to developments in the countryside generally and may express their views to Ministers on any such proposals.

(d) The Tourist Boards which will be created by the Bill now before Parliament have the duty to enlarge tourist traffic in Great Britain as a whole and in the separate countries. They will be referred to again later in this chapter.

(e) The Highlands and Islands Development Board has the duty to prepare, concert, promote, assist and undertake measures for the economic and social development of the Highlands and Islands and they too have wide ranging powers to achieve their objectives in terms of industry, tourism and agriculture.

These bodies are effectively linked to their respective Government Departments who have the responsibility for ensuring that their activities form part of a coherent policy.

The Forestry Commission, the Nature Conservancy and the Red Deer Commissions all have important parts to play in the remoter areas, and there are, of course, many other agencies and private bodies with a direct interest in the separate elements of action, conservation and community life in these areas. Our hope now is that we are gradually creating the machinery of government which will provide a forum in which proposals and difficulties can be comprehensively considered.

It may be argued that there are too many interests and, in particular, too many statutory agencies with overlapping responsibilities. There is point in this criticism and one might forecast that some years hence, when these activities have generated much greater momentum, some legislative action will be desirable to harness them in larger groupings than now. But we should be cautious about the desirability of establishing some kind of unitary authority responsible for the preparation of truly comprehensive plans dealing with all aspects of the problems of particular areas. Ideally, perhaps, plans of this kind should exist but frequently experience tends to show that such plans take an unconscionable time to produce and they are in danger of being overtaken by the march of events while in preparation. More important, perhaps, they become the subject of so much discussion and consultation, that the will to action is eroded. In a period when it is still easily possible to define separate spheres where energetic thinking is required, there is some merit in creating small units dedicated to their particular field.

Administration has been described as the taking of decisions on inadequate information. This was not a cynical observation. The businessman's hunch, the administrator's decision, is often required to let the action proceed and prevent it becoming bogged down in an endless search for information. If the basic information is available, if the decision is taken with understanding and sympathy for the subject, then there may be some chance that the decision will also be right.

SOME BASIC PROBLEMS

Industry
In considering some of the basic problems confronting the administrator in relation to the remoter areas, it may be convenient to use three examples of rural planning in Scotland which help to identify them. The Highlands and Islands, the Borders, the Clyde Estuary have all recently been the subject of intensive study. In their nature they are very disparate situations which throw up some singular and some common problems. They have the common factor of population problems, albeit ranging from the need to stop the drift outwards by attracting industry, to the need to move population in to support the industry which wishes to establish itself. In each, the industry will have to be established in lovely areas and there will be the problem of displacing farmers. In one there will be the need to sacrifice recreational opportunities. In some instances the industries themselves will be unpopular because of the nature of their activities.

These are the self-evident difficulties. The initial brief to the administrator is crystal clear. In a country like Scotland the changing pattern of the older industries involves great human problems of displacement and new opportunities for employment. In the remoter areas change, the lack of earning capacity, and the lack of diversified employment opportunity for families cause a steady drain of population. In these circumstances, the urgent demand on Government is to organise the change, to create new opportunities, and to stem the flow from those great rural areas which are seen by many as essential to the stability of a modern society. It would not be surprising if the administrator was instructed as his first task to create the circumstances in which action can be taken by those who have the energy and the capacity to take it, to create the basis on which any society must live and grow—satisfactory employment opportunities in viable enterprises. This cannot be an instruction to encourage all development, regardless of its effects. Local and national interests involve many complex factors. In any local situation attention must be paid to what may be called the 'existing mosaic of living'. In the national sense we must have great regard for the heritage of our people, our attraction as a tourist country, and our way of life. But always the society must live and grow or the rest has no meaning, except as a museum piece.

Perhaps the most acute dilemma at present is the conflicting demands on agricultural land. All new developments whether in housing, recreation or industry seem to be voracious in their demands for agricultural land of high quality. Sometimes it must almost seem to the agricultural community that developers are wilfully dedicated to using high quality farming land instead of less useful open space. Is this as surprising as might be thought? Is it, perhaps, also true that the very factors which have led farming communities to establish themselves in particular places that seemed good to live in, and then to plough and nourish the soil over the centuries, are the very same factors which lead developers to these places for new forms of activity? Attraction for workpeople, accessibility to centres of population, availability of water from the hills or the sea, equable climate, are also much sought after by modern developers.

How do you arrive at a policy which, in a modern society, desperate almost for new and additional forms of activity, can identify the true long-term balance between agriculture and development? In terms of employment potential, agriculture is to a large extent the victim of its own increasing mechanisation and efficiency, requiring fewer and fewer people, and contributing to the very problem of depopulation in the remoter areas. Major industry capable of being established in the remoter areas is almost by definition a massive user of flat land. While such industry may employ far less people per acre of land required than smaller labour-intensive technological industry, the numbers are, nevertheless, many times what would be involved in the same acreage used for agriculture. The hope also is that these major industries will attract satellite industries which will provide a range of occupations suitable to family units and thereby create viable and stable communities. Most planners are nervous now about the arrival of a single major industry without satellites because of the second generation employment problem. Planned concentration to the point at which all available labour can be absorbed is the goal, but this has its effects in major demands for land in some areas.

The policy of concentration also leads one to ask one of the most difficult questions about the future of the population in the remoter areas. If it is now correctly recognised that stability can only be achieved by a measure of concentration and selection, even that policy is one that demands a great deal of promotion and steering of activity. It is a policy, too, which requires a great deal of financial support in many forms, the social services, the investment grants, the infrastructure costs for houses, roads and schools. There is a tendency now to bring undue harassment to bear on the policy with the demands for support for many places which feel they are faced with a question of survival. How far can we dissipate our energies and our resources without finishing up in a generally unsatisfactory situation? What is the price that can be paid to achieve our objectives in the remoter areas? How far are they prepared to co-operate in some rationalisation of the existing communities?

Tourism
The wider aspects of tourism have been fully dealt with in a separate chapter on this subject. It may, however, be relevant to deal in this particular chapter with the question of the administrative structure required and now being developed for the growth of tourism.

There is increasing recognition that the combined factors of increasing affluence, increasing education, and increased leisure time inevitably lead to a massive increase in holiday taking, whether for short or longer periods. These factors are at work in many countries so that we may expect to have to deal with an enormous increase of activity on the part of the citizens of Britain and with a rapidly rising number of tourists from other countries. The recognition of the economic importance of this activity always comes more slowly in countries which are basically industrial than in others where reliance on tourism is fundamental to the operation of any kind of viable economy. There are many parts of Britain, however, where tourism is as vital to the economy as it is in any other country. Inevitably the remoter areas have come to rely, and will increasingly rely, on tourism, as a very important prop in their local economies.

It was for these reasons that the Government decided to establish a new machinery within Government to enable tourism to be promoted in a more effective way than had been done in the past. The Development of Tourism Bill now before Parliament provides for the creation of new statutory tourist organisations for Britain as a whole (overseas promotion, etc.) and separate tourist boards for England, Scotland and Wales. These boards will have the necessary powers to promote, co-ordinate and assist the tourist industry. Because of the diffuse nature of the industry it will not be possible for these boards to operate effectively without also creating effective regional tourist organisations and local organisations to assist them with their task. The whole operation is seen as one involving a new and more effective dialogue between the statutory organisations, the Government Departments responsible for the infrastructure on which tourism must develop, and the commercial interests who create the amenities and the services on which tourists must rely. The Tourist Bill has been generally welcomed and given the co-operation of all concerned; there seems no reason why Britain as a whole and each of the separate countries should not now make a very significant advance in bringing the economic benefits of tourism in larger measure to the country, and specifically to the remoter areas of Britain.

The same problem of the duality of welcome and resistance will no doubt appear in a number of places. The pressures of tourism are sometimes as unwelcome to those who love particular areas as are any other kinds of industrial development. Everybody concerned with genuine tourism and the countryside must wish to preserve the amenity and the loveliness of the countryside, the historic buildings, the charm of the villages, and all the other things which make for the growth of tourism. At the same time, if the pressures are to be met, if the customers are to be attracted, then there must be significant growth of access to the countryside and of recreational facilities of all kinds both for day and night tourism. In so far as we are able to plan effectively to concentrate growth in particular places, we will at one and the same time make multi-purpose activity which is attractive to all age groups and we will prevent the sporadic spoiling of the countryside. Almost certainly, however, some of these concentrations will, in the view of many people, destroy the quietness that has previously existed there. There are many examples of this kind of development. Once again the question will be one of balance. If, however, it is part of the aim to provide development which is viable in an economic and commercial sense, which is acceptable to the majority of the visitors, then this is the theme which must dominate the approach. The genius which we may hope to find in our planners is to reconcile this theme with the conservation of all that makes tourism truly attractive.

Perhaps, too, we shall need some changes of attitudes in the remoter areas. It is very understandable that people who have for generations made their living by the soil, or the sea, or the hill, should be somewhat dubious about taking to new forms of work which involve the demands of tourists with outlandish standards and demands. But it would be very wrong to connive at a comparison of these traditional and new forms of work which suggested that one of them is somehow less worthy of good people. The outlandish habits and demands of strangers may in themselves help to bridge the gap of change and lead to a pride in standards of planning, amenity, and care for the remote places which would be of great value and which has not always been a feature of this people. The Highlands and Islands Development Board, for example, has already set its hand very forcefully to the bringing of the economic and other benefits of tourism to the Highlands and may have set a pattern already in showing what is possible when effective agencies and resources can be brought together in the remoter areas.

Planning inquiries
When major industrial events are forecast for rural areas, all those who are concerned to have the issues involved properly ventilated and discussed are given an opportunity to do so under planning legislation at a public enquiry. In a democratic society this machinery has a vital part to play in the proper discussion of issues which may have considerable importance and marked long-term effects on local communities. The machinery is fortunately much used—fortunately,

because planners and administrators alike are constantly reminded of the strength of local democracy and of the enduring interest of people in the character of the areas in which they live.

There is some doubt, however, whether the present enquiry machinery is serving its true purpose. The very nature of public enquiries tends to set a scene in which the opponents of development present their case elaborately and vigorously while the case for the proposal, on whose outcome many people in the area may depend, may have to be presented in the nature of things in a defensive way. The national interest in the proposals as part of a great scheme of change is not often argued as such and there may be a tendency, to put it no higher, for the narrower interests in a local situation to dominate the possible outcome. In a national issue some of these difficulties may be overcome when, in appropriate cases, the new *Commissions of Inquiry* provided in the new Planning Bill are used.

SUMMARY

Two of the main objectives that face an administrator concerned with development in dealing with the problems of the remoter areas are:

(*a*) to assist in the achievement of viable economic activity which will provide diversified employment opportunity for whole communities;

(*b*) to increase the opportunity for people in a modern industrial society to enjoy the recreational potential of the remoter areas, and to do these things within a framework, wherever possible, of conservation of the natural heritage and the natural landscape beauty of the different areas.

The difficulties which national policies of this kind may produce when they come to be applied to particular localities have been emphasised in this chapter which also suggests that the people in the remoter areas must decide for themselves whether they accept the objectives and, therefore, the implications. Their case may be weakened by appearing to demand that all the existing communities, however small, should be supported and provided with the facilities of modern infrastructure. The policies themselves seem to be possible of achievement only by selection and concentration and it is necessary for the case to be put in terms which recognise the social and economic facts of the situation.

There is immense interest in the remoter areas and great public sympathy for their difficulties. The machinery of Government designed to enable these problems to be considered and dealt with is elaborate. The opportunity should now be taken to sharpen and define the thinking about realist solutions.

Postscript

THE EDITORS*

The introduction to this symposium sets the stage for three scenes which reveal, in turn, the economic and social framework of the remoter rural areas, some of the attempts that are being made to solve their problems, and the targets to aim at if a drama, which initially shows signs of developing into a tragedy, is to end reasonably happily. It is now the task of the editors to sum up the main points in the twelve chapters and to indicate the lessons which came out of the Conference itself.

The four chapters on the economic and social framework describe the role of agriculture, forestry, manufacturing industry and tourism in the economy of the remote areas. Some of them, notably agriculture, are declining in terms of the employment they offer, with the result that most attempts to reverse the drift from the remoter rural areas will have to depend on the development of manufactures or tourism. In certain localities the growth of fisheries has helped to maintain the rural population, and it was suggested in discussion that this industry should have received more attention in the Conference.

The unit of planning was taken to be the region, but the chapters in Part II show that this is a very flexible term. The region covered by the Highlands and Islands Development Board is nearly half of Scotland, whereas the Rural Development Board which had been proposed for mid-Wales represented scarcely one-sixth of the area of the Principality. The chapter on the Mid-Wales Industrial Development Association confines itself to a description of the industries it is fostering (though the Association acknowledges that in practice industrial development is inextricably linked with general development). In contrast, the Highlands and Islands Development Board deals with all kinds of traditional activities such as agriculture, horticulture, forestry and fishing, as well as fostering new enterprises, especially in tourism and manufacturing.

* The Editors regret the amount of time that has elapsed between the date of the Conference and the publication of this volume.

The many-sided activities of the H.I.D.B., described in Chapter 7, draw attention to the importance of integration in planning. This subject was given prominence at the Conference in several papers, as well as by speakers from the floor. Few developments in the countryside can take place without influencing other features of it. For example, forestry is not merely the use of land for the production of timber: the roads that must be constructed for it can be of use to neighbouring farms, and the forests themselves can add, but not always, to the amenities of the countryside in general and the enjoyment of tourists in particular. Moreover, work in the forest may be available to farm workers in situations where it is possible to make the two activities complementary. Tourism can assist the small farm to remain viable if the farmer and his wife are prepared to accommodate holidaymakers. But the opening up of the countryside also increases the hazards to which farms and forests are exposed by thoughtlessness and ignorance, and sometimes by vandalism, on the part of those who do not possess the countryman's appreciation of the behaviour that it is necessary to observe if the hills and dales are to be enjoyed without damage. And the advantages of integration are sometimes dissipated by the competition which is another feature of the many uses to which the countryside may be put—competition between farming and forestry for land and labour, the devastation of areas of outstanding beauty if industry or mining is introduced into them unscrupulously, and the undermining of the health of crops or livestock by the uncontrolled waste products of industry.

Part III reveals the attention that was paid by the Conference to Policy Objectives. While attention was directed to the *ad hoc* ways in which the state already offers assistance, emphasis was placed on the importance of integration in planning: the difference between integrating the many activities that are part of planning, and co-ordinating sectoral plans *post facto* was stressed in several papers. But the interdependence of disciplines implied by this outlook carries with it the need for subordination of individual interests. This requires more restraint than is always apparent amongst planners who have been trained to regard their own subject as paramount; and some criticism was levelled at systems of training which are content to turn out future professional staff with such parochial viewpoints.

The interdependence of town and country was emphasised.

Traditionally countryfolk have raised their living standards above subsistence level by selling their surplus food to the towns. Food prices are nowadays too low for farmers to continue to do this satisfactorily, and not even government subsidies have stemmed the drift of the young people away from the land. Those that remain have become more dependent on the towns—for their business requirements as well as their market outlets, and such less tangible amenities as education and entertainment.

At the same time increasing affluence and mobility have made it possible for the town dwellers to take advantage of the recreational benefits which the countryside offers them. But to do this satisfactorily the countryside must prepare for its visitors by the provision of adequate facilities—roads suitable for the increased traffic, parking and picnic spaces, shops, accommodation and other conveniences. All these will be required to meet the needs of an increasingly mobile and affluent urban population which inevitably will wish to take advantage of the rural areas for recreation. For the problem is not simply one of improving the situation that exists today: conditions are not static, and if the present trend continues the depopulation of the countryside in the remoter areas will reach the stage where it will no longer be possible to justify the expense of maintaining the minimum amenities just for those who continue to reside there. But if the countryside itself, and not simply its produce, is to be shared with the town dwellers then its future organisation must take into consideration the requirements of its urban visitors as well as its permanent residents. Here are grounds for supporting reorganisation of local government on such lines as the Redcliffe Maud Report proposed for integrating town and country—in spite of the reluctance which rural councils not surprisingly exhibit at agreeing to anything which appears to undermine their authority. Their prejudice is fostered by the bias towards the city outlook that so many planners have developed through their training, and by the advantages the towns often possess for attracting many of the most competent officials. Particular attention is paid to these points in Chapters 11 and 13.

The complexity and urgency of the many problems of remote areas was apparent to all participants at the Conference and will be to the readers of this volume. The basic problem however stemmed from the potential conflict of interest between different groups and the difficulty of devising solutions that are reasonably equitable to all those concerned. At any point in the process of rapid social and economic change, which invariably implies major technological innovations, some individuals or groups get hurt or left behind in the process. On the other hand, some groups manage to avoid or delay the impact of these forces because political organisation tends to be defensive, even though this defensiveness may limit the response to new challenges. And that in brief is what has been happening in the remoter rural areas. Hence, in terms of traditional economic activity the rural areas as a social entity decline because modern technology allows farming to proceed with greatly reduced, and reducing, amounts of hired labour. Indeed, all the signs are that farmers themselves, at least the smaller among them, will also decline in number in the years ahead. At the same time, forestry has not yielded the employment opportunities that were once envisaged for it. The new feature, however, has been the quickening of interest in these areas by the urban population which has already been noted.

Thus with local population in decline and national standards of social provision increasing, the remoter rural areas face special problems unless new and long-term employment opportunities emerge. So far the economic viability of rural industrialisation, even with preferential support from the government, is far from certain.

These special problems arise because the areas are changing their identity even more rapidly than hitherto. The trouble is that, while their old identity is disappearing, their new role is a long while in taking shape. It is not without significance that the recent enquiries and continuing debate about the organisation of local government have led to suggestions for dismantling the existing framework and substituting broader-based units which might be seen to have the merit of providing linkage to cater for the interdependence of urban and rural areas. Essentially populations in remoter areas and those to whom they may be linked in terms of local government will have to shoulder much of the burden of the changes that are occurring. A new framework might well assist in the process. But no matter how good the framework the confidence is also needed to ensure that what is built for the future is not only on firm foundations but is durable and fashioned to modern needs of the community as a whole in developing its new identity.

A further development should be a broader-based approach to the problems. At present there is a multiplicity of organisations with responsibilities for the many aspects of rural problems; transport, education, social services and agriculture all have separate central policies which are seen not necessarily in relation to each other but in relation to their national specialised setting. In this respect, agricultural policies impinging on the remoter areas tend to suffer from a confusion of objectives—social, agricultural and economic. In fact, the time has surely come for a broader-based, rather than piecemeal, approach to the whole of the problems of rural development. Such an approach might well mean the replacement of some outdated institutions by new ones more appropriate to the problems. The same consideration also applies to land-use policy where it is now questionable whether the basic philosophy dominating such policy is any longer appropriate.

A feature of central importance at the Conference was the recognition of the heavy dependence of many of the remote areas on government assistance in one form or another. But the Conference was equally aware that there were others in the queue standing outside the doors of the Treasury. There was, however, enough unanimity of feeling in the discussion to be able to conclude that while Treasury assistance might be needed, it can never be more than a catalyst in helping to achieve long-term solutions. In fact, the outcome will really depend upon achieving a smooth transition from traditional to new status as a result of the energy and determination of those directly concerned with the problems, as well as understanding and support from those individuals and institutions nationally who have direct links and involvement in the future development of these areas.

Thus there are many facets of the problem of the remoter rural areas and it is easy to agree with a concluding remark at the Conference that little that was unanimous came out of it. Yet all points of view received their share of attention and discussion by the Conference members. In presenting the papers in this volume the Editors issue a final warning. The situation is not one that can be left to itself: year by year more and more people leave the rural areas while, at the same time, the traditional institutional framework has been built on the assumption of stable population and reasonable levels of economic activity. If no clear signpost to the ultimate viability of these areas was discovered by the Conference, at least there was agreement that the end justified the search for the road to it.

LIST OF CONTRIBUTORS

Baillie, I. F.   C.M.G., O.B.E., M.A., Senior Research Associate, Agricultural Adjustment Unit, Department of Agricultural Economics, University of Newcastle upon Tyne.*

Cumming, D. G.   B.Sc., Department of Forestry, University of Aberdeen.

Dower, M.   M.A., A.R.I.C.S., A.M.T.P.I., Director, Dartington Amenity Research Trust, Totnes, Devon.

Garbett-Edwards, D. P.   F.C.I.S., Secretary, Mid-Wales Industrial Development Association, Newtown, Montgomeryshire.

Gaskin, Professor M.   D.F.C., M.A., Department of Political Economy, University of Aberdeen.

Grieve, Professor Sir Robert   M.A., M.I.C.E., M.T.P.I., A.M.I.Man.E., Hon.-A.R.I.A.S., Chairman, Highlands and Islands Development Board, 6, Castle Wynd, Inverness.†

Hughes, A. A.   Under Secretary, Scottish Development Department.‡

Jones, J. Morgan   C.B., C.B.E., M.A., Formerly Deputy Chairman Designate, Wales Rural Development Board, Maesnewydd, North Road, Aberystwyth.

Matthews, Professor J. D.   B.Sc., F.R.S.E., Department of Forestry, University of Aberdeen.

Philip, M. S.   M.B.E., M.A., B.Sc., Department of Forestry, University of Aberdeen.

Raeburn, Professor J. R.   Ph.D., M.A., F.R.S.E., Professor of Agriculture and Principal of College, School of Agriculture, University of Aberdeen.

Robinson, Professor D. G.   B.A., M.T.P.I., Professor of Regional Planning, Department of Town and Country Planning, University of Manchester.

Romus, Professor P.   Institute of European Studies, 79, Avenue des Cocoinelles, Boitsfort, Brussels 17, Belgium.

Thomas, J. Gareth   M.A., Registrar, University of Wales, Cathays Park, Cardiff.

Travis, Professor A. S.   B.A., M.T.P.I., Department of Town and Country Planning, Heriot-Watt University and Edinburgh College of Art, 48, Manor Place, Edinburgh.

Williams, Professor W. M.   M.A., Department of Sociology and Anthropology, University College of Swansea.

* Now Secretary of the Thistle Foundation, Edinburgh.
† Now Professor of Town Planning, University of Glasgow.
‡ Now Managing Director, Crudens Ltd., Musselburgh.

INDEX

Aachen, Germany (see Liége)
Aberdeen area, 166, 175
Aberdeen, University of, 45
Aberdeenshire, 7, 11
Aberystwyth, 51, 114, 115, 117
Accommodation for tourists, 79
Aeron estuary, W. Wales, 117
Afforestation (Wales), 127 (see also under Forestry)
Agricultural Adjustment Unit, Univeristy of Newcastle, ix, x
Agriculture Act 1947, 188
Agriculture Act 1957, 111
Agriculture Act 1967, viii, 88, 109, 111
Agriculture and Forestry, 26, 41–43
Agriculture, Development of, 1965, 111
Agriculture and Fisheries for Scotland, Dept. of, 41, 130, 136
Agriculture (Improvement of Roads) Act, 1955, 122
Agriculture (Fisheries and Food), Ministry of, 218
Akenfield (Suffolk), 208
Alcan, 138
Alps, 150
Annan, 33
Antwerp, Belgium, 149
Ardennes, Luxemburg, 149
Area Tourist Organisations, 141
Argyll(shire), 45, 46, 130, 139
Arran, Island of, 193
Aviemore, Invernesshire, 74, 77, 80, 83, 89

Bacon, Edmund, 224
Baillie, I. F., vii
Bala, Mid-Wales, 71
Bari-Taranto, Italy, 157
Barra, Outer Hebrides, 141
Bavaria, Germany, 158
Beacham Report, 1964, on 'Depopulation in Mid-Wales,' 67, 69, 112 f.n., 113
Beauly/Cromarty Firth area, 175, 183

Belgium, 149, 150, 154
Bellingham Rural District, Northumberland, 39
Berriew, Mid-Wales, 114
Birmingham, 68, 77, 131, 193
Black Mountains, S. Wales, 91
Blaenau Ffestiniog, Merioneth, 66
Board of Trade, 68
Borders, Scottish, 228
Brecon (Brecknock) (co.), 51, 92, 112 f.n., 114
Brecon (Brecknock) (t), 71
Brecon Beacons, 91
Brighton, 76
Bristol, 34, 77
British Aluminium Co., 138, 140
British Hotels and Restaurants Association, 88
British Rail, 218
British Waterways Board, 218
Builth Wells, Brecknock, 71
Byrness, Northumberland, 191

Caerws (New Town), 71
Cairngorms Area, 80
Cairngorms Area Report, 83
Cairngorms Sports Development Company, 89
Caithness, 130, 131, 132, 138, 139
Calabria, Italy, 158
Caldrons Farm, 38
Cambrian Range, 127
Cambridge, 76
Campbeltown, Argyll, 141
Canada, 7, 193
Cardiganshire, 51, 92, 112 f.n., 114, 116
Cardigan Bay, 114
Carmarthenshire, 91, 114, 118, 123 f.n.
Castle, Barbara, policy, 80
Cattle, fat, returns from, 14
Central Moorlands Region (Wales), 126, 127
Channel (English), 150
Cheshire, 91